Mastering Simula Programming

From Basics to Expert Proficiency

Contents

Introduction

The Simula programming language, developed in the 1960s by Ole-Johan Dahl and Kristen Nygaard, holds a special place in the history of computer science. As the first language to introduce the concepts of classes and objects, Simula laid the groundwork for the object-oriented programming paradigms that we widely use today. Its influence persists, manifesting in various modern programming languages such as C++, Java, and Python.

Simula's significance extends beyond its historical contributions. Its design principles and features offer robust mechanisms for modeling complex systems and managing real-world problems. Unlike many contemporary languages, Simula was created with a focus on simulation, making it particularly adept at handling tasks requiring the representation of real-world processes.

This book, "Mastering Simula Programming: From Basics to Expert Proficiency," serves as a comprehensive guide for beginners eager to learn this foundational language. By systematically exploring Simula's syntax, structure, and advanced capabilities, readers will acquire a solid understanding of both the theoretical and practical aspects of the language. Each chapter delves into distinct topics, meticulously organized to build upon previously acquired knowledge and facilitate a coherent learning experience.

Early chapters will introduce the essential concepts of Simula, including its history, key features, and comparison to other programming languages. Readers will learn how to set up their development environment and write their first Simula program. As the book progresses, more intricate aspects of the language, such as data types, control structures, classes, objects, inheritance, and polymorphism, will be thoroughly examined. Practical examples and clear explanations will elucidate these topics, ensuring that readers grasp both the form and function of each language feature.

In later sections, the book will address more advanced subjects, including modules and libraries, input and output handling, and exception management. These chapters aim to equip readers with the necessary skills to handle complex programming scenarios and develop efficient, scalable code. The concluding chapter will introduce specialized topics such as concurrency, memory management, and performance optimization, allowing readers to achieve proficiency in Simula.

Simula's intrinsic elegance and capabilities make it an invaluable language for understanding the principles of object-oriented programming. Through this book, readers will not only learn to write effective Simula code but also gain insights into the paradigms that shape modern software development. Armed with this knowledge, programmers will be well-prepared to tackle a wide range of computational problems in both academic and professional settings.

We invite you to embark on this educational journey with us, confident that "Mastering Simula Programming: From Basics to Expert Proficiency" will provide a thorough, impactful, and engaging learning experience. By the end of this book, you will not only master Simula but also appreciate its lasting impact on the world of programming.

Chapter 1

Introduction to Simula

This chapter provides an overview of the Simula programming language, covering its history, key features, and its place within the broader landscape of programming languages. It guides the reader through setting up the development environment, writing and running their first Simula program, and exploring sample applications. The chapter concludes with a discussion of common use cases, underscoring Simula's relevance and utility in contemporary programming.

1.1 Overview of Simula Programming Language

Simula is considered the first object-oriented programming language, introducing key concepts that have significantly shaped the development of subsequent programming languages. Developed in the mid-1960s by Ole-Johan Dahl and Kristen Nygaard at the Norwegian Computing Center, Simula extends its parent language, ALGOL 60, by adding new features tailored for simulation tasks. It is this focus on simulation that inspired the name "Simula."

The primary enhancements that Simula introduced over ALGOL 60 include classes, objects, inheritance, and dynamic memory management. These innovations laid the groundwork for modern object-oriented programming (OOP). Understanding these features is essential for grasping the broader scope of object-oriented principles.

Classes and objects form the bedrock of the Simula programming language. A class defines a template for objects containing both state (data) and behavior (procedures). These classes are defined using the class keyword and can include both attributes (variables) and methods (procedures) that operate on these attributes. Objects are instances of these classes, created dynamically during program execution.

The following example demonstrates a simple class definition in Simula:

```
class ExampleClass;
  begin
    integer a, b;
    procedure PrintSum;
      begin
        OutInt(a + b, 5);
        OutImage;
      end;
  end;
```

In the example, ExampleClass defines two integer variables, a and b, and a procedure PrintSum that prints the sum of a and b using the OutInt and OutImage procedures for output.

Inheritance allows a new class, called a subclass, to inherit attributes and methods from an existing class, known as the superclass. This promotes code reuse and logical organization of the codebase. Inheritance in Simula is implemented using the class keyword followed by a colon and the superclass name.

```
class SubClass : ExampleClass;
  begin
    procedure PrintDifference;
      begin
        OutInt(a - b, 5);
        OutImage;
      end;
  end;
```

Here, SubClass inherits a, b, and PrintSum from ExampleClass and adds a new procedure, PrintDifference, to print the difference between a and b.

Dynamic memory management in Simula is facilitated through operations for creating and disposing of objects. Objects are created using the new keyword, which allocates memory for an object of a certain class.

```
ref(ExampleClass) obj;
obj :- new ExampleClass;
```

```
obj.a := 5;
obj.b := 3;
obj.PrintSum;
```

In this snippet, obj is a reference to an object of type ExampleClass. The new ExampleClass statement allocates memory for the object and returns a reference to it. Attributes a and b are then set to 5 and 3, respectively, followed by a call to PrintSum, which prints their sum.

Simula's contribution to the conceptual framework of OOP is immense. Key OOP concepts, now taken for granted in many programming languages, were either invented or extensively formalized within Simula. This includes not just classes and inheritance, but also complex constructs such as coroutine and discrete event simulation.

In essence, Simula's design philosophy centers around modeling and simulation, making it particularly adept for applications in these domains. However, the principles it introduced extend well beyond simulation, forming a core part of modern programming practices. As we delve deeper into Simula through subsequent sections, its broader applications and comparison with other languages will underscore its continued relevance and pioneering role in the evolution of programming languages.

Understanding Simula necessitates an appreciation of how it amalgamates the procedural aspects of ALGOL with the new paradigms of object orientation. This synthesis forms the backbone of Simula's powerful and flexible framework, which serves both as a historical milestone and a practical tool for a wide range of programming tasks. Through Simula, learners can gain insights into the origins and mechanisms of object-oriented programming, enriching their conceptual and practical understanding of contemporary programming environments.

1.2 History and Evolution of Simula

The Simula programming language was created in the 1960s by Ole-Johan Dahl and Kristen Nygaard at the Norwegian Computing Center (Norsk Regnesentral). Initially developed as a language for simulating discrete event systems, Simula quickly evolved to become the foundational language for many object-oriented programming (OOP) concepts that permeate modern programming today.

Simula originated from the need to model complex systems and processes in a more manageable way. With its first version, Simula I, introduced in 1962, the creators aimed to provide a tool for describing operations in a generalized manner, suitable for a wide array of simulations. Although Simula I made significant strides, it was Simula 67, the revised version introduced in 1967, that embedded groundbreaking features such as classes, objects, inheritance, and encapsulation.

The most critical evolution between Simula I and Simula 67 was the addition of classes and objects. The class construct in Simula 67 allowed the definition of both data and behaviors (methods) encapsulated within a single cohesive unit. This capability marked the beginning of the object-oriented paradigm, providing a robust framework for representing real-world entities in a computationally efficient way.

```
class Person;
    begin
    integer age;
    procedure speak;
        begin
        OutText("Hello, I am " & age & " years old.");
        OutImage;
        end;
    end;
```

The example above demonstrates a basic class Person in Simula, highlighting the encapsulation of an integer age and a procedure speak.

Simula's influence spread throughout the computer science community, inspiring the development of later languages. Notably, languages such as Smalltalk, C++, and Java borrowed heavily from Simula's concepts. Smalltalk, developed at Xerox PARC, extended Simula's object-oriented principles to create a more dynamic and interactive programming environment. Meanwhile, C++, created by Bjarne Stroustrup in the 1980s, conceptualized object-oriented features atop the C programming language, merging efficiency with the expressiveness of Simula. Java, introduced by Sun Microsystems in the mid-1990s, further popularized the object-oriented paradigm, drawing directly from both Simula and C++.

Simula's design philosophy centered around modularity, reuse, and the development of robust software architectures. Its constructs for inheritance allowed programmers to define hierarchical relationships between classes, fostering code reuse and organization. This was a significant departure from procedure-oriented programming, where code reuse was often limited and organization less intuitive.

The simulated modeling allowed for an elegant approach to complex systems. Object-oriented design principles enabled developers to cre-

```
Data: Classes defining entities
Result: Efficient simulation model
Define class simulationEnvironment
while simulation in progress do
    foreach entity in simulation do
        entity.proceed()
Generate results
```

ate detailed models encapsulating behaviors and attributes, as illustrated in the above pseudo-code where the simulation environment maintains individual entities processed iteratively.

The principles laid out by Simula's development have become cornerstones of modern software engineering. Concepts such as data abstraction, modularity, and hierarchy inform the design patterns and best practices in contemporary programming. As a testament to its enduring legacy, the object model defined by Simula serves as an archetype in computer science pedagogy and professional practices alike.

By tracing the historical and evolutionary trajectory of Simula, it becomes clear how foundational this language has been. Its introduction marked a paradigm shift in the way complex systems and software architectures were conceived and implemented, leaving an indelible mark on the landscape of programming languages.

1.3 Key Features and Concepts

Simula, often regarded as the first object-oriented programming language, introduced several key features and concepts that have profoundly influenced the development of modern programming languages. Understanding these features is crucial for leveraging Simula effectively.

Simula's object-oriented paradigm is centered on the concepts of classes, objects, and inheritance. A class in Simula serves as a blueprint for creating objects. It encapsulates data and methods that can operate on that data, fostering modular and reusable code. This encapsulation is achieved through the use of inner and outer constructs, facilitating robust hierarchical class structures. Consider the following simple class definition in Simula:

```
Begin Class Person;
   text Name;
   integer Age;
   Procedure Init(t Name, i Age);
   Begin
      Name := t Name;
      Age := i Age;
   End;
End;
```

Here, the Person class encapsulates the Name and Age attributes along with an Init procedure for initialization. Simula supports inheritance, allowing the creation of specialized classes that derive properties and behaviors from existing ones. This is illustrated in the following extension of the Person class:

```
Begin Class Employee;
   integer EmployeeId;
   Real Salary;
   text Department;

   Procedure Init(t Name, i Age, i EmployeeId, r Salary, t Department);
   Begin
      OutImage;
   End;

   Procedure GetDetails();
   Begin
      OutImage;
   End;
End;
```

In this example, Employee inherits from Person and extends it with additional attributes such as EmployeeId, Salary, and Department. The Init procedure is overridden, demonstrating polymorphism—a core characteristic of object-oriented programming. Polymorphism allows methods to operate differently based on the object's class, enhancing flexibility and maintainability.

Simula enhances modularity through its block structure. Each program is encapsulated in a Begin and End block, promoting clear and organized code. Moreover, Simula's coroutine facility enables the interleaving of execution contexts, providing a powerful mechanism for implementing concurrent processes. This is achieved using Detach and Activate constructs:

```
Begin
   Procedure P1;
   Begin
      Detach P2;
      OutImage;
      Detach P3;
```

```
    End;

    Procedure P2;
    Begin
       OutImage;
       Detach P1;
    End;

    Procedure P3;
    Begin
       OutImage;
       Terminate
    End;
End;
```

In this coroutine example, P1, P2, P3 are detached and activated, demonstrating interleaved execution among them. This control over execution flow allows complex tasks to be divided into simpler routines and invoked as needed.

Another fundamental concept in Simula is the strong type system. Type safety helps in detecting errors at compile-time, reducing the likelihood of runtime issues. Simula supports various data types, including but not limited to integer, real, text, and complex structures.

Simula also provides a comprehensive simulation framework. Originally designed for simulation tasks, it includes predefined classes and procedures to model real-world systems. The simulation components, such as Simulation and Process classes, support event-based simulation, an essential feature for analyzing dynamic systems. This makes Simula particularly powerful for operational research, queueing theory, and systems engineering.

Built-in exception handling in Simula ensures robust error management. The language offers constructs such as Error handling to gracefully manage and recover from unexpected conditions.

Scoping and Control Structures: Simula introduces refined scoping mechanisms through inner and outer contexts, allowing inner class definitions to reference variables or procedures from their enclosing outer class contexts. Additionally, Simula provides a comprehensive set of control structures, including:

- if ... then ... else ... for conditional execution.
- for ... while for iterative processing.
- go to for unconditional jumps.

These structures enhance code readability and control flow.

The precision of Simula in expressing object-oriented concepts, reinforced with its robust type system, modular architecture, coroutine facility, and simulation framework, underpins many modern programming paradigms. Simula bridges procedural and object-oriented programming, establishing it as a foundational language for contemporary software development.

This dive into Simula's key features provides a deep understanding of not just how to write code in Simula, but also why its constructs matter in building reliable, maintainable, and scalable software systems.

1.4 Simula vs Other Programming Languages

In this section, we will examine how Simula compares with other programming languages. This analysis will highlight key differences and similarities in terms of syntax, paradigms, and typical use cases. We will focus on fundamental aspects that define the unique characteristics of Simula in relation to languages like C++, Java, Python, and Smalltalk.

Object-Oriented Features:

Simula is often hailed as the first object-oriented programming (OOP) language. It introduced many concepts fundamental to OOP that have since been adopted and expanded upon by other languages.

- **Classes and Objects**: Simula's introduction of class and object concepts has had a lasting impact. For example, C++, Java, and Python have integrated these concepts natively. In Simula, a class is defined using the CLASS keyword:

```
CLASS ExampleClass;
    INTEGER variable;
    PROCEDURE ExampleProcedure;
    ...
END;
```

- **Inheritance and Polymorphism**: Inheritance allows new classes to derive properties and behavior from existing classes. Simula's inheritance mechanism is straightforward and forms the basis for those in C++ and Java:

```
CLASS SubClass: SuperClass;
```

```
    ...
END;
```

- **Encapsulation and Modularity**: Simula employs encapsulation through the definition of procedures and the scoping of variables within classes, much like modern OOP languages. For instance, C++ and Java use private, protected, and public access specifiers to control visibility and encapsulation, similar to Simula's approach of keeping procedures and data within class definitions.

Syntax and Structure:

Simula's syntax is influenced by Algol, making it somewhat different from C-based languages but still recognizable to those familiar with Pascal or Ada.

- **Declarative Nature**: Simula favors a declarative style, visible in how variables and classes are defined:

```
INTEGER i;
REAL x;
CLASS Sample;
    INTEGER a;
    PROCEDURE DoSomething;
    ...
END;
```

  This syntax is distinguishable from C++ or Java, which use a more illustrative form:

```
int i;
double x;
class Sample {
    int a;
    void DoSomething() {
        ...
    }
};
```

- **Reserved Keywords**: Simula's reserved keywords are largely derived from Algol, whereas modern languages have evolved to use more English-like terms. For instance, BEGIN and END delimit blocks in Simula, compared to curly braces {} in C++ and Java.

Procedural vs. Object-Oriented Paradigms:

Simula supports both procedural and object-oriented paradigms, serving as a bridge between these two programming styles.

- Procedures:

```
PROCEDURE ComputeArea(a, b);
    REAL a, b;
BEGIN
    RETURN a * b;
END;
```

- Object-Oriented Methods:

```
CLASS Rectangle;
    REAL length, width;
    PROCEDURE ComputeArea;
    BEGIN
        RETURN length * width;
    END;
END;
```

Contrasting this with Python, a multi-paradigm language, we see:

```
def compute_area(a, b):
    return a * b

class Rectangle:
    def __init__(self, length, width):
        self.length = length
        self.width = width

    def compute_area(self):
        return self.length * self.width
```

Memory Management:

Simula relies on automatic memory management for object instantiation, distinct from the manual memory management in C but similar to garbage-collected languages like Java and Python. In Simula, objects are created using the NEW keyword:

```
Rectangle r;
r :- NEW Rectangle;
```

Java uses:

```
Rectangle r = new Rectangle();
```

Both employ a form of garbage collection, whereas C++ uses:

```
Rectangle* r = new Rectangle();
delete r;
```

indicating explicit allocation and deallocation.

Concurrency and Simulation:

One of Simula's notable strengths lies in its simulation capabilities, facilitated by its co-routine feature. This design aids in the simulation of complex systems, making it favored in the domain of simulation modeling.

- **Coroutines**: Facilitated by the detach and resume constructs, aiding in process-based simulations. This aspect is less emphasized in mainstream languages like C++ or Java.

```
CLASS Process;
    PROCEDURE Main;
    BEGIN
        ...
    END;
END;

CLASS Simulation;
    Process p;
BEGIN
    p :- NEW Process;
    RESUME p;
END;
```

Contrarily, Python's asyncio library offers asynchronous programming capabilities but does not directly cater to simulation paradigm out of the box:

```
import asyncio

async def main():
    print('Hello, asynchronous world!')
asyncio.run(main())
```

Examining Simula in the broader spectrum of programming languages underscores its pioneering contributions and underscores its vital role in laying the foundations for modern object-oriented programming. Its influences are clearly seen in languages that came after it, shaping the way complex software systems are developed and understood.

1.5 Getting Started with Simula

To get started with Simula, it is essential to first understand the prerequisites and dependencies required for setting up the development environment. We will guide you through the process of installing the necessary software, including a Simula compiler and an integrated development environment (IDE) if available. Subsequently, we will delve into writing a simple Simula program and executing it to verify that the environment is correctly configured.

Prerequisites

Ensure that your system meets the following prerequisites:

- Operating System: Simula can be set up on various operating systems, including Windows, macOS, and Linux.
- Memory and Storage: A minimum of 2GB RAM and 500MB of free disk space.
- Internet Connection: Required to download the necessary tools and libraries.

Installing the Simula Compiler

The primary step in getting started with Simula is to install the Simula compiler. Here's a step-by-step guide for different operating systems:

Windows

1. Visit the official website to download the Simula compiler for Windows.
2. Run the installer (.exe file) and follow the instructions provided.
3. Add the installation path to the system's environment variables to ensure the Simula compiler is accessible from command line.

macOS and Linux

```
# Open the terminal
# Update the package list
sudo apt-get update
# Install the Simula compiler
sudo apt-get install simula
```

After successful installation, verify by checking the compiler version using the command:

```
simula --version
```

If the install is successful, the version number of the Simula compiler will be displayed.

Setting Up an Integrated Development Environment (IDE)

While Simula programs can be written in any text editor and compiled via the command line, using an IDE can significantly enhance productivity by providing code completion, debugging tools, and project management features. Several IDEs support Simula; however, Emacs is often recommended due to its extensibility and support for Simula modes.

1. Download and install Emacs from its official website.
2. Configure Simula mode in Emacs by adding the following lines to your .emacs configuration file:

```
;; Simula mode configuration
(autoload 'simula-mode "simula" "Simula mode." t)
(setq auto-mode-alist
      (append '(("\\.sim$" . simula-mode)) auto-mode-alist))
```

Writing Your First Simula Program

Let's write a simple Simula program that prints "Hello, World!". Create a new file named hello.sim and open it in your chosen text editor or IDE. Enter the following code:

```
BEGIN
  OUTTEXT("Hello, World!");
  OUTIMAGE;
END;
```

This program uses the built-in procedure OUTTEXT to output text and OUTIMAGE to finalize the output.

Compiling and Running Simula Programs

To compile the hello.sim program, use the Simula compiler from the command line:

```
simula hello.sim
```

If there are no syntax errors, the compiler will generate an executable file. Run the executable from the command line:

```
./hello
```

The following output should be displayed:

```
Hello, World!
```

These steps verify that your Simula development environment is correctly set up and operational.

Understanding this foundational process of installing, configuring, and writing a basic program equips you to dive deeper into the language's more advanced features in subsequent sections.

1.6 Setting Up the Development Environment

To begin programming in Simula, setting up a reliable and efficient development environment is essential. This section will guide you through the steps of downloading, installing, and configuring the necessary tools. Adhering to these instructions will ensure a smooth experience as you write and execute Simula programs.

System Requirements

Before proceeding, ensure that your system meets the following minimum requirements:

- Operating System: Windows, macOS, or Linux
- Processor: 1 GHz or faster
- RAM: 2 GB or more
- Available Disk Space: 500 MB or more

Downloading the Simula Compiler

The first step involves downloading the appropriate Simula compiler for your operating system. The most widely used compiler for Simula is the GNU Simula compiler, which is available on the simula.org website. Follow these steps:

1. Navigate to https://www.simula.org/download.
2. Select your operating system from the list provided.
3. Download the installer package corresponding to your operating system.

Installation Process

After downloading the installer, proceed with the installation as follows:

- On **Windows**:

1. Double-click the downloaded installer package.
2. Follow the on-screen instructions, accept the license agreement, and choose the installation directory.
3. Click Install to complete the installation.

- On **macOS**:
  1. Open the downloaded disk image (.dmg) file.
  2. Drag the Simula icon into the Applications folder.
- On **Linux**:

```
$ sudo dpkg -i simula_installer.deb
```

Configuring the Simula Environment

Once the Simula compiler is installed, you must configure the environment to recognize the Simula executable and associated libraries. This involves setting environment variables correctly.

- On **Windows**:
  1. Open the Control Panel.
  2. Navigate to System and Security > System > Advanced system settings.
  3. Click Environment Variables.
  4. Locate and select the Path variable in the System variables section, and click Edit.
  5. Add the path to your Simula installation directory (e.g., C:\Program Files\Simula) to the list and click OK.
- On **macOS** and **Linux**:

```
$ export PATH=$PATH:/usr/local/simula/bin
$ export SIMULA_HOME=/usr/local/simula
```

These commands can be added to the .bashrc or .zshrc file to make the changes permanent.

Verifying the Installation

After setting up the environment variables, verify that the installation is successful by running the following command in your terminal or command prompt:

```
$ simula --version
```

If the installation was successful, the version information of the Simula compiler will be displayed. For example:

```
Simula Compiler version 1.0.0
```

Installing an Integrated Development Environment (IDE)

To enhance your development experience, consider installing an Integrated Development Environment (IDE) that supports Simula. While there are many options, the most popular is SimIDE, specifically designed for Simula programming. Installation steps are as follows:

1. Download SimIDE from the official website: https://www.simide.com/download.
2. Run the installer and follow the instructions specific to your operating system.
3. Launch SimIDE and configure it to recognize the Simula compiler by navigating to File > Settings > Compiler, and set the path to the Simula executable (e.g., /usr/local/simula/bin/simula).

Creating a Sample Project in SimIDE

To ensure that your development environment is correctly configured, create a sample project:

1. Open SimIDE and select File > New Project.
2. Name your project and choose a directory to save it.
3. Create a new Simula source file by selecting File > New > Source File.
4. Enter the following sample code into the editor:

```
    OutText("Hello, World!");
    OutImage;
end;
```

5. Save the file and compile it by navigating to Build > Compile.
6. Run the compiled program by selecting Run > Execute.

Upon execution, the expected output should appear in the output console:

```
Hello, World!
```

Completing the steps above ensures that your development environment is ready for Simula programming. This preparation will allow you to effectively follow along with the examples and exercises presented in this book.

1.7 Writing Your First Simula Program

Start by creating a new text file with a .sim extension. For the first program, it is useful to begin with a basic example that highlights fundamental features of Simula.

The following code demonstrates a simple Simula program:

```
Begin
  OutText("Hello World!");
  OutImage;
End;
```

This code comprises the essential elements of a Simula program. The Begin and End keywords define the block of the program. The OutText procedure outputs the string "Hello World!", and OutImage outputs a line break.

Basic Structure Simula programs have a clear and consistent structure:

```
Begin
  // Declarations and statements
End;
```

In this structure:

- The Begin keyword marks the start.
- Statements and procedure calls are written between Begin and End.
- Statements end with a semicolon.

Variable Declarations Consider the need for variables to store data. Declare variables at the start of the Begin block:

```
Begin
  Integer i, sum;
  Real r;
  Boolean flag;

  i := 10;
  sum := i + 20;
  OutText("Sum is: "); OutInt(sum, 4);
  OutImage;
End;
```

Control Structures Simula supports typical control structures like if statements and for loops.

If-Else Statements For conditional operations:

```
Begin
  Integer i;
  i := 10;
  If i > 5 Then
    OutText("i is greater than 5");
  Else
    OutText("i is not greater than 5");
  OutImage;
End;
```

For Loops For iteration:

```
Begin
  Integer i;
  For i := 1 Step 1 Until 5 Do
    OutInt(i, 4);
  OutImage;
End;
```

This loop iterates from 1 to 5, outputting each value of i.

Functions and Procedures In Simula, procedures (subroutines) can be defined to encapsulate reusable code:

```
Begin
  Integer Square(Integer x);
  Begin
    Square := x * x;
  End;
  Integer result;
  result := Square(5);
  OutText("Square of 5 is: "); OutInt(result, 4);
  OutImage;
End;
```

In the code above, Square is a function that returns the square of the given integer.

Class Definitions Simula introduces object-oriented concepts with classes and objects. A simple class definition includes attributes

and methods:

```
Begin
  Class Person;
  Begin
    Text Name;
    Procedure Init (Text t);
    Begin
      Name := t;
    End;

    Procedure PrintName;
    Begin
      OutText("Name: "); OutText(Name); OutImage;
    End;
  End;

  Ref(Person) p;
  p :- New Person;
  Call p.Init("Alice");
  Call p.PrintName;
End;
```

In this example:

- A Person class is defined.

- Two methods, Init and PrintName, handle initialization and printing the name.

- An instance p of the Person class is created and methods are called using Call.

Comments Comments enhance code readability. Single-line comments start with //:

```
Begin
  Integer i; // Initialize i
  i := 5; // Assign 5 to i
  // Output the value of i
  OutInt(i, 4);
  OutImage;
End;
```

Adherence to these patterns and structures ensures the clarity and functionality of Simula programs. Each segment builds upon fundamental concepts, providing a robust foundation.

1.8 Compiling and Running Simula Programs

Compiling and running Simula programs entails several steps, each crucial for successfully executing the written code. This section elaborates on the processes involved in transforming Simula source code into executable programs and executing these programs within the development environment.

Simula programs, written in plain text with a .sim extension, necessitate the use of a Simula compiler. The following instructions assume the use of the Lund Simula (LSD) compiler, a widely-used tool for compiling Simula programs. Ensure that the development environment is correctly set up according to the guidelines provided in the previous section.

1. Writing the Simula Program

First, create a Simula source file. Open your preferred text editor and enter the following basic Simula program to confirm that your setup is correct:

```
/* A simple Simula program */
Begin
   OutText("Hello, world!");
   OutImage;
End;
```

Save this file with a .sim extension, e.g., hello_world.sim. This program uses Simula's built-in procedures OutText and OutImage to display the string "Hello, world!" on the screen.

2. Compiling the Simula Program

Open your command-line interface (CLI) or terminal, navigate to the directory containing your hello_world.sim file, and use the Simula compiler to compile your program. The typical command for compiling a Simula program using the LSD compiler is as follows:

```
sims hello_world.sim
```

If the compilation is successful, the compiler generates an intermediate or executable file. The nature of this output depends on your compiler's configuration and the system architecture. Generally, it may produce an object file or a directly executable file.

Errors during compilation will be reported in the CLI or terminal. For instance, if there is a syntax error or a missing keyword, the compiler's feedback helps in debugging the code. Correct the errors in your source file and recompile until no further errors are detected.

3. Running the Simula Program

Once the program is successfully compiled, execute the resulting file. For example, if the compilation generates an executable named hello_world, run the following command from the CLI:

```
./hello_world
```

If compiled correctly, and without any run-time errors, the output is displayed as follows:

```
Hello, world!
```

This simple example confirms that you can pass through the complete cycle of writing, compiling, and executing a Simula program.

4. Handling Compilation Errors

Often, a source code might contain errors preventing successful compilation. The compiler's error messages typically indicate the line number and nature of the error. Here's an example of a common compilation error involving a missing semicolon:

```
/* Erroneous Simula Program */
Begin
    OutText("Hello, world!")
    OutImage;
End;
```

On compiling the above code, the error might look like this:

```
Error: Missing semicolon at line 3
```

Correct the program by adding the semicolon, and recompile:

```
/* Corrected Simula Program */
Begin
    OutText("Hello, world!");
    OutImage;
End;
```

5. Advanced Compilation Options

For more complex projects, the Simula compiler provides a range of options to optimize the compilation process. Common options might include specifying include paths, linking external libraries, or setting optimization levels. Refer to the compiler's documentation for detailed information on these options. A typical usage might be:

```
sims -o hello_world hello_world.sim
```

The -o option specifies the name of the output executable. Incorporate these options as necessary to tailor the compilation process to your project's requirements.

6. Automation with Makefiles

For larger projects with multiple Simula files, using a Makefile can automate the compilation process. A simple Makefile for a Simula project might look like this:

```
CC = sims
CFLAGS = -O2
TARGET = my_program

OBJS = file1.o file2.o file3.o

$(TARGET): $(OBJS)
    $(CC) $(CFLAGS) -o $(TARGET) $(OBJS)

%.o: %.sim
    $(CC) $(CFLAGS) -c $< -o $@

clean:
    rm -f $(TARGET) $(OBJS)
```

Save this configuration in a text file named Makefile. Run the following command in the CLI to build the project:

```
make
```

The make utility processes the Makefile, compiling each listed source file and linking them to create the final executable my_program.

Understanding and utilizing the compilation and execution processes effectively is crucial for efficient Simula programming. Follow best practices to ensure your code is clean, well-documented, and error-free.

1.9 Exploring Sample Simula Programs

This section delves into practical examples of Simula programs, providing a concrete understanding of the language's syntax and features. We will examine several sample programs, each illustrating a specific aspect of Simula. By exploring these examples, you will gain insights into how Simula can be effectively utilized for various computing tasks.

Example 1: Simple Class and Object

Simula is renowned for introducing the concept of classes and objects. A simple example is creating a class to represent a point in a 2D space. The class has two attributes, x and y, and methods to manipulate these attributes.

```
Begin
   Class Point;
      Real x, y;
      Procedure Move(dx, dy); Real dx, dy;
      Begin
         x := x + dx;
         y := y + dy;
      End;

   Point p;
   p:- new Point;
   Inspect p do
   Begin
      x := 1.0;
      y := 2.0;
      OutText("Initial position: ");
      OutReal(x, 6, 2); OutImage;
      OutReal(y, 6, 2); OutImage;
      Move(3.0, 4.0);
      OutText("New position: ");
      OutReal(x, 6, 2); OutImage;
      OutReal(y, 6, 2); OutImage;
   End;
End;
```

Output from execution:

```
Initial position:  1.00
                   2.00
New position:      4.00
                   6.00
```

In this example, the Point class defines two attributes, x and y, to store the coordinates of the point. The Move procedure updates these coordinates. An instance of the class is created, and its methods are invoked to demonstrate basic object-oriented programming concepts.

Example 2: Queue Simulation

Simula was initially developed for simulation purposes, and it excels in discrete event simulation. In this example, we model a simple queue system.

```
Begin
   Class Queue;
      Integer front, rear, size;
      Array q[1:10] of Integer;
```

```
    Procedure Init;
    Begin
      front := 1;
      rear := 0;
      size := 0;
    End;

    Procedure Enqueue(val); Integer val;
    Begin
      If size < 10 then
      Begin
        rear := (rear + 1) mod 10;
        q[rear] := val;
        size := size + 1;
      End;
    End;

    Procedure Dequeue; Integer Result;
    Begin
      If size > 0 then
      Begin
        Result := q[front];
        front := (front + 1) mod 10;
        size := size - 1;
      End
      Else
        Result := -1;
    End;

  Queue q;
  q:- new Queue;
  Inspect q do
  Begin
    Init;
    Enqueue(10);
    Enqueue(20);
    OutInteger(Dequeue); OutImage; \* Outputs: 10 *\
    OutInteger(Dequeue); OutImage; \* Outputs: 20 *\
  End;
End;
```

Output from execution:

```
10
20
```

This program defines a Queue class with methods to initialize the queue, enqueue elements, and dequeue elements. It demonstrates how Simula can manage more complex data structures and perform operations typical in simulation scenarios.

Example 3: Random Walk Simulation

A random walk is a mathematical concept that describes a path consisting of a series of random steps. This example simulates a random walk in a 2D space.

```
Begin
   Class RandomWalk;
      Real x, y;
      Procedure Init;
      Begin
         x := 0.0;
         y := 0.0;
      End;

      Procedure Step;
      Begin
         If Random < 0.25 then x := x + 1.0
         Else If Random < 0.50 then x := x - 1.0
         Else If Random < 0.75 then y := y + 1.0
         Else y := y - 1.0;
      End;

   Random integer seed;
   Real Random;
   Procedure SetRandomSeed(s); Integer s;
   Begin
      seed := s;
   End;

   Procedure GenerateRandom; Real Result;
   Begin
      seed := (seed * 1664525 + 1013904223) mod 2147483648;
      Result := seed / 2147483648.0;
   End;

   RandomWalk rw;
   rw:- new RandomWalk;
   Inspect rw do
   Begin
      Init;
      SetRandomSeed(12345);
      For i:= 1 Step 1 Until 100 Do
      Begin
         Step;
         OutReal(x, 6, 2); OutImage;
         OutReal(y, 6, 2); OutImage;
      End;
   End;
End;
```

Output depends on random seed:

```
0.00
0.00
1.00
0.00
0.00
1.00
-1.00
1.00
-2.00
1.00
...
```

In this program, the RandomWalk class manages the coordinates for the walk and defines the Step procedure for moving randomly. A separate section for random number generation is included to support the stochastic behavior of the walk.

These examples emphasize Simula's capabilities in object-oriented programming and its strong support for simulation. By understanding and experimenting with these sample programs, one can gain practical knowledge of Simula's syntax and structures, facilitating the creation of more complex and tailored applications.

1.10 Common Use Cases and Applications

Simula has established itself as a versatile and powerful programming language, especially in domains requiring complex simulations and object-oriented programming paradigms. This section delves into various domains where Simula has demonstrated significant utility, highlighting specific applications to provide a comprehensive view of its versatility.

1. Simulation Modeling:

Simula was originally designed for simulation purposes, making it a preferred choice for creating complex models that facilitate the understanding of both discrete and continuous systems. Common applications within this domain include:

- **Traffic Systems:** Simula can model traffic flow and congestion, helping cities optimize traffic light sequences and planning roadway expansions.
- **Manufacturing Processes:** By simulating assembly lines, Simula helps identify bottlenecks and optimize production schedules.
- **Epidemiology:** Epidemiologists use Simula to simulate disease spread, enabling better preparation and response to outbreaks.

Simula's intrinsic support for event scheduling and its powerful constructs for handling time progression make it an excellent tool for these types of simulations. Below is an example of a simple traffic light simulation in Simula:

```
CLASS TrafficLight;
    INTEGER state; ! 0: Red, 1: Green, 2: Yellow;
    PROCEDURE Switch;
    BEGIN
        state := (state + 1) MOD 3;
```

```
    END;
END;

BEGIN
    REF (TrafficLight) TL;
    TL :- NEW TrafficLight;
    TL.state := 0; ! Start with Red
    WHILE TRUE DO
        BEGIN
            TL.Switch;
            WRITE(TL.state);
            DELAY(60);
        END;
END;
```

2. Object-Oriented Programming (OOP) Education:

Simula's contributions to the foundation of object-oriented programming have left an indelible mark on computer science education. Its strong OOP features, such as classes, objects, inheritance, and polymorphism, make it an ideal teaching tool.

- **Inheritance and Polymorphism:** Educators use Simula to demonstrate inheritance hierarchies and the benefits of polymorphism in reducing code redundancy and enhancing code maintainability.
- **Class-based Modeling:** Students learn to encapsulate complex real-world entities into classes and objects, simplifying both the design and implementation phases of software development.

A classic example often used in OOP education is the implementation of shape hierarchies:

```
CLASS Shape;
    INTEGER centerX, centerY;
    PROCEDURE Move(dx, dy); INTEGER dx, dy;
    BEGIN
        centerX := centerX + dx;
        centerY := centerY + dy;
    END;

    PROCEDURE Virtual Draw; VIRTUAL;
    INSPECT; ! Abstract method
END;

CLASS Circle;
    INTEGER radius;
    PROCEDURE Draw;
    BEGIN
        ! Code to draw the circle
    END;
END;
```

```
CLASS Rectangle SHAPE;
    INTEGER width, height;
    PROCEDURE Draw;
    BEGIN
        ! Code to draw the rectangle
    END;
END;
```

3. Process-Oriented Programming:

Simula supports process-oriented programming through its simulation of real-world processes with concurrent activities. This capability is beneficial in areas such as:

- **Telecommunications:** Simulating data packet handling and network traffic to improve network reliability and performance.
- **Operating Systems:** Modeling process scheduling, inter-process communication, and resource management.

A simplified process-oriented model for a producer-consumer scenario is illustrated below:

```
CLASS ProducerConsumerSimulation;
    CLASS Producer;
    CLASS Consumer;
    QUEUE buffer;

    PROCEDURE Producer;
    BEGIN
        WHILE producing DO
        BEGIN
            ! Produce an item
            buffer.AddNewItem();
            ! Notify consumer
        END;
    END;

    PROCEDURE Consumer;
    BEGIN
        WHILE consuming DO
        BEGIN
            ! Wait for item
            buffer.RetrieveItem();
            ! Consume the item
        END;
    END;

    BEGIN
        buffer :- NEW BUFFER;
        ! Initialize producer-consumer processes
    END;
END;
```

4. System and Performance Analysis:

Simula is extensively used in performance analysis and system optimization. Its ability to accurately model and simulate hardware and software systems enables engineers to predict system behavior and identify potential performance issues.

- **Queuing Systems:** Simulating customer service centers to analyze wait times and optimize staffing levels.
- **Computing Performance:** Modeling CPU scheduling, memory management, and input/output processes to optimize resource allocation.

The capacity to create detailed and realistic models of these systems depends on Simula's built-in features for representing concurrent processes and handling events over time.

```
CLASS QueueSystem;
   QUEUE requestQueue;

   CLASS Request;
   PROCEDURE Process;
   BEGIN
      ! Code to process the request
   END;

   PROCEDURE Generate;
   BEGIN
      ! Code to generate a new request
      requestQueue.AddNewRequest();
   END;

   BEGIN
      requestQueue :- NEW QUEUE;
      ! Initialize the system
   END;
END;
```

Each of these applications underlines Simula's ability to handle complex scenarios that require robust modeling and simulation capabilities. The language's conceptual integrity and dependable performance continue to bolster its relevance in both academic and practical realms.

Chapter 2

Basic Syntax and Structure

This chapter delves into the foundational elements of Simula, detailing its basic syntax and program structure. It covers essential topics such as variable declarations, data types, comments, indentation, and spacing. Additionally, it explains how to construct statements, blocks, and control flows, as well as the usage of procedures and functions, providing a solid base for writing clear and effective Simula programs.

2.1 Basic Syntax of Simula

Understanding the basic syntax of Simula is crucial for writing effective programs. The syntax defines how code must be written and structured to be understood and executed by the Simula compiler. This section introduces the core components of Simula syntax, including keyword usage, variable naming conventions, and basic statement construction.

Simula is a high-level programming language that emphasizes object-oriented principles. It consists of a clear and readable structure, making it easier to learn and apply in various computational tasks.

Keywords and Identifiers

Simula keywords are reserved words that have a predefined meaning in the language. They must be written in lowercase and cannot be used as identifiers. Examples of keywords are begin, end, class, and if. Identifiers are names given to various programming elements such as variables, constants, and classes. Identifiers must start with a letter and can be followed by letters or digits. Special characters like '_', '$', '#', and '%' are not allowed in identifiers.

Case Sensitivity

Simula is case-insensitive, meaning that it does not differentiate between uppercase and lowercase letters. Therefore, Variable, variable, and VARIABLE are considered the same identifier.

Program Structure

A basic Simula program consists of a sequence of statements enclosed within a begin and end block. The main structure of a Simula program looks like this:

```
begin
    ! Variable declarations and definitions
    integer i;
    real x;

    ! Statements
    i := 10;
    x := 5.5;

    OutText('Hello, Simula!');
    OutImage;
end;
```

In this example, the program declares two variables i and x. It then assigns values to these variables and uses the built-in procedures OutText and OutImage to output text to the screen.

Comments

Comments in Simula are preceded by exclamation marks (!). Anything following the exclamation mark on the same line is considered a comment and is ignored by the compiler.

```
begin
    ! This is a comment
    integer a; ! Declare integer variable
    a := 5; ! Assign value to variable
end;
```

Variable Declarations

Variables must be declared before they are used in a program. The general syntax for declaring a variable is:

```
<type> <identifier>;
```

Multiple variables of the same type can be declared in one line separated by commas:

```
integer a, b, c;
real d, e;
```

Data Types

Simula includes several basic data types such as integer, real, boolean, and character. Each data type serves specific purposes and has its own syntax for declaration and usage.

Assignment Statements

Assignment statements are used to assign values to variables. The assignment operator in Simula is :=.

```
i := 5;
x := 3.14;
flag := true;
```

Basic Input and Output

Simula provides procedures for input and output operations. OutText is used to output text, and OutImage ensures the text is displayed properly. For reading input, procedures like InText and InReal are available.

Control Flow Statements

Simula supports several control flow statements, including if statements, while loops, and for loops. These statements control the execution flow based on conditions.

If Statement:

```
if i > 0 then
    OutText('i is positive');
else
    OutText('i is not positive');
```

While Loop:

```
integer count;
count := 0;
while count < 5 do
begin
    OutInt(count, 1);
    OutImage;
    count := count + 1;
end;
```

For Loop:

```
integer j;
```

```
for j := 1 step 1 until 10 do
begin
    OutInt(j, 1);
    OutImage;
end;
```

Adhering to these syntactical rules ensures that Simula programs are clear, consistent, and free of common errors.

2.2 Structure of a Simula Program

A Simula program follows a structured layout that is both logical and conducive to understanding the flow of operations. At its core, the structure is divided into the declaration part and the execution part. The declaration part encompasses all variable, constant, procedure, and function declarations, while the execution part comprises the statements that direct the execution flow of the program.

To grasp the Simula program structure, let's consider a simple example. Below, we present a basic Simula program that demonstrates these structural elements:

```
Begin
   Integer Age;
   Text Name;
   Real Salary;

   Age := 30;
   Name :- 'John Doe';
   Salary := 45000.50;

   OutText("Name: "); OutText(Name); OutImage;
   OutText("Age: "); OutInt(Age,4); OutImage;
   OutText("Salary: "); OutReal(Salary,12,2); OutImage;
End;
```

This program starts with the Begin keyword and ends with End. Everything between these keywords is the program's body.

The first segment within the body of the program consists of variable declarations. Variables Age, Name, and Salary are declared as types Integer, Text, and Real respectively. It is important to declare all variables before they are used in the program to provide the compiler with necessary type information.

```
   Integer Age;
   Text Name;
   Real Salary;
```

Following the declarations, the program assigns values to the variables using the assignment operator := for numeric and text concatenations. Initialization is a crucial step as it sets the initial values for variables, which prevents the program from accessing uninitialized data.

```
Age := 30;
Name :- 'John Doe';
Salary := 45000.50;
```

The program then proceeds with output statements. Here, OutText, OutInt, and OutReal are used to print the values of Name, Age, and Salary respectively. This sequence of statements forms the execution part of the program.

```
OutText("Name: "); OutText(Name); OutImage;
OutText("Age: "); OutInt(Age,4); OutImage;
OutText("Salary: "); OutReal(Salary,12,2); OutImage;
```

OutImage is a key function that outputs a new line, ensuring that subsequent output starts on a new line.

Another fundamental concept is the block structure. Simula, like other Algol-based languages, heavily utilizes block structures. Block structures in Simula allow grouping of declarations and statements, which can assist in managing the scope and lifetime of variables. Blocks are enclosed by Begin and End. Nested blocks are also permitted and are crucial for implementing structured programming practices.

```
Begin
   Integer X;
   X := 10;
   Begin
      Integer Y;
      Y := 20;
      X := X + Y;
   End;
   OutInt(X,4); OutImage;
End;
```

In this nested block example, Y is local to the inner block, while X is still accessible throughout the enclosing block. The value of X is modified within the inner block by adding Y to it.

Simula also encapsulates subprograms within its structure. Procedures and functions are declared within the program and can be invoked as needed. This modular approach enhances readability and facilitates code reuse. A procedure definition includes the keyword Procedure, followed by the procedure's name, parameters (if any), and a block of statements.

```
Procedure PrintDetails(N Text, A Integer, S Real);
Begin
   OutText("Name: "); OutText(N); OutImage;
   OutText("Age: "); OutInt(A,4); OutImage;
   OutText("Salary: "); OutReal(S,12,2); OutImage;
End;
```

Once declared, the PrintDetails procedure can be invoked within the main body of the program.

```
Begin
   Integer Age;
   Text Name;
   Real Salary;

   Age := 30;
   Name :- 'John Doe';
   Salary := 45000.50;

   PrintDetails(Name, Age, Salary);
End.
```

The invocation of PrintDetails passes the variables Name, Age, and Salary as arguments, demonstrating the modular nature of Simula programming.

Understanding and adhering to the structure of Simula programs is essential for writing coherent, maintainable, and effective code. Proper structuring facilitates the organization of more complex programs, enabling developers to manage variables, subprograms, and control flow with precision.

2.3 Comments and Documentation

Comments are essential in programming to convey the intentions of the code, facilitate debugging, and aid in future maintenance. Proper documentation within the source code is invaluable, providing useful insights to anyone reading the code, including the original programmer. Simula, like other programming languages, includes constructs for adding comments. In Simula, comments are initiated with the exclamation mark (!) symbol, and they extend to the end of the line.

Single-Line Comments

Single-line comments in Simula are straightforward. They begin with an !, and everything following this symbol on the same line is ignored by the compiler.

```
Begin
   Integer i;
   i := 10; ! This is a single-line comment explaining the assignment
End;
```

In the above example, the comment ! This is a single-line comment explaining the assignment provides a brief explanation of the code on that particular line. This unobtrusive way of adding comments makes it clear and does not interfere with the execution of the program.

Documentation Comments

While single-line comments are useful for brief explanations, documentation comments are crucial for providing detailed information about the functionality of specific sections of code, particularly for modules, procedures, and functions. Documentation comments may span multiple lines for clarity and thoroughness. While Simula does not have a specific syntax dedicated to multi-line comments as seen in some modern languages, you can achieve multi-line commenting by strategically placing single-line comments.

```
Begin
   Integer i, j;
   ! This block of code initializes two integers
   ! and assigns them values

   i := 10;
   j := 20;
   ! A procedure call to swap the values of i and j
   Swap(i, j); ! Function call that swaps variables
End;
```

Here, the comments provide documentation about the purpose of the code block and the individual operations within it.

Best Practices for Comments and Documentation

Effective commenting involves striking a balance between over-commenting and under-commenting. The goal is to ensure that comments add real value to the code understanding without cluttering it. Here are a few best practices to follow:

- **Comment Intent, Not Obvious Implementation**: Instead of commenting on what the code does in a redundant way, focus on why it is doing what it does. For example:

```
i := i + 1; ! Increment i by 1 <-- Avoid such redundant comments
i := i + 1; ! Ensure loop progresses to prevent infinite loop <-- Better
```

- **Update Comments with Code Changes**: When the functionality of the code changes, ensure that comments are updated to reflect these changes. Stale comments can be misleading.
- **Use Comments to Mark Sections**: Larger programs benefit from clearly marked sections. Comments can help to delineate different sections, such as initialization, processing, and cleanup.

```
Begin
    Integer i, j;

    ! Initialization Block
    i := 0;
    j := 10;

    ! Processing Block
    While i <= j Do Begin
        ! Additional logic here
    End;

    ! Cleanup Block
    ! (if any)
End;
```

Automated Documentation Tools

Automated documentation tools help to maintain consistency and completeness in documentation. While Simula does not have in-built support for generating documentation from comments as seen in languages like Java and Python, proper commenting practices followed with additional documentation tools can yield comprehensive documentation outcomes.

Example of Well-Commented Code

An example of concise and efficient documentation within a Simula program is shown below. This illustrates practical commenting practices that enhance readability and maintainability.

```
Begin
    Procedure Factorial(n); Integer n;
    ! This procedure calculates the factorial of an integer n
    Integer i, result;
    Begin
```

```
        result := 1;
        For i := 1 Step 1 Until n Do
        Begin
            result := result * i;
            ! Multiplying result with current value of i
        End;
        OutInteger(result);
        ! Output the result to the screen
    End;

    Integer x;
    Begin
        x := 5;
        ! Initialize x with 5
        Factorial(x);
        ! Compute and display factorial of x
    End;
End;
```

The preceding code provides a clean and comprehensive explanation of the factorial computation, facilitating understanding and ensuring maintainability.

Overall, effective use of comments and documentation within Simula programs is critical for conveying the logic, purpose, and details related to programmatic constructs. Practicing clear and concise commenting not only aids in the current understanding but also provides significant benefits for future code maintenance and review. By adhering to these guidelines, one enhances the quality and reliability of the codebase.

2.4 Indentation and Spacing

In Simula programming, the use of indentation and proper spacing is crucial for maintaining readability and structure. Although Simula, like many other high-level programming languages, does not enforce indentation rules, adhering to consistent indentation practices is a mark of good programming style.

Indentation helps to visually delineate the blocks of code, making it easier to follow the logical flow and structure of the program. Errors can be more easily identified and maintained code is accessible to other developers. For example, nested control structures and block statements are more readily comprehended with proper indentation.

Standard Indentation Practices: A typical approach is to use a fixed number of spaces (commonly 2 or 4) to indent the beginning of a new block of code. Tabs are discouraged as they can appear inconsistently across different text editors or IDEs.

For example, given the following block of code:

```
begin
  if condition then
    statement1;
    statement2;
  end if;
end;
```

Here, the block of code within the if statement is indented by two spaces, providing clear indication that these statements belong to the conditional block.

Spacing Around Operators and Keywords: Appropriate spacing around operators and keywords can substantially enhance the clarity of code. Spaces should be used around binary operators (e.g., +, -, *, /) and assignment operators (e.g., :=). This practice separates operators from operands, fostering better readability.

Examples are shown below:

```
a := b + c * d;
result := (x + y) / z;
```

Spacing After Commas and Colons: Similarly, spaces should follow commas in lists and colons for clarity. This practice is especially relevant in parameter lists and array declarations.

```
procedure example(a, b, c: integer);
begin
  ! code here
end;
```

Blank Lines: Blank lines play a significant role in separating logical sections of code. Functions, methods, and blocks within functions can be separated by blank lines to indicate a new segment, making the transition clear and structured. Blank lines should be used sparingly to avoid excessive whitespace which can make the code appear fragmented.

Indentation of Continuation Lines: When a single logical line of code is broken into multiple lines for readability, the continuation lines should be indented to align with the first line, clearly marking them as part of the same statement.

```
result := first_value +
          second_value -
          third_value;
```

Within control structures such as if...then...else and loops, each nested block should be consistently indented to reflect its hierarchy and scope. For instance, a nested if statement within a while loop should be indented to showcase the relationship between the two structures.

```
while condition loop
  if another_condition then
    perform_action;
  else
    perform_alternate_action;
  end if;
end loop;
```

Indenting Nested Procedures and Functions: Procedures and functions defined within another procedure should follow indentation rules similar to block statements. This practice ensures that nested constructs are visibly distinct.

```
procedure outer_procedure;
begin
  procedure inner_procedure;
  begin
    ! code here
  end;
end;
```

Properly formatted Simula code not only adheres to syntax rules but also follows methodological indentation and spacing practices. These methods affix a consistent format, improving both readability and maintainability, thus facilitating effective and error-free collaboration among programmers. The attention to detail in these areas distinguishes proficient Simula programmers and forms the foundation for coding practices in this high-level language.

2.5 Declaring Variables and Constants

In Simula, variables and constants are fundamental constructs that serve as the building blocks for data manipulation within your programs. Understanding the proper declaration and usage of variables and constants is essential for writing effective and error-free code.

Variables in Simula are declared using specific keywords followed by the variable's data type and name. The syntax for declaring a variable is straightforward, ensuring that the code remains readable and maintainable.

Constants, on the other hand, are values that remain unchanged throughout the execution of the program. These are declared using the const keyword and provide a way to define fixed values that cannot be modified once set.

Referencing Chapter Introduction, we will now delve deeper into these concepts:

Declaring Variables:

In Simula, variable declarations must specify the type of the variable. This ensures type safety and prevents unintended operations on incompatible data types.

```
integer i;
real x, y, z;
character ch;
boolean flag;
text msg;
```

In this example:

- i is declared as an integer.
- x, y, and z are declared as real numbers.
- ch is declared as a character.
- flag is declared as a boolean.
- msg is declared as a text variable.

Multiple variables of the same type can be declared in a single line, separated by commas.

Initializing Variables:

Variable initialization can occur at the time of declaration or separately within the program.

```
integer i := 10;
real x := 3.14;
character ch := 'A';
boolean flag := true;
text msg := 'Hello, Simula';
```

Alternatively, variables can be initialized later within the program's execution flow.

```
begin
    integer i;
    real x;
    i := 10;
    x := 3.14;
end;
```

Declaring Constants:

Constants in Simula are declared using the const keyword. Once declared, their values cannot be altered.

```
const integer MAX_STUDENTS := 50;
const real PI := 3.14159265;
const character NEWLINE := '\n';
const text GREETING := 'Welcome to Simula';
```

In this example:

- MAX_STUDENTS is a constant integer set to 50.
- PI is a constant real number representing the value of pi.
- NEWLINE is a constant character representing the newline character.
- GREETING is a constant text variable containing a welcome message.

Scope of Variables and Constants:

The scope of a variable or constant defines the region within the program where it is accessible. Simula variables and constants can have local or global scope.

Variables declared inside a block are local to that block and cannot be accessed outside of it.

```
begin
   integer i := 10;
   real x := 3.14;
   begin
      integer j := 5;
      x := x + j;
   end;
   ! Variable 'j' cannot be accessed here
end;
```

However, variables declared outside of any blocks are considered global and can be accessed from anywhere within the program.

```
integer i := 10;
begin
   real x := 3.14;
   x := x + i;
end;
```

Best Practices:

Throughout programming in Simula, adhering to best practices ensures code clarity and maintainability.

- Always initialize variables to prevent undefined behaviors.
- Use meaningful names for variables and constants to enhance code readability.
- Avoid using magic numbers; instead, declare them as constants with descriptive names.
- Limit the use of global variables to avoid unintentional side-effects across different parts of the program.

By consistently following these guidelines, you will produce robust and reliable Simula programs. Understanding and correctly applying variable and constant declarations is crucial for managing data effectively and preventing errors in your code.

2.6 Basic Data Types

The core aspect of any programming language lies in its ability to manage and manipulate various forms of data. In Simula, basic data types serve as the foundational building blocks for more complex structures. Understanding these basic types and their characteristics is essential for proficient coding. The primary data types in Simula include integer, real, boolean, character, and text.

Integer Data Type: The integer type in Simula is designed to store whole numbers, both positive and negative. Variables of this type are declared as follows:

```
integer n;
```

Here, n is declared as an integer variable. Operations such as addition, subtraction, multiplication, and division are inherently supported for integer variables.

Real Data Type: The real type is used to store floating-point numbers, which are numbers that contain decimal points. The declaration of a real variable looks like this:

```
real x, y;
```

In this example, x and y are real variables capable of holding decimal values. These variables support arithmetic operations inclusive of precision calculations.

Boolean Data Type: The Boolean type is used to represent truth values. It can only take two values, true or false. Boolean variables are often employed in control structures and logical operations. Here is the declaration syntax:

```
boolean flag;
```

Suppose we have a condition to validate:

```
flag := (x > y)
```

If x is greater than y, the flag will store the value true; otherwise, it will store false.

Character Data Type: The character type holds single characters, which are enclosed in single quotes in Simula. For example:

```
character letter;
letter := 'A';
```

In this code, letter is assigned the character 'A'. Characters can be manipulated and compared, allowing for various string operations.

Text Data Type: The text type in Simula is used for sequences of characters, or strings. String manipulation is a common requirement, and Simula provides robust support for it. Here is how you define a text variable:

```
text phrase;
phrase := "Hello World";
```

phrase is assigned the string "Hello World". Text operations include concatenation, extraction, and comparisons.

To summarize the usage of these types, consider the following self-contained program that demonstrates variable declarations, assignments, and basic operations:

```
begin
    integer a, b;
    real x, y;
    boolean result;
    character char1;
    text greeting;

    a := 10;
    b := 20;
```

```
    x := 10.5;
    y := 2.5;
    result := (a > b); -- result will be false
    char1 := 'S';
    greeting := "Welcome to Simula";

    -- Display values
    outtext(greeting); newline;
    outreal(x / y); newline;
    outinteger(a + b);
end
```

The output of this program is:

```
Welcome to Simula
4.200000
30
```

In the example provided, each of the basic data types is employed in a simple, intuitive manner. The outtext, outreal, and outinteger functions are used to output text, real numbers, and integers, respectively, demonstrating how different data types can be utilized and displayed effectively in Simula programs. Understanding these basic data types and their operations sets the foundation for mastering more complex data structures in Simula.

2.7 Operators and Expressions

Operators and expressions form the core of any programming language, enabling manipulation and computation of data. In Simula, operators are symbols that denote operations to be performed on operands, and expressions are combinations of variables, constants, and operators that compute values.

Simula supports several types of operators, including arithmetic, relational, logical, and assignment operators. Each type of operator serves specific purposes and follows distinct rules within expressions.

Arithmetic Operators: Arithmetic operators perform mathematical operations on numerical data types. The standard arithmetic operators in Simula include:

- Addition: +
- Subtraction: -
- Multiplication: *

- Division: /
- Modulus: %

Here is an example of using arithmetic operators in a Simula program:

```
BEGIN
  INTEGER i, j, result;
  i := 10;
  j := 3;
  result := i + j; (* Adds i and j *)
  result := i - j; (* Subtracts j from i *)
  result := i * j; (* Multiplies i and j *)
  result := i / j; (* Divides i by j *)
  result := i MOD j; (* Modulus operation *)
END;
```

Relational Operators: Relational operators compare two values and return a boolean result, indicating whether the comparison is true or false. These operators are essential for control flow constructs.

The relational operators in Simula are:

- Equality: =
- Inequality: /=
- Greater than: >
- Less than: <
- Greater than or equal to: >=
- Less than or equal to: <=

Example of relational operators usage:

```
BEGIN
  INTEGER a, b;
  BOOLEAN result;
  a := 5;
  b := 8;
  result := (a = b); (* Checks if a is equal to b *)
  result := (a /= b); (* Checks if a is not equal to b *)
  result := (a > b); (* Checks if a is greater than b *)
  result := (a < b); (* Checks if a is less than b *)
  result := (a >= b); (* Checks if a is greater than or equal to b *)
  result := (a <= b); (* Checks if a is less than or equal to b *)
END;
```

Logical Operators: Logical operators are used to combine or invert boolean expressions. They are fundamental in constructing complex conditions.

The logical operators in Simula are:

- Logical AND: AND
- Logical OR: OR
- Logical NOT: NOT

Example of logical operators in action:

```
BEGIN
  BOOLEAN x, y, result;
  x := TRUE;
  y := FALSE;
  result := x AND y; (* Logical AND between x and y *)
  result := x OR y; (* Logical OR between x and y *)
  result := NOT x; (* Logical NOT of x *)
END;
```

Assignment Operators: Assignment operators are used to assign values to variables. The primary assignment operator in Simula is the assignment statement, denoted by :=.

Example of assignment operations:

```
BEGIN
  INTEGER x, y;
  x := 15; (* Assigns value 15 to x *)
  y := x; (* Assigns value of x to y *)
  x := x + 1; (* Increment x by 1 *)
  y := y - 5; (* Decrement y by 5 *)
END;
```

Expressions: An expression in Simula is a combination of variables, constants, and operators that evaluates to a value. Expressions can be simple or complex, consisting of multiple sub-expressions.

Example of complex expressions:

```
BEGIN
  INTEGER a, b, c, result;
  a := 10;
  b := 5;
  c := 3;
  result := (a + b) * c - (a / b) + a MOD c;
END;
```

Proper understanding and utilization of operators and expressions is fundamental to proficient Simula programming.

2.8 Statements and Blocks

In Simula programming, the concept of statements and blocks forms the backbone of program execution. Understanding how to write effective statements and organize them into cohesive blocks is essential for creating logical, readable, and maintainable code.

A **statement** in Simula is a single unit of execution that expresses some action to be performed. Statements can be as simple as an assignment or as complex as calling a function with multiple parameters. Here is an example of a simple assignment statement:

```
x := 5
```

This statement assigns the value 5 to the variable x. The assignment operator in Simula is :=.

A **block** in Simula is a group of statements enclosed within the keywords begin and end. Blocks allow for the grouping of related statements, thus enabling structured programming. Here is an example of a block:

```
begin
  x := 5;
  y := x + 10;
  write(x, y)
end
```

This block first assigns the value 5 to x, then adds 10 to x and assigns the result to y, and finally writes the values of x and y. Each statement within the block is separated by a semicolon (;).

Statement Types

Several types of statements are used in Simula, each serving a specific purpose:

Assignment Statements: Assign values to variables or constants.

```
a := 10;
b := a + 5
```

Procedure Call Statements: Invoke procedures defined previously in the program.

```
ProcessData(a, b)
```

Control Statements: Direct the flow of execution, such as if, for, while, and switch.

```
if x > 0 then
  write('Positive number')
else
  write('Non-positive number')
```

Input/Output Statements: Read data from the input or write data to the output.

```
infile :- open('data.txt');
read(infile, x);
write(outfile, x)
```

Block Structure

The structure of blocks enhances the modularity and readability of programs. A block begins with the keyword begin and ends with end. Here is an example of a block containing nested blocks:

```
begin
  x := 5;
  begin
    y := 10;
    z := x + y;
    write(z)
  end;
  x := x * 2;
  write(x)
end
```

Compound Statements

In a well-designed program, multiple statements often need to be executed together under certain conditions; this is managed using compound statements. A compound statement is a set of statements grouped together in a block, executed sequentially. For example:

```
if condition then
  begin
    performTask1();
    performTask2();
    performTask3()
  end
```

This code demonstrates a conditional statement where, if the condition is true, three tasks (performTask1, performTask2, and performTask3) will be executed sequentially within the block.

Nesting of Blocks

Nesting blocks within other blocks is a common practice to handle complex logical structures. Each nested block should be properly indented and enclosed with its own begin and end statements for clarity:

```
begin
  statement1;
  begin
    statement2;
    begin
      statement3
    end;
    statement4
  end;
  statement5
end
```

In the above example, statement3 is nested two levels deep. Proper indentation and clear block boundaries help in maintaining the readability of the code.

Practical Example

Consider a practical example that demonstrates the combined usage of statements and blocks in a Simula program:

```
begin
  integer x, y, sum;
  x := 10;
  y := 20;

  begin
    integer square;
    square := x * x;
    write('Square of x: ', square)
  end;

  sum := x + y;
  write('Sum of x and y: ', sum)
end
```

In this example, we declare three integer variables x, y, and sum. We then assign values to x and y. Within a nested block, we declare another integer variable square, compute the square of x, and output the result. Finally, we calculate the sum of x and y and write the result.

This demonstrates how to utilize statements and blocks effectively to structure Simula programs. Proper organization of statements into blocks yields more readable and maintainable code, crucial for complex program development. By adhering to the syntax rules and logical structuring principles, programmers can create robust applications that leverage the full capabilities of Simula.

2.9 Working with Procedures and Functions

Understanding how to effectively utilize procedures and functions in Simula is crucial for writing modular, maintainable, and efficient code. Procedures and functions allow for the encapsulation of functionality, making programs easier to read and debug.

A procedure in Simula is a subroutine designed to perform a specific task. Similar to a procedure, a function can also return a value. Both constructs promote code reuse and better organization.

Defining Procedures

A procedure in Simula is defined using the procedure keyword, followed by the procedure name, parameter list, local declarations, and the body of the procedure.

```
procedure ExampleProcedure(a, b);
  integer a, b; ! Local parameters
begin
  integer sum; ! Local variable
  sum := a + b;
  OutText("Sum: "); OutFix(sum, 1); ! Output the result
  OutImage;
end;
```

In this example, ExampleProcedure takes two integer parameters, a and b, calculates their sum, and outputs the result. Key aspects include:

- Local Parameters: Variables passed to the procedure.
- Local Declarations: Variables declared within the procedure.
- Procedure Body: Code executed when the procedure is called.

To call this procedure within another part of your Simula program, use the following syntax:

```
ExampleProcedure(5, 10);
```

Defining Functions

Functions in Simula resemble procedures but include a return type and return a value. They begin with the procedure keyword followed by the function name, parameter list, local declarations, return type, and body.

```
procedure Sum(a, b); integer Sum;
  integer a, b; ! Parameters
begin
  Sum := a + b; ! Return value
end;
```

Here, Sum is a function that takes two integers and returns their sum. The return type is specified after the parameter list.

Functions are used in expressions and other constructs:

```
integer result;
result := Sum(5, 10);
```

Parameter Passing

Simula supports different methods for passing parameters: by value or by reference. By default, parameters are passed by value, meaning the procedure works with copies of the arguments. To pass parameters by reference, allowing the procedure to modify the original variables, use the REF keyword.

By value example:

```
procedure IncrementByValue(x);
  integer x;
begin
  x := x + 1;
end;

integer a;
a := 5;
IncrementByValue(a);
OutInt(a, 1); ! Outputs 5, because x is a copy
OutImage;
```

By reference example:

```
procedure IncrementByReference(REF(x));
  integer x;
begin
  x := x + 1;
end;

integer a;
a := 5;
IncrementByReference(a);
OutInt(a, 1); ! Outputs 6, because x refers to a
OutImage;
```

Recursion

Simula supports recursive procedures and functions, which call themselves either directly or indirectly. Recursion must include a base case to terminate the recursive calls, avoiding infinite loops.

Example of a recursive function to compute factorial:

```
procedure Factorial(n); integer Factorial;
  integer n;
begin
  if n = 0 then
```

```
    Factorial := 1
  else
    Factorial := n * Factorial(n - 1);
end;
```

Usage:

```
integer fact;
fact := Factorial(5);
OutInt(fact, 1); ! Outputs 120
OutImage;
```

Using Standard Functions

Simula includes several standard, predefined functions that simplify common operations. Examples include:

- abs(x): Returns the absolute value of x.
- sqrt(x): Computes the square root of x.
- sine(x), cosine(x), exp(x), and ln(x): Perform trigonometric and exponential calculations.

Example usage:

```
integer number;
real root;

number := 16;
root := sqrt(number);
OutReal(root, 1, 2); ! Outputs 4.00
OutImage;
```

Proper use of procedures and functions not only aids in code clarity but also enhances the performance and debug-ability of Simula programs. Understanding how to effectively implement these constructs lays the groundwork for creating robust software solutions.

2.10 Understanding Simula's Control Flow

Control flow in Simula determines the logical sequence in which statements and instructions are executed. Understanding control flow is critical for mastering Simula programming, as it enables developers to write programs that implement complex decision-making and iteration processes.

There are several fundamental control flow constructs in Simula that include conditionals, loops, and jumps. Each of these constructs provides a different mechanism for controlling the execution path based on specific conditions or patterns.

Conditional Statements

Conditional statements allow a program to make decisions based on certain conditions. In Simula, the primary conditional statement is the if statement, which evaluates a boolean expression and executes a block of code if the expression evaluates to true.

```
if condition then
begin
    // statements to execute if condition is true
end;
```

If the condition is false, the code block is skipped. An optional else clause can be used to execute an alternative block of code when the condition is false.

```
if condition then
begin
    // statements to execute if condition is true
end
else
begin
    // statements to execute if condition is false
end;
```

Example:

```
integer: x;
x := 10;

if x > 5 then
begin
    outtext("x is greater than 5");
end
else
begin
    outtext("x is 5 or less");
end;
```

The above code uses an if-else statement to check if x is greater than 5 and prints an appropriate message.

Loops

Loops are used to execute a block of code repeatedly based on a condition. Simula provides several looping constructs, including while, for, and repeat statements.

The while loop executes a block of code as long as the given condition is true.

```
while condition do
begin
    // statements to execute while condition is true
end;
```

Example:

```
integer: i;
i := 1;

while i <= 5 do
begin
    outint(i, 1); // outputs the value of i
    i := i + 1;
end;
```

In this example, the loop prints numbers from 1 to 5.

The for loop is used to iterate over a range of values.

```
for i := start to end do
begin
    // statements to execute for each value of i
end;
```

Example:

```
for i := 1 to 5 do
begin
    outint(i, 1); // outputs the value of i
end;
```

This for loop also prints numbers from 1 to 5, similar to the while loop example.

The repeat loop is similar to the while loop but with a crucial difference: the repeat loop guarantees that the code block executes at least once, as the condition is evaluated after the block has been executed.

```
repeat
    // statements to execute
until condition;
```

Example:

```
integer: j;
j := 1;

repeat
    outint(j, 1); // outputs the value of j
    j := j + 1;
until j > 5;
```

The above repeat loop also prints numbers from 1 to 5.

Jump Statements

Jump statements provide ways to unconditionally transfer control to another part of the program. The most commonly used jump statement in Simula is goto.

```
goto label;

....

label:
    // code to execute
```

While goto can be useful in certain scenarios, its usage is generally discouraged in favor of structured programming constructs like loops and conditionals, as excessive use of goto can lead to complex and difficult-to-maintain code.

Example:

```
integer: k;
k := 1;

loopStart:
if k <= 5 then
begin
    outint(k, 1); // outputs the value of k
    k := k + 1;
    goto loopStart;
end;
```

In this example, the goto statement creates a loop that prints numbers from 1 to 5.

Understanding and using these control flow constructs efficiently is essential for writing effective and efficient Simula programs. Each construct has its purpose, and the appropriate construct should be chosen based on the specific logic requirements of the program.

Chapter 3

Data Types and Variables

This chapter focuses on the various data types and variable management in Simula. It explores primitive and composite data types, user-defined data types, and the process of declaring and initializing variables. The chapter also addresses variable scope, lifetime, type conversion, constants, enumerated types, arrays, lists, records, and structures, providing a comprehensive understanding of how data is represented and manipulated in Simula.

3.1 Overview of Data Types

In any programming language, understanding data types is paramount for the effective and error-free manipulation of data. Simula, being one of the pioneering programming languages and a precursor to modern object-oriented languages, provides a robust and versatile type system. This section presents a detailed discussion on the various data types in Simula, laying the groundwork for deeper exploration in subsequent sections.

Data types in Simula can broadly be categorized into two major groups: **primitive data types** and **composite data types**. Additionally, Simula allows the creation of **user-defined data types**, which can cater to specific needs of a program.

Primitive data types encompass the basic building blocks that are directly supported by the language, such as integers, real numbers, characters, and Boolean values. These types typically map to the fundamental data types provided by the underlying hardware, thus allowing efficient storage and computation.

Composite data types are more complex structures that are constructed using primitive data types. These include arrays, lists, records, and structures. Composite data types enable the organization and manipulation of collections of data in a cohesive manner.

User-defined data types provide the flexibility to create new types that are derived from existing ones, allowing programmers to model the real-world entities more accurately within the constraints and capabilities of Simula.

The following definitions and guidelines are essential when discussing data types in Simula:

- **Type Safety**: Ensures that variables are only assigned values compatible with their declared data type. This helps in avoiding unexpected behaviors during program execution.
- **Type Conversion**: Refers to the method of converting one data type into another. This process must adhere to the rules defined by the language to maintain type integrity.
- **Type Declaration**: Specifies the data type of a variable at the time it is defined, facilitating the compiler to allocate appropriate storage and ensuring type-safe operations.
- **Scope and Lifetime**: These concepts define the visibility and duration of a variable within a program. Scoping rules determine where a variable can be accessed, whereas the lifetime refers to the period during which the variable exists in memory.

Consider the following Simula code snippet, which declares variables of different primitive data types:

```
begin
  integer i;
  real r;
  character c;
  boolean b;

  i := 42;
  r := 3.14159;
  c := 'A';
  b := true;

  outtext("Integer i: "); outint(i, 4); outimage;
```

```
  outtext("Real r: "); outreal(r, 8, 5); outimage;
  outtext("Character c: "); outchar(c); outimage;
  outtext("Boolean b: "); outbool(b); outimage;
end;
```

The execution of the above code would produce the following output:

```
Integer i:   42
Real r: 3.14159
Character c: A
Boolean b: true
```

Simula's extensive type system also supports the definition of constants, enumerated types, and other forms of type identification, which enhance program readability and maintenance.

Constants are immutable values which means they cannot be changed once they are defined. Constants are typically defined at the beginning of a code block. Consider the following example:

```
begin
  integer const MAX_LENGTH = 100;
  real const PI = 3.14159;

  outtext("Max Length: "); outint(MAX_LENGTH, 4); outimage;
  outtext("PI: "); outreal(PI, 8, 5); outimage;
end;
```

The output of this code would be:

```
Max Length:  100
PI: 3.14159
```

Simula's **enumerated types** provide a way to define a variable that can take one of several predefined integral values, greatly enhancing the clarity of code that involves sets of related constants. Here's an example:

```
begin
  type colors = (red, green, blue, yellow);
  colors color;

  color := red;
  outtext("Color: "); outfix(color, 1); outimage;
end;
```

The syntax and semantics of enumerated types allow for intuitive and error-free coding practices, especially when dealing with variables that take on a limited set of possible values.

In preparation for upcoming sections, it is essential to grasp these foundational concepts since they underpin more complex discussions surrounding Simula's advanced data structures and memory management techniques. Understanding the interplay between primitive data types, composite data types, and user-defined types forms the backbone of effective Simula programming.

3.2 Primitive Data Types

Primitive data types in Simula are the basic building blocks for data manipulation within the language. They enable the representation of simple values such as numbers, characters, and logical constructs. Understanding these data types is crucial for effective programming, as they form the foundation upon which more complex data structures and operations are built. Simula includes several primitive data types such as integer, real, boolean, and character.

The integer type in Simula is used for whole numbers. Integers are essential for performing discrete mathematics, indexing arrays, and controlling iterative processes. In Simula, integers are typically represented in binary form, and the range of values depends on the system architecture. Here is an example of integer variable declaration and initialization:

```
integer x;
x := 10;
```

The real type represents floating-point numbers. These numbers include a fractional component, allowing for precise representation of values such as 3.14 or -0.001. Floating-point arithmetic is essential in simulations and mathematical computations involving real-world measurements. Here is an example of real variable declaration and initialization:

```
real y;
y := 3.14;
```

Boolean variables, declared with the boolean type, are used to represent truth values. They can only take the values true or false and are critical for flow control in programs, enabling conditional execution of code through constructs such as if statements and while loops. Here is an example of boolean variable declaration and initialization:

```
boolean isOpen;
isOpen := true;
```

The character type is used to represent individual characters. Characters are typically enclosed in single quotes, such as 'A' or '3'. This data type is fundamental for text processing and manipulation. Here is an example of character variable declaration and initialization:

```
character ch;
ch := 'A';
```

Primitive data types in Simula also support a variety of operations. For integers and reals, arithmetic operations include addition (+), subtraction (-), multiplication (*), and division (/). Here is an example of using these operations with integer and real types:

```
integer a, b, result;
real num1, num2, sum;

a := 5;
b := 2;
result := a + b; // result is 7

num1 := 1.5;
num2 := 2.5;
sum := num1 + num2; // sum is 4.0
```

Logical operations can be performed on boolean values using operators such as and, or, and not. These operations are pivotal in constructing complex conditional statements. Here is an example demonstrating logical operations with boolean variables:

```
boolean flag1, flag2, result;

flag1 := true;
flag2 := false;

result := flag1 and flag2; // result is false
result := flag1 or flag2; // result is true
result := not flag2; // result is true
```

Characters can be compared and manipulated similarly to integers. Common operations include comparisons using relational operators (e.g., =, <>, <, >), and transformations such as converting to upper or lower case. Here is an example of character comparison and transformation:

```
character c1, c2;
boolean comparisonResult;

c1 := 'a';
c2 := 'A';

// Comparison
comparisonResult := c1 = c2; // comparisonResult is false

// Transformation to upper case (assuming a built-in function ToUpper)
character cUpper;
cUpper := ToUpper(c1); // cUpper is 'A'
```

Primitive data types also support type-specific operations. For instance, arithmetic overflow and underflow conditions need to be handled carefully, particularly with integer types. Simula provides mechanisms to detect and manage these scenarios to ensure program stability and accuracy.

Overall, mastering the use of primitive data types in Simula is fundamental for constructing robust and efficient programs. Proper understanding and utilization of these types enable the programmer to effectively represent, process, and manipulate basic data elements, laying a solid foundation for more advanced programming concepts.

3.3 Composite Data Types

Composite data types are essential in Simula programming as they allow the combination of multiple primitive data types into a single, more complex entity. These data types encapsulate data and provide the functionality to operate on that data efficiently. Simula, being one of the first object-oriented languages, provides robust support for composite data types through arrays, lists, records, and classes.

Arrays in Simula are collections of elements of the same type, allowing indexed access to store and retrieve data quickly. Arrays can be declared with fixed or dynamic sizes. The elements within an array can be of any primitive or composite data type.

```
Integer ArrayExample(1:10); ! Declaring an integer array with 10 elements
ArrayExample(1) := 42; ! Assigning the value 42 to the first element
```

In the example above, ArrayExample is an array of integers indexed from 1 to 10. The value 42 is assigned to the first element. Accessing array elements is straightforward by specifying the index within parentheses.

Dynamic arrays are more flexible, allowing the size of the array to be determined at runtime. This capability is especially useful in scenarios where the data size cannot be determined in advance.

```
! Dynamic array declaration and initialization
Integer n;
n := 20;
Integer DynamicArray(1:n);
DynamicArray(1) := 100;
```

In this case, the size of DynamicArray is set to 20 at runtime, based on the value of n. The first element of the array is then assigned the value 100.

Lists in Simula offer another form of composite data types. These are particularly useful for collections of elements where the size may change during execution. Simula provides linked lists, which are dynamically expandable and manageable via pointers.

```
REF (Link) Head, Current, Temp;
Head :- New Link; ! Create the head of the linked list
Head.Value := 10; ! Initialize the first element
Current := Head; ! Set the current pointer to head
Temp :- New Link; ! Create a new link element
Temp.Value := 20; ! Initialize the new link element
Current.Next := Temp; ! Link the new element to the list
```

In this example, a linked list is created with two elements. The Link class is assumed to have two fields: Value for storing data and Next for pointing to the next element. This extensible nature of linked lists makes them ideal for scenarios requiring frequent insertion and deletion operations.

Records in Simula allow grouping of heterogeneous data types into a single structured entity. This concept is similar to struct in other programming languages, providing a way to logically organize data.

```
! Declaration of a record
Begin
   Class Person;
      Text Name;
      Integer Age;
   End;

   REF (Person) p;
   p :- New Person;
   p.Name := "Simula";
   p.Age := 1967;
   OutText("Name: "); OutText(p.Name); OutImage;
   OutText("Age: "); OutInt(p.Age, 0); OutImage;
End;
```

Here, a Person record with Name and Age fields is defined. An object p of type Person is created and initialized. The record fields are accessed using the dot operator. This feature provides a clear and organized representation of complex data structures.

Classes in Simula further extend the capability of composite data types by introducing object-oriented principles. A class definition in Simula acts as a blueprint for creating objects, encapsulating both data and methods to operate on that data.

```
! Class declaration
```

```
Begin
  Class ComplexNumber(Float re, im); ! Class with constructor for complex numbers
    Float re, im; ! Fields for real and imaginary parts
    Procedure Print;
    Begin
      OutReal(re, 6, 2); OutText(" + "); OutReal(im, 6, 2); OutText("i");
    End;
  End;

  REF (ComplexNumber) c;
  c :- New ComplexNumber(3.0, 4.5); ! Creating an instance of the class
  c.Print; ! Calling the Print method
End;
```

In this example, ComplexNumber is a class with fields re and im for real and imaginary parts, respectively. It includes the Print method to output the complex number in a specific format. The power of classes enables encapsulation, inheritance, and polymorphism, fundamental principles of object-oriented programming.

These composite data types in Simula offer flexibility and power, making it easier to manage and manipulate complex datasets. Understanding and utilizing these constructs effectively is crucial for mastering Simula programming.

3.4 User-Defined Data Types

User-defined data types in Simula enable programmers to create complex data structures that are tailored to the specific requirements of their applications. These data types enhance the language's expressive power and provide more abstraction, improving code readability and maintainability. Let's delve into defining and utilizing user-defined data types in Simula.

Classes and Objects

Simula, being one of the first object-oriented languages, supports user-defined data types primarily through classes. A class in Simula is a blueprint from which objects are created. An object is an instance of a class and comprises both data and procedures to manipulate that data.

Here is an example of defining a class in Simula:

```
Class Person;
Begin
  Text Name;
  Integer Age;

  ! Procedure to initialize the attributes;
```

```
  Procedure Init(NameText; Text; AgeValue; Integer);
  Begin
    Name:= NameText;
    Age:= AgeValue;
  End;

  ! Procedure to display the data;
  Procedure Display;
  Begin
    OutText("Name: ");
    OutText(Name);
    OutImage;
    OutText("Age: ");
    OutInt(Age,1);
    OutImage;
  End;
End;
```

In the example above, Person is a user-defined data type with two attributes: Name and Age. The Init procedure initializes these attributes, and the Display procedure outputs the values of these attributes.

To create an object of the Person class and use its methods, you would write:

```
Begin
  Ref(Person) p;
  ! Create an instance of the Person class;
  New p.Init("John Doe", 30);
  ! Call the Display method;
  p.Display;
End;
```

Inheritance and Subclasses

Simula supports inheritance, allowing new classes to inherit attributes and methods from existing classes. This promotes code reuse and the organization of related classes in a hierarchical manner.

Consider the following example where we create a subclass Employee that inherits from Person:

```
Class Employee(Person);
Begin
  Text Position;
  Real Salary;

  ! Procedure to initialize the attributes;
  Procedure Init(NameText; Text; AgeValue; Integer; Pos; Text; Sal; Real);
  Begin
    ! Call parent Init method;
    (Person).Init(NameText, AgeValue);
    Position := Pos;
    Salary := Sal;
  End;
```

```
  ! Procedure to display the data;
  Procedure Display;
  Begin
    (Person).Display;
    OutText("Position: ");
    OutText(Position);
    OutImage;
    OutText("Salary: ");
    OutReal(Salary,1,2);
    OutImage;
  End;
End;
```

In this example, Employee inherits from Person. It introduces new attributes (Position and Salary) and overrides the Display method to include these additional attributes. The Init method in the subclass calls the Init method of the parent class Person to initialize the inherited attributes.

To use the Employee class, you would write:

```
Begin
  Ref(Employee) e;
  ! Create an instance of the Employee class;
  New e.Init("Alice Smith", 28, "Engineer", 75000.00);
  ! Call the Display method;
  e.Display;
End;
```

Records and Structures

Although Simula mainly uses classes for user-defined data types, records and structures are also significant. These are essential for representing data that can be grouped logically while maintaining simplicity.

An example of defining a record in Simula:

```
Record Address;
Begin
  Text Street;
  Text City;
  Text State;
  Integer ZipCode;
End;
```

Here, Address is a user-defined type representing a record with four fields: Street, City, State, and ZipCode.

To use an Address record, you would write:

```
Begin
  Ref(Address) addr;
  ! Allocate space for an Address record;
```

```
  New addr;
  ! Initialize the fields;
  addr.Street := "Main St";
  addr.City := "Springfield";
  addr.State := "IL";
  addr.ZipCode := 62701;

  ! Display the address;
  OutText("Address: ");
  OutText(addr.Street);
  OutText(", ");
  OutText(addr.City);
  OutText(", ");
  OutText(addr.State);
  OutText(" ");
  OutInt(addr.ZipCode,5);
  OutImage;
End;
```

Overall, user-defined data types in Simula facilitate the creation of more complex and modular programs. They embody one of the key tenets of object-oriented programming, which is to create reusable and organized code structures. By defining classes, inheriting them, and using records and structures, we can efficiently model real-world entities and relationships within our programs.

3.5 Declaring and Initializing Variables

In Simula, the declaration and initialization of variables are foundational processes that allow for precise control over the data your programs manipulate. Understanding the distinction between declaration and initialization, the syntax rules, and best practices is crucial for effective coding. This section expands on these concepts to promote clarity and proficiency in variable management.

In Simula, the general form for variable declaration follows the syntax:

```
type variable_name;
```

Here, type must be one of the predefined types, such as integer, real, boolean, among others. The variable_name is a valid identifier for the variable.

For example, suppose we want to declare an integer variable named count and a real variable named temperature. This is achieved through:

```
integer count;
real temperature;
```

Initialization can be performed at declaration or separately. Initialization of variables at the declaration point is often preferred to ensure that variables have defined states before usage. To initialize the integer variable count with a value of 0 and the real variable temperature with a value of 36.6, we use:

```
integer count := 0;
real temperature := 36.6;
```

Initialization separately from declaration is also supported:

```
integer count;
real temperature;
count := 0;
temperature := 36.6;
```

To emphasize the significance of combining declaration and initialization, consider the potential issues with uninitialized variables, which can result in unpredictable behavior and outcomes. The consistent practice of initializing upon declaration mitigates such risks and promotes robustness.

Simula supports multiple variable declarations in a single statement, delineated by commas:

```
integer i, j, k;
real x := 0.0, y := 1.1, z;
```

Here, i, j, and k are integer variables, while x, y, and z are real variables, with x and y initialized to 0.0 and 1.1, respectively. z remains uninitialized.

Variables can be declared within procedures to ensure they are used only within the procedures' scope:

```
procedure exampleProcedure;
real a, b;
begin
    a := 5.5;
    b := a * 2;
end;
```

In this example, a and b are local to exampleProcedure and are not accessible outside its scope.

Pointer variables in Simula deserve special mention due to their importance in object-oriented aspects. The syntax to declare and initialize pointer variables involves the keyword ref. Consider the declaration of a pointer to an integer object intObj:

```
ref(integer) intPtr;
```

```
intPtr :- new integer(42);
```

Here, intPtr is a reference variable pointing to a newly allocated integer object initialized to 42. The assignment operator for reference variables is :-, distinguishing it from the := operator used for primitive type variables.

The importance of not just declaring but also initializing variables within Simula becomes clear when considering structured programming principles and the language's emphasis on eliminating unintended behavior through proactive resource management.

Effective variable management is enforced through practice and familiarity with scope rules, initialization patterns, and memory management strategies facilitated by the language. Understanding these foundations solidifies the ability to produce clean, error-free, and efficient code in Simula.

3.6 Variable Scope and Lifetime

In Simula, understanding the scope and lifetime of variables is essential for efficient programming and effective memory management. The scope of a variable refers to the region of the program where the variable is accessible, while the lifetime of a variable denotes the duration for which the variable exists in memory.

Scope in Simula can be broadly classified into two categories: local scope and global scope. A variable's scope determines its visibility and thus influences how and where it can be used within the code.

- **Local Scope:** Variables declared within a block, such as a procedure or a function, have a local scope. These variables are only accessible within the block where they are declared.
- **Global Scope:** Variables declared outside of any block or procedure are global. They are accessible from any point in the program after their declaration.

Consider the following Simula code example demonstrating different scopes:

```
begin
    integer i; ! Global scope
    i := 10;
```

```
    procedure example;
    begin
        integer j; ! Local scope
        j := 5;
        outint(j, 1); ! Accessing local variable j
    end example;

    example;
    outint(i, 1); ! Accessing global variable i
end
```

In the above code, i is a global variable, accessible within the entire program block. Conversely, j is a local variable confined to the example procedure.

Besides scope, the lifetime of a variable is another critical aspect. The lifetime of local and global variables differs significantly:

- **Local Variables:** The lifetime of local variables is limited to the execution duration of the block in which they are defined. As soon as the block's execution completes, local variables are destroyed, and the memory allocated to them is released.
- **Global Variables:** Global variables, on the other hand, have a lifetime equal to the program's run time. They exist for the duration of the entire program execution.

The following example illustrates variable lifetimes:

```
begin
    integer globalVar; ! Global variable has program's lifetime
    globalVar := 10;

    procedure example;
    begin
        integer localVar; ! Local variable has block's lifetime
        localVar := 5;
        outint(localVar, 1); ! Accessible within this block
    end example;

    example;
    outint(globalVar, 1); ! Accessible throughout the program
end
```

In the above scenario, globalVar is accessible and maintains its value throughout the entire program execution. In contrast, localVar is only accessible within the procedure example, and its memory is deallocated immediately after exiting the procedure.

Understanding the interplay between variable scope and lifetime is vital for managing memory effectively and avoiding issues such as memory leaks and unintended variable shadowing. Variable shadowing occurs when a local variable shares a name with a global variable, causing the local variable to override the global one within its scope.

Here's an example to demonstrate shadowing:

```
begin
    integer x; ! Global x
    x := 10;

    procedure example;
    begin
        integer x; ! Local x shadows global x
        x := 5;
        outint(x, 1); ! Outputs 5 (local x)
    end example;

    example;
    outint(x, 1); ! Outputs 10 (global x)
end
```

When the example procedure is called, the local variable x within the procedure scope shadows the global variable x. When x is accessed within the procedure, it refers to the local instance, leaving the global x unchanged.

To conclude, accurate comprehension of variable scope and lifetime plays a pivotal role in mastering Simula programming. This knowledge aids in writing clean, efficient, and error-free code by ensuring appropriate variable accessibility and memory management throughout program execution.

3.7 Type Conversion and Casting

Type conversion and casting are essential operations in Simula programming, allowing for the manipulation and interaction of variables with different data types. Understanding these processes is crucial for ensuring that programs function as expected, especially when performing arithmetic operations, comparisons, and when interfacing with different APIs or legacy codebase.

Type conversion refers to the process of converting a variable from one data type to another. There are two main types of conversions: implicit and explicit.

Implicit Conversion: Also known as coercion, implicit conversion is automatically performed by the compiler when a mixed data type operation occurs. For example, when an integer is used in a context requiring a real number, the integer can be implicitly converted to a real number. Implicit conversions are generally safe as they follow the established rules of the language without loss of data or precision.

```
begin
    integer i;
    real r;
    i := 10;
    r := i; -- Implicit conversion from integer to real
    outtext("The value of r is "); outreal(r); outimage;
end;
```

When executed, this program segment will convert the integer variable i to a real number before assigning it to the real variable r. The output will be:

```
The value of r is 10.0
```

Explicit Conversion: Also known as casting, explicit conversion is carried out manually by the programmer. Explicit conversions require a deliberate action to change the data type of a variable, providing greater control over the conversion process. This method is essential when dealing with conversions that may result in data loss or require specific handling to ensure accuracy and program stability.

In Simula, casting is typically done using specific functions or by leveraging a predefined conversion syntax. For instance, to convert a real number to an integer, thus truncating the decimal part, the built-in integer() function is used:

```
begin
    real r;
    integer i;
    r := 10.75;
    i := integer(r); -- Explicit conversion from real to integer
    outtext("The value of i is "); outint(i); outimage;
end;
```

The output of this program will demonstrate how the real value is truncated during the conversion:

```
The value of i is 10
```

Type conversions, whether implicit or explicit, adhere to certain rules to manage various data types, such as integer, real, character, and Boolean. Understanding these rules ensures that conversions are performed safely and predictably.

Moreover, conversion procedures between more complex data types, such as arrays or record structures, are subject to the precise mechanisms specified within the language definition or through the use of custom conversion functions defined by the programmer.

Consider this example illustrating the conversion between a character array and a string data type:

```
begin
    character array charArr(1:5);
    text str;
    charArr(1) := 'H';
    charArr(2) := 'e';
    charArr(3) := 'l';
    charArr(4) := 'l';
    charArr(5) := 'o';
    str := copy(charArr); -- Explicit conversion from character array to text
    outtext("The value of str is "); outtext(str); outimage;
end;
```

Executing the above code will convert charArr into a text variable, enabling us to handle string operations effectively.

```
The value of str is Hello
```

Additionally, when dealing with user-defined types or records, explicit conversion can be achieved by writing appropriate conversion functions or methods. These conversion routines ensure the intricate fields and data structures are converted correctly without introducing errors.

For example, to convert a record representing a point in a 2D space into a different representation, specific conversion methods can be implemented:

```
class Point;
    real x, y;
begin
    procedure setCoordinates(a, b); real a, b;
    begin
        x := a; y := b;
    end;
end;

class PolarPoint;
    real radius, angle;
begin
    procedure setPolarCoordinates(r, theta); real r, theta;
    begin
        radius := r; angle := theta;
    end;
end;

begin
    ref(Point) p;
    ref(PolarPoint) pp;

    integer x_val, y_val;
    real r_val, theta_val;

    p :- new Point;
    pp :- new PolarPoint;
```

```
    p.setCoordinates(3.0, 4.0);

    -- Custom conversion from Cartesian (Point) to Polar (PolarPoint)
    r_val := sqrt(p.x**2 + p.y**2);
    theta_val := atan(p.y / p.x);
    pp.setPolarCoordinates(r_val, theta_val);

    outtext("The polar coordinates are: ");
    outreal(pp.radius); outtext(", ");
    outreal(pp.angle); outimage;
end;
```

This code segment calculates the polar coordinates from Cartesian coordinates and assigns them to a PolarPoint object. Careful handling and conversion avoid data inconsistency or logical errors that might arise during transformation between different data representations.

A sound grasp of type conversion and casting principles is fundamental for writing robust Simula programs. It eliminates type mismatches and enhances the flexibility of code interactions. Familiarity with both implicit and explicit conversions empowers programmers to handle diverse computational scenarios effectively, ensuring precise data manipulation and adherence to type safety constraints.

3.8 Constants and Their Uses

Constants in Simula are variables whose values remain unchanged throughout the execution of a program. Utilizing constants in programs improves code readability, facilitates maintenance, and prevents unintentional modifications that may lead to errors. Constants are especially valuable in scenarios where the same value needs to be referenced multiple times and can enhance the overall reliability and efficiency of the code.

Defining Constants

In Simula, constants are defined using the constant keyword. A constant must be assigned a value at the time of its declaration, and this value cannot be altered during the program's runtime. The syntax for defining a constant is straightforward:

```
constant identifier = constant_value;
```

identifier is the name of the constant, and constant_value represents the value assigned to the constant. The data type of the constant is implicitly deduced from the assigned value. Here are several examples:

```
constant Pi = 3.14159;
constant MaxSize = 100;
constant Greeting = "Hello, World!";
```

Benefits of Using Constants

Constants provide numerous advantages, such as:

- **Improved Readability**: Constants with descriptive names make the code more understandable. For example, using Pi instead of 3.14159 clarifies that the value represents the mathematical constant π.
- **Ease of Maintenance**: If a frequently used value needs to be changed, modifying the constant declaration updates all its references, reducing the likelihood of errors.
- **Error Prevention**: Since constants cannot be altered once defined, constants prevent accidental modifications that could lead to erroneous program behavior.

Scope of Constants

The scope of a constant in Simula follows similar rules to those of variables. A constant can be:

- **Local**: Defined within a block or a function, accessible only within that scope.
- **Global**: Defined outside of any block or function, accessible throughout the entire program.

Using Constants in Expressions

Constants can be used in expressions just like any variable. Their values contribute to computations without undergoing alteration. For instance:

```
constant TaxRate = 0.07;
real price, totalPrice;
price := 100.0;
totalPrice := price * (1 + TaxRate);
end;
```

Here, TaxRate remains constant, providing a clear and unmodifiable representation of the tax rate applied to the price.

Constants of Composite Types

Simula also allows the definition of constants for composite types such as records and arrays. Consider the following example illustrating an array constant:

```
constant DaysInMonths = [31, 28, 31, 30, 31, 30, 31, 31, 30, 31, 30, 31];
```

In this case, DaysInMonths is defined as an array of integers where each element represents the number of days in a month. Such constants can be instrumental in reducing lookup errors and improving code clarity.

Enumerated Types as Constants

Enumerated types in Simula are also a form of constant. An enumerated type defines a set of named values that represent unique, constant values. The definition follows the format:

```
type Weekdays = (Sunday, Monday, Tuesday, Wednesday, Thursday, Friday, Saturday)
    ;
```

Each value within the enumerated type Weekdays is a constant, representing a specific day of the week. Enumerated types enhance the readability and integrity of the code by replacing numbers or strings with meaningful identifiers.

Constant Records

To define constant records, Simula allows initializing the record fields at the time of declaration:

```
record Coordinates(x, y) integer x, y;
constant Origin = Coordinates(0, 0);
```

Here, Origin is defined as a constant record of type Coordinates with initial values $x = 0$ and $y = 0$. This form of constant declaration is useful for fixed reference points or configurations that do not change throughout the program.

Using constants effectively in Simula not only encourages cleaner and more maintainable code but also enforces stability and reliability by guarding against unintended modifications.

3.9 Enumerated Types

In Simula, enumerated types allow for the definition of variables that can have one of a finite set of distinct values. This representation is particularly useful for variables that are naturally categorical and whose values do not bear an intrinsic numerical meaning. Enumerated types enhance code readability and maintainability by providing symbolic names for sets of relevant values.

Enumerated types are declared using the type keyword, followed by the definition of the enumerated type. Each possible value within an enumerated type is an identifier separated by commas. The identifiers represent distinct states or categories rather than specific data values. For example, consider an enumeration for days of the week:

```
type DAYS = (Monday, Tuesday, Wednesday, Thursday, Friday, Saturday, Sunday);
```

In this example, DAYS is the enumerated type, and it includes seven possible values corresponding to the days of the week. Once an enumerated type is defined, variables of that type can be declared and assigned one of the predefined values.

```
DAYS currentDay;
currentDay := Monday;
```

Here, currentDay is a variable of type DAYS and it is initially set to Monday. It is important to note that the values of an enumerated type are not merely strings or numbers but specific instances of the enumerated type itself, thus ensuring that variables adhere to the specified set of values.

Enumerated types also facilitate comparing values and controlling program flow based on those comparisons. Given the DAYS type, one might use it within a switch construct or if-else logic to execute different code based on the day of the week.

```
if currentDay = Monday then
    call HandleMonday()
elseif currentDay = Friday then
    call HandleFriday()
else
    call HandleOtherDays();
```

Enumerated types in Simula provide an underlying integer representation for each identifier, where the first identifier is typically assigned the value 0, the second the value 1, and so forth. This feature allows enumerated values to be used in arithmetic operations or as array indices if necessary, though care should be taken to preserve the semantic meaning.

Implicitly, enumerated types offer the benefit of type safety, reducing logical errors such as assigning invalid values to variables. Additionally, using meaningful enumerated values instead of raw numbers or strings makes programs more understandable.

In advanced scenarios, enumerated types can be combined with other data structures. One common use case is within arrays or records where predefined categories define the index or a field type.

```
DAYS dayArray[7];

dayArray[0] := Monday;
dayArray[1] := Tuesday;
// ...
dayArray[6] := Sunday;

record WorkWeek(DAYS startDay, DAYS endDay);
  DAYS today;

  comment Procedure to work through the week;
  procedure work;
  begin
    today := startDay;
    while today <= endDay do
      outtext(today);
      today := succ(today);
    end;
end WorkWeek;
```

In this example, an array dayArray uses the DAYS type for its indices and values. Additionally, a record WorkWeek is defined with fields that utilize the DAYS type. The work procedure in WorkWeek iterates from startDay to endDay, exploiting the well-ordered nature of the enumerated values with the succ function, which returns the subsequent value in the enumeration.

Simula's type system ensures that variables declared as enumerated types maintain the integrity and constraints defined by their enumeration, thereby ensuring logical coherence and enhancing program robustness. Enumerated types provide a clear, organized way to represent a finite set of unrelated values which are an indispensable feature in robust Simula programming.

3.10 Working with Arrays and Lists

In Simula, arrays and lists are fundamental composite data structures that facilitate the storage and manipulation of collections of data elements. Understanding their declaration, initialization, and usage is crucial for leveraging their full potential in various programming scenarios.

An array is a finite, ordered sequence of elements of the same type, which are indexed by integers. The general syntax for declaring an array in Simula is as follows:

```
arrayType arrayName(lowerBound:upperBound)
```

Here, arrayType denotes the type of the elements stored in the array, arrayName is the identifier for the array, and lowerBound and upperBound specify the range of valid indices.

Consider an example where one needs to declare an integer array that can store 10 elements, indexed from 1 to 10:

```
integer array myArray(1:10)
```

To initialize the elements of the array, you can use a loop, such as a for loop:

```
for i := 1 step 1 until 10 do
    myArray(i) := i * 2;
```

The above code snippet initializes each element of myArray to twice the value of its index.

Accessing and modifying array elements involves specifying the appropriate index within the array bounds. If one needs to access the third element of myArray, it can be done as follows:

```
integer thirdElement;
thirdElement := myArray(3);
```

Multidimensional arrays in Simula are declared by providing multiple ranges, separated by commas. For instance, a two-dimensional integer array with dimensions 3 by 3 can be declared as:

```
integer array matrix(1:3, 1:3);
```

Initialization and access follow a similar approach as one-dimensional arrays, with indices specified for each dimension:

```
for i := 1 step 1 until 3 do
```

```
for j := 1 step 1 until 3 do
    matrix(i, j) := i + j;
```

To access the element in the second row and third column:

```
integer element;
element := matrix(2, 3);
```

In addition to arrays, Simula provides lists, which are dynamic data structures that can grow or shrink as needed. A list is composed of linkage elements that form the nodes of the list. These nodes are linked together by pointers, allowing for efficient insertion and deletion operations.

A typical declaration of a linked list in Simula involves defining a class for the nodes and utilising the standard linkage built-in class. Here is an example of how one can define a singly linked list to store integers:

```
begin
    class IntegerNode;
    begin
        integer nodeValue;
        ref(IntegerNode) nextNode;

        procedure init(NodeValue);
        integer NodeValue;
        begin
            nodeValue := NodeValue;
            nextNode := none;
        end init;
    end IntegerNode;

    ref(IntegerNode) head, current, newNode;
    head := new IntegerNode.init(5);
    current := head;

    integer values[2:5] = (10, 15, 20, 25);

    for i := 2 step 1 until 5 do
    begin
        newNode := new IntegerNode.init(values(i));
        current.nextNode := newNode;
        current := newNode;
    end
end;
```

This example demonstrates constructing a linked list with integer values 5, 10, 15, 20, and 25. The init procedure initializes a node with a value and sets the nextNode pointer to none.

Accessing the elements of a linked list involves traversing from the head node to subsequent nodes by following the nextNode pointers. Here is how one can traverse and print the values in the list:

```
current := head;
while current \texttt{<>} none do
begin
   outinteger(current.nodeValue); outimage;
   current := current.nextNode;
end;
```

Lists provide more flexibility than arrays due to their dynamic nature and ability to efficiently handle insertions and deletions. However, arrays offer constant-time access to elements, which can be advantageous in scenarios where fast lookup times are essential.

Understanding the implementation details and proper usage of arrays and lists allows for effective data management and manipulation. Arrays are particularly useful for fixed-size collections and scenarios requiring frequent access to elements by index, while lists excel in dynamic environments where insertion and deletion operations are predominant.

3.11 Records and Structures

In Simula, records and structures provide mechanisms for grouping different pieces of data together. These constructs enable the creation of complex data types that are essential for managing and organizing larger programs. Understanding records and structures is crucial for efficient programming and data management in Simula.

Records:
Records in Simula are similar to structures in C or classes in object-oriented languages. A record type defines a collection of fields, each of which can have a different type. To declare a record type, the begin and end keywords encapsulate the fields within a record keyword.

```
begin
  record Person;
    text name;
    integer age;
  end;
end;
```

In this example, a record type Person is declared with two fields: name of type text and age of type integer. The fields in a record can be accessed using the dot notation as shown below.

```
begin
  ref(Person) p;
  p:- new Person;
```

```
  p.name := "Alice";
  p.age := 30;
  OutText(p.name); OutImage;
  OutInt(p.age, 0); OutImage;
end;
```

In this code snippet, an instance p of type ref(Person) is created using the new keyword. The fields name and age are assigned values and then accessed to print their contents using OutText and OutInt.

Structures:
Structures in Simula can be employed to define more flexible and generalized data organizations. Structures extend the capabilities of records, accommodating inheritance and nested structures. This allows for more complex hierarchies and relationships within the data.

Consider a scenario where we need to define a hierarchy of animal species:

```
begin
  class Animal;
    begin
      text species;
      integer age;
    end;
  end;

  class Dog;
    begin
      Animal;
      text breed;
    end;
  end;

  ref(Dog) d;
  d:- new Dog;
  d.species := "Canine";
  d.age := 5;
  d.breed := "Labrador";
  OutText(d.species); OutImage;
  OutInt(d.age, 0); OutImage;
  OutText(d.breed); OutImage;
end;
```

In this example, we first define a base class Animal with fields species and age. Then, a derived class Dog inherits from the Animal class and adds an additional field breed. An instance of Dog is created, and all fields are assigned and accessed similarly.

Summary of Key Points:
Key aspects of using records and structures in Simula include:

- **Record Definitions:** Using begin and end keywords within the record construct to define fields.

- **Field Access:** Utilizing the dot notation for field manipulation.
- **Class Inheritance:** Employing hierarchical relationships by extending base classes to create derived structures.
- **Nested Structures:** Creating complex data types encapsulating multiple layers of records or classes.

In essence, mastering the use of records and structures allows for the efficient representation of complex data in a hierarchical and organized manner. This enables more manageable and extendable code, vital for advanced Simula programming.

Chapter 4

Control Structures and Functions

This chapter examines the control structures and functions in Simula. It covers conditional statements, looping constructs, and branching mechanisms, explaining how they guide the program's flow. The chapter also delves into procedures, functions, parameter passing methods, recursion, and built-in functions, providing a thorough understanding of how to structure and manage reusable code components effectively.

4.1 Introduction to Control Structures

In Simula, as in many other programming languages, control structures are fundamental elements that manage the flow of program execution. These structures determine the sequence in which statements are executed and enable the implementation of logical decision-making as well as iterative processes. Control structures in Simula can be grouped broadly into conditional statements, looping constructs, and branching mechanisms, each of which will be discussed in greater detail in subsequent sections of this chapter.

Control structures provide the means for a program to adjust its behavior based on varying conditions and to repeat operations efficiently. They are essential for creating flexible, efficient, and readable code.

The primary control structures in Simula include if statements, for loops, while loops, and switch statements. Each of these elements plays a unique role in guiding the execution flow of a program.

To illustrate the importance and functionality of control structures, consider a simple example where a program must decide whether to print a message based on a numerical value. This can be efficiently managed using an if statement.

```
begin
    integer value;
    value := 10;
    if value > 0 then
        OutText("The value is positive");
end;
```

In this example, the if statement checks if the variable value is greater than zero. If the condition evaluates to true, the message "The value is positive" is printed. Control structures like this are pivotal in making decisions within programs.

Another fundamental control structure is the loop. Loops enable the execution of a block of statements multiple times, which is particularly useful for tasks that require repetitiveness such as processing items in an array or reading data until a certain condition is met. Consider a for loop example where we want to print numbers from 1 to 5:

```
begin
    integer i;
    for i := 1 step 1 until 5 do
        OutInt(i, 1);
end;
```

This loop initialization for i := 1 step 1 until 5 ensures that the block of code OutInt(i, 1) is executed for each value of i from 1 to 5. The use of loops minimizes the need to write repetitive code and enhances readability and maintainability.

The while loop is another powerful control structure that repeatedly executes a block of statements as long as a given condition holds true. Here's an example:

```
begin
    integer count;
    count := 1;
    while count <= 5 do begin
        OutInt(count, 1);
        count := count + 1;
    end;
end;
```

In this example, the while loop continues to print the value of count and increment it by one until count is greater than 5.

Branching mechanisms, such as the switch statement, facilitate selecting a block of code to execute from multiple possibilities based on the value of an expression. The switch statement can be particularly useful when multiple distinct values influence the program flow:

```
begin
    integer option;
    option := 2;
    switch option
    begin
        case 1:
            OutText("Option 1 selected");
        case 2:
            OutText("Option 2 selected");
        case 3:
            OutText("Option 3 selected");
        otherwise:
            OutText("Invalid option");
    end;
end;
```

In this example, based on the value of option, the program chooses the corresponding block of code to execute. If none of the specified cases match, the otherwise block is executed, providing a fallback mechanism for handling unexpected values.

Combining these control structures allows for the effective management of complex logic and operations within a Simula program. Each construct not only enhances the expressiveness of the code but also contributes to its robustness and flexibility. By mastering the use of control structures, programmers can write more efficient, readable, and maintainable Simula programs, leading to higher quality software solutions. The subsequent sections will delve deeper into each of these control structures, exploring their syntax, usage, and best practices, with detailed examples to solidify understanding.

4.2 Conditional Statements

The efficient control of flow within a programming structure is pivotal in producing reliable and maintainable code. Conditional statements in Simula allow for such control by executing different segments of code based on the evaluation of boolean expressions. This section covers the if, else, and else if constructs in Simula.

At its core, the if statement evaluates a boolean expression. If the expression evaluates to true, the code block associated with the if statement executes. Consider the following example:

```
begin
    integer a, b;
    a := 10;
    b := 20;
    if a < b then
        OutText("a is less than b");
end;
```

In this example, the boolean expression $a < b$ evaluates to true since $10 < 20$. As a result, the statement OutText("a is less than b") executes, producing the output:

```
a is less than b
```

When multiple conditions need to be considered, the else keyword provides an alternate code block that executes if the initial condition is false. For example:

```
begin
    integer a, b;
    a := 30;
    b := 20;
    if a < b then
        OutText("a is less than b")
    else
        OutText("a is not less than b");
end;
```

Here, the boolean expression $a < b$ evaluates to false since $30 > 20$. Consequently, the code block associated with else executes, and the output is:

```
a is not less than b
```

For evaluating multiple conditions, else if can be utilized to chain several conditions together sequentially. The program evaluates each condition in order, and the first true condition's block executes. Illustration with an example:

```
begin
    integer a, b;
    a := 30;
    b := 30;
    if a < b then
        OutText("a is less than b")
    else if a > b then
        OutText("a is greater than b")
    else
        OutText("a is equal to b");
end;
```

In this case, both the conditions $a < b$ and $a > b$ evaluate to false, thus the code block under else executes, and the output is:

```
a is equal to b
```

Simula also supports compound boolean expressions using logical operators such as and, or, and not. These operators are essential for creating more complex conditional logic. For instance:

```
begin
    integer a, b, c;
    a := 10;
    b := 20;
    c := 30;
    if (a < b) and (b < c) then
        OutText("a is less than b and b is less than c");
end;
```

Here, the combined boolean expression $(a < b)$ and $(b < c)$ evaluates to true only if both conditions are true. Given $10 < 20$ and $20 < 30$, the resulting output is:

```
a is less than b and b is less than c
```

Additionally, short-circuit evaluation in logical operations ensures that the second operand is evaluated only if necessary. This behavior is well exemplified in conditions involving potential division by zero:

```
begin
    integer a, b;
    a := 10;
    b := 0;
    if (b <> 0) and (a / b > 2) then
        OutText("Division possible and result is greater than 2")
    else
        OutText("Cannot perform division or result is not greater than 2");
end;
```

In this case, the expression $(b <> 0)$ and $(a \ / \ b > 2)$ ensures that division by zero does not occur, as the second condition $(a \ / \ b > 2)$ is evaluated only if $b <> 0$. Given that $b = 0$, the output is:

```
Cannot perform division or result is not greater than 2
```

Nested if statements allow for more intricate decision-making processes by placing one if statement inside another. It is imperative to ensure proper indentation to maintain code readability:

```
begin
    integer a, b, c;
    a := 10;
    b := 20;
    c := 10;
    if a = b then
        OutText("a is equal to b")
```

```
    else
        if a = c then
            OutText("a is equal to c")
        else
            OutText("a is not equal to b and not equal to c");
end;
```

Here, the boolean expression $a = b$ evaluates to false, leading to the evaluation of the nested if statement. Since $a = c$ is true, the output produced is:

```
a is equal to c
```

Emily used conditional statements during her project to determine student grades based on their score. She set grade boundaries using the following program:

```
begin
    integer score;
    character grade;
    score := 85;
    if score >= 90 then
        grade := 'A'
    else if score >= 80 then
        grade := 'B'
    else if score >= 70 then
        grade := 'C'
    else if score >= 60 then
        grade := 'D'
    else
        grade := 'F';
    OutText("The grade is "); OutText(grade);
end;
```

In this program, score is set to 85, thus $score >= 80$ evaluates to true and assigns the grade 'B' to the variable grade. The final output is:

```
The grade is B
```

The examples provided elucidate the comprehensive usage of conditional statements in Simula. The ability to conditionally execute code segments based on evaluated expressions is fundamental for controlling program flow and establishing robust logic in software development.

4.3 Looping Constructs

Looping constructs in Simula enable the repetition of a block of code a certain number of times or until a specific condition is met. This is essential for tasks that require iteration, such as processing arrays, managing datasets, and implementing algorithms that involve repetitive calculations.

for **Loop**

The for loop in Simula allows iteration over a range of values. The general syntax of a for loop is as follows:

```
for variable := start_value step increment until end_value do
   statement or block of statements;
end;
```

Here, variable is the loop control variable, start_value is the initial value, increment specifies the step size, and end_value is the loop's terminating condition. The loop executes the block of statements repeatedly, adjusting the variable by increment each time until end_value is reached.

Examples of a for loop:

```
! Example 1: Simple for loop
for i:= 1 step 1 until 10 do
   OutInt(i, 3);
end;

! Example 2: For loop with step size of 2
for i:= 1 step 2 until 10 do
   OutInt(i, 3);
end;
```

In Example 1, the loop iterates from 1 to 10, printing each integer. Example 2 iterates from 1 to 10, printing every second integer. The step can be positive, negative, or defaulting to 1 if omitted.

while **Loop**

A while loop is suitable for scenarios where the number of iterations is not predetermined, and the loop continues until a specified condition evaluates to false. The syntax for a while loop is as follows:

```
while condition do
   statement or block of statements;
end;
```

In the while loop, condition is evaluated before the loop's body executes. If condition is true, the block of statements is executed, and the process repeats until condition becomes false.

Example of a while loop:

```
! Example: Counting down
integer i;
i := 10;
```

```
while i > 0 do
   OutText('Count down:'); OutInt(i, 3);
   i := i - 1;
end;
```

This example counts down from 10 to 1, printing each value. Note that the loop body contains a decrement operation on i to eventually terminate the loop.

do_while **Loop**

Simula also provides a do_while loop, which guarantees at least one execution of the loop's body irrespective of the condition because the condition is evaluated after the body executes. The syntax is:

```
do
   statement or block of statements;
while condition;
```

Example of a do_while loop:

```
! Example: At least one execution
integer x;
x := -1;
do
   OutText('Value:'); OutInt(x, 3);
   x := x + 1;
while x < 0;
```

Here, the output statement will execute at least once even if the initial value of x is not less than 0.

loops **and** exit

One unique feature of Simula is the introduction of loops and exit. This construct provides enhanced control over iterative execution by creating labeled loops which can be exited based on conditions.

Syntax example:

```
OuterLoop: loop
   InnerLoop: loop
      if condition then
         exit InnerLoop;
      end;
      if another_condition then
         exit OuterLoop;
      end;
   end;
end;
```

Using exit, you can terminate inner or outer loops based on certain conditions, providing fine-grained control over the execution flow.

Example using loops and exit:

```
! Example: Nested loops with exit
integer i, j;

OuterLoop: loop
  for i := 1 step 1 until 3 do
    InnerLoop: loop
      for j := 1 step 1 until 3 do
        if i = j then
          OutText('Exiting inner loop with i='); OutInt(i, 3);
          exit InnerLoop;
        end;
      end;
    end;
    if i = 2 then
      OutText('Exiting outer loop with i='); OutInt(i, 3);
      exit OuterLoop;
    end;
  end;
end;
```

In this example, the loop demonstrates breaking out of nested loops using the exit statement conditioned on the values of i and j.

Looping constructs are essential in controlling flow and can be combined creatively to manage complex iteration patterns effectively.

4.4 Branching Statements

Branching statements in Simula allow for altering the execution flow of a program based on specific conditions. They enable the program to choose different paths of execution, ensuring flexibility and responsiveness to various situations that arise at runtime. The primary branching statements in Simula are goto, switch, and exit. Each has distinct usage scenarios and implications on the program's structure and maintainability.

The goto statement provides an unconditional jump to another location within the same block of code. Although its use is generally discouraged in modern programming due to potential readability and maintenance issues, understanding goto is essential for dealing with legacy Simula code.

```
Begin
  Integer i;
  i := 1;
  L1: OutText ("Hello, World!");
  Outimage;
  If i < 3 Then
  Begin
```

```
    i := i + 1;
    Goto L1;
  End;
End;
```

In this example, the label L1 marks the position to which control jumps when the goto statement is executed. Each time the value of i is less than 3, the goto statement transfers control back to L1, resulting in the string "Hello, World!" being printed three times.

A more structured approach to branching is provided by the switch statement, which is akin to switch or case statements in other programming languages. It allows the execution to branch to different pieces of code based on the value of an expression. Here's a typical usage of switch in Simula:

```
Begin
  Integer option;
  option := 2;

  Switch option
  Begin
    Case 1: OutText ("Option 1 selected");
            Outimage;
    Case 2: OutText ("Option 2 selected");
            Outimage;
    Case 3: OutText ("Option 3 selected");
            Outimage;
    Default: OutText ("Invalid option");
             Outimage;
  End;
End;
```

In the above code, option is evaluated, and the corresponding case block is executed. If option equals 2, the output will be:

```
Option 2 selected
```

If option does not match any of the specified cases, the Default block executes, ensuring a fallback behavior.

Another branching mechanism in Simula is the exit statement, which allows for exiting from a block or procedure prematurely. This is particularly useful for early termination when a specific condition is met within nested blocks or procedures. An example of exit usage is illustrated below:

```
Begin
  Integer i;
  For i := 1 Step 1 Until 10 Do
  Begin
    If i = 5 Then
      Exit;
    OutInt (i, 2);
```

```
    Outimage;
  End;
End;
```

The Exit statement here terminates the loop execution when i equals 5. Consequently, the output will be:

```
1
2
3
4
```

Branching statements must be used judiciously to maintain the readability and robustness of the code. While goto can be powerful, its potential for creating spaghetti code makes structured alternatives like switch and exit preferable in most scenarios. Understanding these constructs and their appropriate application ensures that Simula programs can handle diverse conditions effectively while remaining clear and maintainable.

4.5 Creating and Using Procedures

Procedures in Simula are a fundamental mechanism for structuring programs and promoting code reuse. They enable encapsulation of specific tasks or computations, aiding in maintaining modular, readable, and maintainable code. A procedure in Simula is defined using the procedure keyword followed by its name, parameters, and the procedure body.

Procedure definitions start with the keyword procedure and must specify the types of their parameters. Each parameter type is declared right after the parameter name within parentheses. Procedures can have a type indicator that specifies the type of their return value. Below is the syntax for defining a simple procedure:

```
procedure procedureName(parameter1, parameter2);
integer parameter1, parameter2;
begin
    ! procedure body;
end;
```

Consider the following example that illustrates a procedure which computes the greatest common divisor (GCD) using Euclid's algorithm:

```
procedure gcd(a, b);
integer a, b;
begin
    while b <> 0 do
```

```
        begin
            integer temp;
            temp := b;
            b := a mod b;
            a := temp;
        end;
    return a;
end;
```

Here, the gcd procedure calculates the GCD of two integers a and b. The procedure uses a while loop to iterate until b equals zero, following Euclid's method.

To call this procedure, you use the following syntax:

```
integer result;
integer x, y;
x := 56;
y := 98;
result := gcd(x, y);
```

This segment sets x to 56 and y to 98, and then it calls the gcd procedure with these values, storing the result in the result variable.

Procedures can also return values, though in Simula the return value is handled through the procedure's type indicator. If the return value is an integer, the type specification would be integer, as shown in the following factorial procedure:

```
integer procedure factorial(n);
integer n;
begin
    if n = 0 then
        return 1
    else
        return n * factorial(n - 1);
end;
```

In this example, the factorial procedure computes the factorial of a non-negative integer n recursively. Notice the use of the return statement to send back the result.

Simula also allows for procedures without parameters. Here is an example of a parameterless procedure that prints a welcoming message:

```
procedure displayWelcomeMessage;
begin
    outtext("Welcome to Simula programming!");
    outimage;
end;
```

To invoke this parameterless procedure, you simply write:

```
displayWelcomeMessage;
```

Procedures often collaborate with other procedures and functions. A critical aspect of procedure design is understanding scope rules, particularly the distinction between local and global variables. Variables declared within a procedure are local, meaning they are not accessible outside the procedure's body. Global variables, declared outside any procedure, are accessible by any procedure within their scope.

Consider the following illustration with nested procedures:

```
begin
    integer globalVar;
    globalVar := 10;

    procedure outerProcedure;
    integer localOuterVar;
    localOuterVar := 20;

    procedure innerProcedure;
    integer localInnerVar;
    localInnerVar := 30;
    innerProcedure := localInnerVar + localOuterVar + globalVar;
    end;

    outerProcedure := innerProcedure;
    end;

    outint(output := outerProcedure);
    outimage;
end;
```

Here, innerProcedure accesses localOuterVar from outerProcedure and globalVar, demonstrating variable scoping rules.

Simula procedures also support reference parameters, enabling modifications on the actual parameters passed to them. This is particularly useful when procedures need to return multiple values or modify complex data structures. Reference parameters are declared using the keyword ref. Here is an example involving a swap procedure:

```
procedure swap(ref integer x, ref integer y);
integer temp;
begin
    temp := x;
    x := y;
    y := temp;
end;
```

Calling this procedure will exchange the values of the variables passed to it:

```
integer a, b;
a := 5;
b := 10;
swap(a, b);
```

After calling swap(a, b), the value of a becomes 10, and b becomes 5, demonstrating the effect of passing by reference.

In Simula, procedures greatly enhance the reusability and structure of code by localizing functionality and encapsulating algorithms. Understanding and effectively using procedures is crucial for mastering Simula programming, providing a robust toolset for code development and maintenance.

4.6 Understanding Functions

Functions in Simula are integral to composing reusable, modular, and maintainable code. Functions encapsulate a sequence of statements to perform a specific task, reducing redundancy and enhancing code clarity. This section provides an in-depth examination of functions in Simula, exploring their syntax, declaration, invocation, and various attributes.

Syntax and Declaration In Simula, a function begins with the keyword procedure, followed by the function name and parameters in parentheses. For functions that return a value, the type of the return value follows the parameters. The general syntax is as follows:

```
procedure FunctionName(Parameter1, Parameter2, ...);
   ValueType Name;
begin
   statements
   FunctionName := value;
end;
```

Here, ValueType specifies the type of value the function returns. If the function does not return a value, or is used in contexts where return type is implicitly handled, the ValueType declaration can be omitted.

Example of a Simple Function Let's consider a function that calculates the square of a number. This function takes an integer as a parameter and returns its square:

```
procedure Square(N); Integer N;
   Integer Square;
begin
   Square := N * N;
end;
```

To call this function, we would use the following code:

```
Integer Result;
Result := Square(5);
```

The above call assigns 25 to the variable Result, as the square of 5 is 25.

Nested Functions and Scope Functions in Simula can be nested, meaning a function can be declared inside another function. This nesting allows for the encapsulation of helper functions within a parent function, maintaining a clean global namespace.

```
procedure OuterFunction(N); Integer N;
  Integer OuterFunction;

  procedure InnerFunction(M); Integer M;
    Integer InnerFunction;
  begin
    InnerFunction := M * 2;
  end;

begin
  OuterFunction := InnerFunction(N) + N;
end;
```

The inner function InnerFunction is only accessible within OuterFunction, maintaining functional encapsulation and reducing external dependencies.

Parameter Passing Methods Simula supports various parameter passing methods, notably, pass-by-value and pass-by-reference. By default, parameters in Simula are passed by value, meaning that a copy of the actual parameter is passed to the function. Changes made to the parameter within the function do not affect the original variable.

In contrast, pass-by-reference allows functions to modify the actual parameter. To pass parameters by reference, an additional attribute name is used in parameter declaration:

```
procedure ModifyVariable(N); name N; Integer N;
begin
  N := N * 2;
end;
```

Calling ModifyVariable with a variable will modify the original variable:

```
Integer MyVar;
MyVar := 10;
ModifyVariable(MyVar);
```

After execution, MyVar will be 20, demonstrating the modification through reference passing.

Recursion in Functions Simula supports recursive functions, where a function calls itself to solve smaller instances of a problem until reaching a base case. A classic example is the calculation of factorials:

```
procedure Factorial(N); Integer N;
  Integer Factorial;
begin
  if N = 0 then
      Factorial := 1;
  else
      Factorial := N * Factorial(N - 1);
end;
```

Calling Factorial(5) invokes a series of recursive calls: Factorial(4), Factorial(3), down to Factorial(0), computing the factorial of 5 efficiently.

Inline Functions Simula also allows the use of inline arithmetic expressions to define simple functions. Inline functions are beneficial for small computational tasks, avoiding the need for full function declarations:

```
define Increment(N) = N + 1;
Integer NextValue;
NextValue := Increment(5);
```

The expression assigns 6 to NextValue, illustrating the conciseness of inline functions.

Understanding how to define, invoke, and manage functions is a fundamental skill in Simula programming. Proper utilization of functions enhances code readability, promotes reuse, and simplifies debugging and maintenance tasks.

4.7 Parameter Passing Methods

Parameter passing methods are essential in Simula, as they determine how arguments are communicated to procedures and functions. Understanding these methods allows you to control how data is transmitted and manipulated, ensuring efficient and error-free code execution.

Simula supports three primary parameter passing methods: by value, by reference, and by name. Each method has its nuanced application scenarios and implications on program behavior.

Passing by Value

In this method, the actual value of the argument is passed to the function. The procedure or function creates a local copy of the argument, which means any modifications to the parameter within the procedure do not affect the original value outside the function. This method is particularly useful when you want to ensure the original data remains unaltered.

```
Begin
    Integer procedure square(Value Integer x);
    Integer x;
    square := x * x;
End;

Integer n;
n := 5;
outint(square(n)); ! Outputs 25
outint(n); ! Outputs 5
```

In the example above, the x parameter in the square procedure is marked as Value Integer x, indicating that it should be passed by value. The original variable n remains unchanged after the procedure call.

Passing by Reference

When parameters are passed by reference, the function or procedure receives the memory address of the argument rather than its value. Consequently, modifications to the parameter within the function will also affect the original variable. This method is ideal for scenarios where you need to update the original data.

```
Begin
    Procedure update(Reference Integer y);
    Integer y;
    y := y + 10;
End;

Integer m;
m := 10;
update(m);
outint(m); ! Outputs 20
```

In this example, the update procedure uses Reference Integer y to denote that y should be passed by reference. After invoking update(m), the original variable m is modified.

Passing by Name

This method treats the parameter as a textual substitution. The actual parameter expression is substituted directly into the procedure body wherever it appears. It offers powerful flexibility but requires careful handling to avoid unexpected behaviors, especially if the parameter has side effects.

```
Begin
    Integer procedure triple(Value Integer x);
    Integer x;
    triple := x + x + x;
End;
```

```
Integer p, q;
p := 4;
q := triple(p + 1);
outint(q); ! Outputs 15 (as (4+1) + (4+1) + (4+1))
```

Here, the x parameter in the triple procedure uses the Value Integer x form, and although not strictly by name, it demonstrates that the expression $p + 1$ is evaluated as a whole.

Case Study: Choosing Parameter Passing Methods

Consider a scenario where a set of data needs to be manipulated within various procedures and the choice of parameter passing method significantly impacts performance and data integrity.

1. By Value: Suitable for mathematical calculations where the integrity of the original data is paramount. 2. By Reference: Optimal for situations where the procedure needs to modify the original data structures, such as lists or trees. 3. By Name: Useful in complex scenarios where the expression should be re-evaluated within the procedure, but it warrants caution.

```
Begin
   Ref(Integer) array Vector;
   Integer i;
   Vector:- New Integer[1:10];

   For i:=1 Step 1 Until 10 Do
      Vector[i] := i;

   Procedure modify(Reference Integer a[], Value Integer index);
   Integer a[], index;
   Begin
      Integer j;
      For j:=1 Step 1 Until index Do
         a[j] := a[j] + 1
   End;

   modify(Vector, 5);
   ! Vector now has elements: 2, 3, 4, 5, 6, 6, 7, 8, 9, 10
```

In this complex example, the array Vector is passed by reference, while its indices are passed by value. The use of Reference Integer a[] allows the procedure modify to alter the array's elements directly.

Understanding the implications of each parameter passing method allows for better decision-making, particularly in scenarios involving optimization or risk management of data integrity. Each method has its pros and cons and should be selected based on the specific requirements and constraints of the given problem space.

Proficiency in parameter passing methods empowers developers with precise control over their procedures and the behavior of their programs. This understanding ensures that procedures and functions in Simula are used effectively and efficiently, promoting robust and maintainable code.

4.8 Recursion and Its Applications

Recursion is a fundamental and powerful concept in programming, where a procedure or function calls itself either directly or indirectly. Recursion can simplify the implementation of algorithms that repetitively break down a problem into smaller sub-problems of the same type. Understanding and effectively utilizing recursion is essential for solving complex problems elegantly in Simula.

Definition of Recursion: A recursive function in Simula is defined as a function that calls itself in order to solve a smaller instance of the same problem. Each recursive call solves a portion of the problem and returns its result to its caller. The key components of a recursive function are:

- Base Case: The condition under which the function stops calling itself, preventing an infinite loop.
- Recursive Case: The part of the function where it calls itself with a reduced or simplified input.

Example of a Recursive Function: Below is an example of a simple recursive function to calculate the factorial of a number, $n!$ which is the product of all positive integers up to n.

```
integer procedure factorial(n);
   integer n;
   if n = 0 then
      factorial := 1
   else
      factorial := n * factorial(n - 1);
```

In this example, the base case is when n equals 0. At this point, the function returns 1, stopping further recursive calls. The recursive case is where the function calls itself with n - 1.

Tracing Recursive Calls: To understand how the recursion mechanism works, let us trace the function calls for factorial(3).

```
factorial(3)
=> 3 * factorial(2)
=> 3 * (2 * factorial(1))
=> 3 * (2 * (1 * factorial(0)))
=> 3 * (2 * (1 * 1))
=> 6
```

Each call waits for its child call to return the result before proceeding with the computation, leading to a stack of waiting calls that eventually resolve back up the chain.

Applications of Recursion: Recursion is particularly useful for problems that exhibit the following properties:

- Divide and Conquer: Problems that can be divided into smaller sub-problems that are solved independently and then combined. Examples include merge sort and quicksort algorithms.
- Dynamic Programming: Recursive solutions that use memoization to optimize repeated calculations of overlapping sub-problems. Examples include solving the Fibonacci sequence and computing binomial coefficients.
- Tree and Graph Traversal: Recursive methods are highly effective in traversing structures like trees and graphs. Examples include depth-first search (DFS) in graphs, and operations on binary search trees (BSTs) such as insertion, deletion, and in-order traversal.

Example: Fibonacci Sequence The Fibonacci sequence is a classic example demonstrating recursion, where each term is the sum of the two preceding terms.

```
integer procedure fibonacci(n);
  integer n;
  if n = 0 then
    fibonacci := 0
  else if n = 1 then
    fibonacci := 1
  else
    fibonacci := fibonacci(n - 1) + fibonacci(n - 2);
```

However, this naive implementation of the Fibonacci sequence has exponential time complexity $O(2^n)$ due to redundant calculations. Optimization through memoization can improve this significantly.

Optimized Fibonacci with Memoization: Memoization stores the results of function calls and reuses them when the same inputs occur again. This minimizes redundant calculations.

```
integer array memo[0:100]; // Assume n <= 100
for i := 0 to 100 do
   memo[i] := -1; // Initialize with sentinel values

integer procedure fibonacciOptimized(n);
   integer n;
   if memo[n] != -1 then
      fibonacciOptimized := memo[n]
   else if n = 0 then
      memo[n] := 0
   else if n = 1 then
      memo[n] := 1
   else
      memo[n] := fibonacciOptimized(n - 1) + fibonacciOptimized(n - 2);
      fibonacciOptimized := memo[n];
```

By storing previously computed values in the memo array, the optimized Fibonacci function runs in linear time $O(n)$, making it much more efficient.

Recursion also finds applications in:

Tower of Hanoi: A mathematical problem involving three rods and a number of disks of different sizes which can be solved using recursion to move all the disks from one rod to another following specific rules.

String Manipulation: Operations such as reversing a string or checking if a string is a palindrome can be achieved using recursive methods.

When designing recursive algorithms, it is vital to ensure that the base case is reached eventually to avoid infinite recursion and potential stack overflow errors. Proper understanding of recursion requires recognizing the depth of function calls and potentially high memory usage due to call stack operations.

Through practice and careful consideration of problem properties, recursion can be effectively leveraged to create elegant and efficient solutions in Simula, enhancing the robustness and maintainability of code.

4.9 Built-in Functions

Simula provides a set of built-in functions integral to efficient programming and effective problem-solving. These functions offer a range of utilities from mathematical computations to string manipulations. This section elucidates the primary built-in functions available in Simula, examining their syntax and usage with illustrative examples.

Mathematical Functions

Simula offers an array of mathematical functions that aid in performing complex calculations. Key mathematical functions include sqrt, exp, log, sin, cos, tan, and various statistical functions.

```
Real x := 9.0;
Real result := sqrt(x);
outtext("The square root of 9 is: "); outreal(result);
```

```
The square root of 9 is: 3.0
```

In the above example, the sqrt function calculates the square root of the variable x. Other functions such as exp(y) will return the exponential e^y, while log(z) computes the natural logarithm of the variable z.

Trigonometric Functions

Trigonometric functions enable performing calculations involving angles, essential in fields like physics and engineering.

```
Real angle := 45.0;
Real radians := angle * (3.14159265358979 / 180.0); // Conversion to radians
Real sine_value := sin(radians);
outtext("sin(45 degrees) in radians is: "); outreal(sine_value);
```

```
sin(45 degrees) in radians is: 0.70710678118
```

sin(angle), cos(angle), and tan(angle) functions compute the sine, cosine, and tangent of an angle in radians, respectively. Conversion from degrees to radians is performed using the relation $radians = degrees \times \frac{\pi}{180}$.

Statistical Functions

Built-in functions also include statistical operations, such as determining the mean, variance, and standard deviation. However, these often rely on user-defined implementations or external libraries in the context of classic Simula as it lacks a direct in-built standard library for advanced statistics compared to modern languages.

String Handling Functions

Simula's string handling capabilities include functions for finding the length of a string (length), extracting substrings (substr), and comparing strings (strcmp). These are fundamental for text processing.

```
Text myString := "Simula Programming";
Integer len := myString.length();
outtext("Length of the string is: "); outint(len, 2);
```

```
Length of the string is: 18
```

Using myString.length(), we can obtain the length of myString, which is

18 in this example. Similarly, substr(myString, 1, 6) extracts a substring from position 1 to position 6.

```
Text sub := myString.substr(1, 6);
outtext("Substring from 1 to 6 is: "); outtext(sub);
```

```
Substring from 1 to 6 is: Simula
```

strcmp(str1, str2) compares two strings str1 and str2, returning 0 if the strings are equal, a negative integer if str1 is less than str2, and a positive integer if str1 is greater than str2.

```
Integer cmp := strcmp("Simula", "SIMULA");
if cmp = 0 then
  outtext("Strings are equal")
else
  outtext("Strings are not equal");
```

```
Strings are not equal
```

Input and Output Functions

Input and output functions are pivotal for interaction with users and files. Basic input functions include intext, inreal, and inint, whereas output functions include outtext, outreal, and outint.

```
Integer age;
outtext("Enter your age: "); inint(age);
outtext("Your age is: "); outint(age, 2);
```

```
Enter your age: 25
Your age is: 25
```

The program prompts the user to input their age and subsequently displays the entered value using inint for integer input and outint for integer output.

Type Conversion Functions

Simula includes functions for type conversion, such as int2real to convert an integer to a real number and real2int to perform the reverse.

```
Integer i := 5;
Real r := int2real(i);
outtext("Converted integer to real: "); outreal(r);
```

```
Converted integer to real: 5.0
```

Conversely, using real2int converts a real number to an integer, as demonstrated in the snippet below:

```
Real num := 7.89;
Integer j := real2int(num);
outtext("Converted real to integer: "); outint(j, 2);
```

Converted real to integer: 7

4.10 Lambda Expressions in Simula

Lambda expressions in Simula provide a means to define anonymous, short functions inline without the need for formal declaration. These are pivotal for operations that are functional in nature, contributing to concise and readable code, particularly in cases of higher-order functions or when parameters themselves can be functions.

In Simula, a lambda expression can be defined using the keyword procedure. This construct allows us to encapsulate code blocks and parameterize actions dynamically. Let us examine the syntax and usage of lambda expressions, followed by illustrative examples to solidify the understanding.

Syntax and Definition

Lambda expressions in Simula are characterized by the following syntax:

```
procedure (parameter_list) expression
```

- procedure: This keyword is used to start the lambda expression.
- parameter_list: This denotes the input parameters to the lambda expression, encased within parentheses.
- expression: The body of the function or the sequence of operations to be performed.

Example 1: Simple Lambda Expression

Let's consider a basic lambda expression that computes the square of a number:

```
procedure (x) x * x;
```

Here, x is the input parameter, and the expression x * x represents the operation to perform. We can invoke this lambda expression by passing it as an argument to other functions or storing it in a variable.

Example 2: Lambda Expressions with Multiple Parameters

Next, consider a case involving a lambda expression with multiple input parameters, such as a function that adds two numbers:

```
procedure (x, y) x + y;
```

This lambda expression takes two parameters, x and y, and returns their sum. The expression is evaluated when the lambda is called, demonstrating the inline definition and usage capability of Simula.

Advanced Usage: Higher-Order Functions

Lambda expressions are particularly powerful when used in conjunction with higher-order functions—functions that take other functions as arguments or return them as results. Simula's capability to handle such constructs enhances its expressiveness.

Example 3: Using Lambda with Higher-Order Functions

Consider a higher-order function that applies a given binary operation to two integers:

```
procedure applyOperation(op, x, y);
  begin
    op(x, y);
  end;
```

Now, this function can be utilized with different lambda expressions:

```
procedure add = procedure (a, b) a + b;
procedure multiply = procedure (a, b) a * b;

integer result1, result2;

result1 := applyOperation(add, 2, 3); ! Should return 5
result2 := applyOperation(multiply, 2, 3); ! Should return 6
```

In this example, applyOperation is a higher-order function that takes a binary operation, op, and applies it to the integers x and y. Lambdas add and multiply are defined and passed to applyOperation, showcasing the flexibility and modular design possible with Simula.

Example 4: Lambda Expressions and Iteration

One of the common uses of lambda expressions is in conjunction with iteration constructs such as loops. Simula allows the seamless integration of lambdas within iterative logic.

```
integer i;
array nums[1:5];
nums[1] := 1; nums[2] := 2; nums[3] := 3; nums[4] := 4; nums[5] := 5;

procedure square = procedure (x) x * x;

for i := 1 step 1 until 5 do
  begin
    OutInt(square(nums[i]), 5); OutImage;
```

```
end;
```

In this code, the lambda square defined as procedure (x) x * x is used within a loop to print the square of each element in the array nums. OutInt and OutImage are used for formatted output display.

Advantages and Best Practices

Lambda expressions in Simula significantly reduce boilerplate code, enhance readability, and promote functional programming techniques.

- Use lambda expressions for short, single-purpose functions that do not require formal declarations.
- Implement higher-order functions to leverage the flexibility of lambdas in complex operations.
- Ensure lambda expressions are kept simple and avoid overly complex logic that can hinder clarity.

Lambda expressions are an essential feature in the arsenal of Simula programming tools. By allowing compact and practical function definitions, they contribute to producing clean, efficient, and maintainable code. Their integration into everyday programming enables advanced functional paradigms and optimizes the expressive power of Simula.

4.11 Error Handling in Functions

Error handling in functions is an essential aspect of robust software development in Simula. Ensuring that functions can gracefully handle errors and exceptional situations not only enhances the reliability of the software but also aids in debugging and maintenance. This section will delve into the techniques and constructs available for implementing error handling in Simula functions.

Simula, like many programming languages, provides mechanisms for error detection, error propagation, and error recovery. In the context of functions, error handling primarily involves managing unexpected conditions that may arise during the execution of a function. Let's explore these concepts in detail.

1. Basic Error Handling Techniques

Basic error handling in Simula involves checking conditions and using standard control structures to manage errors. A simple and common method is the use of conditional statements to validate input parameters and intermediate results within a function. If an error or invalid condition is detected, the function can return a specific error code or perform corrective actions.

```
PROCEDURE Divide(NUM, DENOM); REAL NUM, DENOM;
  IF DENOM = 0 THEN
    BEGIN
      OutText("Error: Division by zero");
      RETURN -1;
    END;
  ELSE
    RETURN NUM / DENOM;
```

In the above procedure Divide, the condition DENOM $= 0$ is checked to prevent a division by zero. If this condition is met, an error message is printed and a sentinel value (-1) is returned, indicating the occurrence of an error.

2. Using GLOBAL and LOCAL Variables for Error States

Another approach to error handling involves the use of GLOBAL and LOCAL variables to maintain and communicate error states. This approach allows for more comprehensive error information to be conveyed between functions.

```
GLOBAL INTEGER G_ErrorCode;

PROCEDURE SafeDivide(NUM, DENOM); REAL NUM, DENOM;
BEGIN
  IF DENOM = 0 THEN
    BEGIN
      G_ErrorCode := 1001; /* Setting an error code for division by zero */
      RETURN 0;
    END;
  ELSE
    BEGIN
      G_ErrorCode := 0; /* No error */
      RETURN NUM / DENOM;
    END;
END;
```

In this example, G_ErrorCode is a GLOBAL variable used to store the error code. By checking the value of G_ErrorCode after calling SafeDivide, other parts of the program can determine if an error occurred and take appropriate action.

3. Exception Handling Constructs

Simula supports exception handling through the use of predefined and user-defined exceptions. Exceptions provide a more structured and powerful way to handle errors and exceptional conditions.

```
EXCEPTION DivisionByZero;

PROCEDURE RobustDivide(NUM, DENOM); REAL NUM, DENOM;
BEGIN
  IF DENOM = 0 THEN
    RAISE DivisionByZero;
  RETURN NUM / DENOM;
END;

TRY
  RealResult := RobustDivide(10, 0);
CATCH DivisionByZero:
  OutText("Caught an exception: Division by zero");
CATCHALL:
  OutText("Caught an unexpected exception");
END;
```

In the code above, the RobustDivide procedure raises an exception DivisionByZero when a division by zero is attempted. The TRY block encloses the call to RobustDivide, and the CATCH blocks are used to handle the DivisionByZero exception specifically, as well as any other unexpected exceptions (CATCHALL).

4. Defining Custom Exceptions

Defining and using custom exceptions enhances the readability and manageability of your code by clearly specifying different types of errors that might occur.

```
EXCEPTION InvalidParameter, CalculationError;

PROCEDURE ComputeValue(X); REAL X;
BEGIN
  IF X < 0 THEN
    RAISE InvalidParameter;
  ELSE IF X > 100 THEN
    RAISE CalculationError;
  RETURN SQRT(X);
END;

TRY
  RealResult := ComputeValue(150);
CATCH InvalidParameter:
  OutText("Input parameter is invalid");
CATCH CalculationError:
  OutText("Calculation error occurred");
END;
```

In this code, two custom exceptions InvalidParameter and CalculationError are defined. Within the ComputeValue procedure, these exceptions are raised under specific conditions. The TRY block and subsequent CATCH blocks illustrate how different exceptions are managed, allowing the program to handle each error condition appropriately.

By employing the techniques outlined in this section, developers can create functions that not only handle errors more effectively but also increase the robustness and maintainability of their Simula programs.

Chapter 5

Classes and Objects

This chapter explores the principles of classes and objects in Simula. It covers the definition and creation of classes and objects, along with class members such as fields and methods. Topics include constructors, destructors, encapsulation, object lifetime, access specifiers, static members, and object relationships like association, aggregation, and composition, providing foundational knowledge of object-oriented programming in Simula.

5.1 Introduction to Classes and Objects

The concepts of classes and objects form the cornerstone of object-oriented programming in Simula. Understanding these concepts is essential for leveraging the full capabilities of the language. This section elucidates the foundational ideas surrounding classes and objects, providing a comprehensive overview that will set the stage for more advanced topics in subsequent sections.

A *class* is a blueprint for creating objects. It defines a set of attributes and methods that the created objects will possess. In Simula, a class encapsulates data (fields) and functions (methods) that operate on the data, promoting modularity and reuse.

Using the following simplified example, we illustrate the creation of a minimal class and object in Simula:

```
Begin
```

```
  Class Vehicle;
    Integer wheels;
    Real speed;
    Procedure SetSpeed(new_speed); Real new_speed;
      Begin
        speed := new_speed
      End of SetSpeed;
    Procedure DisplayDetails;
      Begin
        OutText("Wheels: & wheels & Speed: & speed); NewLine
      End of DisplayDetails;
  End of Vehicle;
End;
```

In the example above, the Vehicle class is defined with two fields, wheels and speed, and two methods, SetSpeed and DisplayDetails.

The *object* is an instance of a class. When an object is instantiated, it inherits the structure and behavior defined by the class but operates independently. Each object maintains its own state (values of fields) and behavior (methods).

To create an object of the Vehicle class and interact with it, one writes:

```
Begin
  Vehicle myCar;
  myCar :- New Vehicle;
  myCar.wheels := 4;
  myCar.SetSpeed(100.0);
  myCar.DisplayDetails;
End;
```

The myCar object, an instance of the Vehicle class, is created and initialized. The method SetSpeed sets the speed field, and the DisplayDetails method prints the details of the object.

```
Wheels: 4 Speed: 100.0
```

In object-oriented programming, classes encourage the reuse of code and the principle of "don't repeat yourself" (DRY). They promote encapsulation, where internal state and functionality are hidden from the outside and accessed through defined methods.

Another significant aspect of classes and objects in Simula is the use of *constructors* and *destructors* for managing the lifecycle of objects. The constructor initializes the object, while the destructor cleans up resources when the object is no longer needed. Although constructors and destructors will be discussed in detail in later sections, the following provides a brief introduction:

```
Begin
  Class Vehicle;
    Integer wheels;
```

```
      Real speed;
      ! Constructor
      Vehicle;
         Begin
            wheels := 0;
            speed := 0.0;
         End of Vehicle;
      ! Destructor
      Destructor;
         Begin
            OutText("Destroying Vehicle"); NewLine
         End of Destructor;
      Procedure SetSpeed(new_speed); Real new_speed;
         Begin
            speed := new_speed
         End of SetSpeed;
      Procedure DisplayDetails;
         Begin
            OutText("Wheels: "& wheels & " Speed: " & speed); NewLine
         End of DisplayDetails;
   End of Vehicle;
End;
```

The constructor Vehicle ensures that fields are initialized, and the destructor prints a message when the object is destroyed. This further strengthens the reliability and maintainability of the program by ensuring that objects are always in a valid state.

The principles of classes and objects serve as a foundation for many advanced features in object-oriented programming, such as inheritance, polymorphism, and dynamic binding. Understanding these basics is crucial for proficiency in Simula and other object-oriented languages. This section has laid the groundwork for exploring these constructs in the context of Simula, and the following sections will build on this knowledge to delve into more complex interactions and functionalities integral to mastering Simula programming.

5.2 Defining Classes

In Simula, the definition of classes provides the blueprint for creating objects. A class encapsulates data and behavior, defining members such as fields and methods, which represent the object's state and operations, respectively. The syntax and structure used to define a class in Simula are critical for constructing functional and efficient object-oriented programs.

A basic class definition in Simula utilizes the class keyword followed by the class name and an optional parameter list. The class body is enclosed within begin and end statements. Here is a simple example of a class definition:

```
class Point(x, y);
begin
    real x, y;
end Point;
```

In this example, Point is a class with two parameters, x and y, which represent the coordinates of a point in a two-dimensional space. The parameters x and y are declared as real types inside the class body.

Class Members

Class members in Simula consist of fields and methods. Fields store the object's data, while methods define the operations that can be performed on the object's data.

Fields

Fields, also known as instance variables, are declared within the class body and can be of any data type, such as integer, real, boolean, or other classes. Fields represent the properties or state of the object. For example:

```
class Circle(radius);
begin
    real radius;
    real Pi := 3.14159;

    real area;
    real circumference;
end Circle;
```

In the Circle class, radius is a parameter representing the radius of the circle. The fields area and circumference are declared to store the computed values for the circle's area and circumference. The Pi field is initialized to the constant value 3.14159, demonstrating field initialization during declaration.

Methods

Methods in Simula are procedures or functions defined within a class that operate on the class's fields. Methods define the behavior of the objects created from the class. Here is an example of adding methods to the Circle class:

```
class Circle(radius);
begin
    real radius;
    real Pi := 3.14159;

    real area;
```

```
    real circumference;

    procedure ComputeArea;
    begin
        area := Pi * radius * radius;
    end ComputeArea;

    procedure ComputeCircumference;
    begin
        circumference := 2 * Pi * radius;
    end ComputeCircumference;
end Circle;
```

In this example, two methods, ComputeArea and ComputeCircumference, are defined within the Circle class. These methods compute the area and circumference of the circle using the radius field, and store the results in the area and circumference fields.

Constructors and Initialization

Constructors in Simula are special methods called during the creation of an object to initialize fields. Simula does not have explicit constructor syntax like some other languages, but initialization can be performed in the class body.

Let's illustrate this by initializing the fields in the Circle class:

```
class Circle(radius);
begin
    real radius;
    real Pi := 3.14159;

    real area := Pi * radius * radius;
    real circumference := 2 * Pi * radius;

    procedure ComputeArea;
    begin
        area := Pi * radius * radius;
    end ComputeArea;

    procedure ComputeCircumference;
    begin
        circumference := 2 * Pi * radius;
    end ComputeCircumference;
end Circle;
```

Here, area and circumference are initialized when the Circle object is created. The expressions for field initialization are evaluated using the parameter radius.

Encapsulation and Access Control

Simula supports encapsulation by restricting access to class members. This can be managed using access specifiers like public, protected, and private.

To control access to the class members, fields and methods can be declared with these access specifiers. Access specifiers allow the designer to hide the implementation details and provide controlled interfaces for interacting with the object.

For instance, consider the following Circle class with access control:

```
class Circle(radius);
begin
    real radius; ! Public field by default
    real Pi := 3.14159;

    private real area := Pi * radius * radius;
    private real circumference := 2 * Pi * radius;

    public procedure PrintMeasurements;
    begin
        outtext("Area: "); outreal(area); outimage;
        outtext("Circumference: "); outreal(circumference); outimage;
    end PrintMeasurements;
end Circle;
```

Here, the fields area and circumference are declared as private, preventing direct access from outside the class. The method PrintMeasurements is declared as public, allowing external code to call this method and obtain the circle's measurements.

Example

Let's combine these concepts in an example program that demonstrates defining and using the Circle class:

```
begin
    ref(Circle) myCircle;
    ! Create a Circle object with radius 5
    myCircle :- new Circle(5);

    ! Call public method to print measurements
    myCircle.PrintMeasurements;
end;
```

Executing this program will produce the following output:

```
Area: 78.53975
Circumference: 31.4159
```

5.3 Creating Objects

Creating objects in Simula involves the instantiation of a defined class, bringing into existence an instance that encompasses the attributes and behaviors delineated by the class. This process establishes the template by which objects are defined, acting as foundational constructs in object-oriented programming.

To create an object, one must first define a class, followed by instantiating that class. Consider the following example where we define a class Person:

```
Begin
  Class Person;
    Begin
    Text name;
    Integer age;
    Procedure init(nm Text, ag Integer);
      Begin
      name := nm;
      age := ag;
      End of init;
    End of Class Person;
End;
```

Upon defining the class Person, we can instantiate objects of this class using the New keyword. The creation of objects typically involves invoking a constructor, which in Simula, initializes the object with specific states.

```
Begin
  Ref(Person) p1, p2;
  p1 :- New Person("Alice", 30);
  p2 :- New Person("Bob", 25);
End;
```

In this snippet, p1 and p2 are references to objects of class Person, instantiated with initial values "Alice", 30 for p1 and "Bob", 25 for p2. Here, p1 and p2 are dynamically allocated objects with their respective attributes initialized via the init procedure.

When an object is created, Simula allocates memory dynamically for the object, and the constructor initializes its attributes. The New keyword is followed by the class name and the parameters that the constructor requires.

Further elaborating on the dynamic allocation, Simula ensures automatic garbage collection, thus relieving the programmer from manual memory management. This prevents common programming errors like memory leaks.

```
p1.name = Alice
p1.age = 30
p2.name = Bob
p2.age = 25
```

It is essential to highlight the powerful abstraction capability facilitated by object creation. Each instance of the class Person retains independent copies of the name and age, allowing diverse states among objects of the same class.

Objects in Simula are accessed through references, which means that a reference can point to different objects or even be made null. This can be demonstrated by reassigning an object reference:

```
Ref(Person) p3;
p3 :- p1; -- p3 now references the same object as p1
p3:- Void; -- p3 is now null
```

This flexibility underscores the importance of object-oriented paradigms in managing complex systems through encapsulated state and behavior.

To summarize, object creation in Simula involves defining a class, utilizing the New keyword to instantiate objects of this class, and initializing object attributes through constructors. This process enables the deployment of robust object-oriented designs in Simula programs.

5.4 Class Members: Fields and Methods

In Simula, a class is defined by its members, which broadly classify into fields (also known as attributes or instance variables) and methods (also known as functions or procedures). These members collectively determine the properties and behaviors of the objects instantiated from the class.

A field of a class in Simula holds data that pertains to the objects of the class. Fields can be of various data types like integer, real, boolean, text, etc. A field can be static or instance-based, where static fields share the same value across all instances of the class, whereas instance-based fields are unique to each object.

The syntax for defining a field within a Simula class is straightforward. Here's an example that demonstrates the definition of two fields, length and width, in a Rectangle class:

```
Class Rectangle;
   Begin
      ! Fields;
      Real length, width;
   End;
```

In the above example, length and width are defined as fields with the Real data type. These fields hold the dimensions of rectangular objects instantiated from the Rectangle class.

Methods in Simula are used to define behaviors or operations that can be performed on the objects of the class. Methods are essential for implementing the functionality associated with the encapsulated data. Methods can be classified as instance methods or class methods, just like fields.

Here's an example that adds a method named Area to the Rectangle class, which calculates the area of the rectangle:

```
Class Rectangle;
  Begin
    ! Fields;
    Real length, width;

    ! Method to calculate area;
    Real Procedure Area;
      Begin
        Area := length * width;
      End Area;
  End;
```

In this example, the Area method is defined to calculate and return the area of the rectangle. The method multiplies the values of the fields length and width to compute the area.

Encapsulation is a fundamental principle of object-oriented programming that Simula supports through its class definitions. Encapsulation involves bundling the data (fields) and the methods that operate on the data into a single unit (the class), and restricting access to some of the object's components. This is achieved using access specifiers, which will be discussed in detail in a later section of this chapter.

Instance methods can access and modify the instance fields of the class, whereas static methods operate at the class level and can manipulate static fields. Here's an example illustrating the introduction of a static field and a static method:

```
Class Circle;
  Begin
    Real radius;
    Ref(Circle) Class count;

    ! Static field to keep track of number of Circle objects;
    Integer NumberOfCircles;

    ! Static method to increment the circle count;
    Procedure IncrementCount;
      Begin
        Integer count;
        count := NumberOfCircles + 1;
        NumberOfCircles := count;
      End IncrementCount;
```

```
        ! Constructor for Circle;
        Procedure CircleConstructor(Real r);
          Begin
            radius := r;
            IncrementCount;
          End CircleConstructor;
    End Circle;
```

Here, the Circle class declares a static integer field NumberOfCircles to track the number of instances of Circle created. The static method IncrementCount increments the NumberOfCircles count whenever a new instance of Circle is constructed using the CircleConstructor method.

Methods can also be overloaded, which means that multiple methods in the same class can have the same name but different parameter lists. This allows for flexibility in how methods of the same name can behave differently based on the arguments they receive. Here's an example:

```
Class Sample;
  Begin
    ! Overloaded methods;
    Text Procedure Print(Ref(Integer) num);
      Begin
        OutText("Integer: " & num & "\n")
      End Print;

    Text Procedure Print(Ref(Real) num);
      Begin
        OutText("Real: " & num & "\n")
      End Print;

    Text Procedure Print(Ref(Text) str);
      Begin
        OutText("Text: " & str & "\n")
      End Print;
  End Sample;
```

In the above example, the Print method is overloaded to handle Integer, Real, and Text types. Depending on the parameter type passed to the Print method, the appropriate version of the method gets invoked.

Comprehension of class members, both fields, and methods, is crucial for mastering object-oriented programming in Simula. Fields represent the state of an object, while methods define its behavior. The intricate interaction between fields and methods, along with their scope and lifetime, forms the cornerstone of effective class design in Simula.

5.5 Constructors and Destructors

Constructors and destructors are key components in the lifecycle of an object. In Simula, they play a crucial role in initializing and cleaning up resources respectively. Understanding how to effectively use constructors and destructors ensures that objects are set up correctly and resources are handled properly, preventing issues such as memory leaks.

A constructor is a special method that is automatically invoked when an object of a class is created. It initializes the object's fields and performs any setup required. Conversely, a destructor is a method that is called when an object is destroyed, which is typically when it goes out of scope or is explicitly deleted. Destructors free any resources that the object may have acquired during its lifetime.

Here is a detailed look into how constructors and destructors are defined and used in Simula:

Constructors: A constructor in Simula is defined within a class and has the same name as the class itself. It can take parameters to initialize an object's state, enabling the creation of objects with specific attributes right at the moment of their instantiation.

Consider the following example where we define a class Person with a constructor:

```
CLASS Person;
  BEGIN
    TEXT name;
    INTEGER age;

    PROCEDURE Person(nm); TEXT nm;
      COMMENT This is the constructor for the Person class;
      name := nm;
      age := 0;
    END;
  END;
```

In this example, the constructor Person takes a TEXT argument nm which is used to initialize the name field of the Person object. The age field is set to a default value of 0. The special comment indicates the purpose of the constructor to enhance readability.

Destructors: A destructor is a method meant to release resources that the object may have acquired during its lifetime. In Simula, destructors are defined with the keyword PROCEDURE followed by any necessary cleanup code. While destructors are less common in early object-oriented languages due to automated memory management, they can be crucial when dealing with resources like files or network connections.

Here is an enhanced example of the Person class with a destructor:

```
CLASS Person;
  BEGIN
    TEXT name;
    INTEGER age;

    PROCEDURE Person(nm); TEXT nm;
      COMMENT This is the constructor for the Person class;
      name := nm;
      age := 0;
    END;

    PROCEDURE finalize;
      COMMENT This is the destructor for the Person class;
      OUTTEXT("Destroying object: " & name); Outimage;
      ! Here we could include code to release resources if any;
    END finalize;

  END;
```

In this example, the finalize procedure acts as the destructor. It provides a simple output message to indicate that the object is being destroyed. The use of OUTTEXT for output and Outimage to finalize the line provides a straightforward illustration of a destructor's functionality.

Constructor Overloading: Simula also supports constructor overloading, allowing multiple constructors within a class, each with different parameter lists. This enables objects to be initialized in various ways.

```
CLASS Person;
  BEGIN
    TEXT name;
    INTEGER age;

    PROCEDURE Person(nm); TEXT nm;
      name := nm;
      age := 0;
    END;

    PROCEDURE Person(nm, ag); TEXT nm; INTEGER ag;
      name := nm;
      age := ag;
    END;
  END;
```

Here, the Person class has two constructors: one that takes only the name and sets age to 0, and another that takes both a name and an age. This provides flexibility in object creation.

Explicit Destructor Invocation: While destructors are typically called automatically, there may be situations where an explicit invocation is necessary to promptly release resources.

```
REF(Person) p1;
p1 :- NEW Person("Alice", 30);
CALL p1.finalize; ! Explicitly calling the destructor.
p1 :- NONE; ! Setting reference to NONE to ensure the object gets cleaned up.
```

In this case, the destructor finalize is explicitly invoked using the CALL statement, ensuring resources are promptly released before resetting the reference.

: Understanding and utilizing constructors and destructors in Simula enables effective object initialization and cleanup. Constructors ensure that objects are properly set up with necessary initial values, while destructors handle cleanup tasks, ensuring that resources are managed efficiently. Proper usage of these functionalities is essential for robust and maintainable code.

5.6 Encapsulation and Data Hiding

Encapsulation and data hiding are fundamental concepts in object-oriented programming (OOP) that deal with restricting access to certain components of an object to ensure controlled interaction and maintain the integrity of the object's state.

Encapsulation refers to the bundling of data and the methods that operate on that data within a single unit, i.e., a class in Simula. This enables the grouping of attributes (data fields) and behaviors (methods) to be treated as a single cohesive unit. By encapsulating these elements, it is possible to expose a limited interface to interact with the object's data while keeping the internal implementation and state hidden from the outside world.

Data Hiding is a mechanism to restrict direct access to some of the object's components. This can be achieved by using access specifiers such as private, protected, and public to regulate the visibility of class members. By hiding the internal state and requiring all interactions to occur through methods, we can ensure that the object behaves in a controlled and predictable manner.

In Simula, access specifiers are utilized to define the visibility and accessibility of class members. The public members are accessible from anywhere within the program, protected members are accessible within the defining class and its subclasses, and private members are accessible only within the defining class.

Encapsulation and data hiding are illustrated through the following example:

```
\\ Define a class with encapsulation and data hiding
class BankAccount;
private:
    real balance;

public:
    procedure deposit(amount); real amount;
    begin
        balance := balance + amount;
    end;

    procedure withdraw(amount); real amount;
    begin
        if amount <= balance then
            balance := balance - amount
        else
            outtext("Insufficient funds."); outimage;
    end;

    procedure getBalance; real out balance;

begin
    balance := 0.0;
end BankAccount;
```

In the above code:

- The class BankAccount encapsulates the attribute balance and the methods deposit, withdraw, and getBalance.
- The balance attribute is declared as private, thereby hiding it from the outside world.
- The methods deposit and withdraw are declared as public, allowing controlled access to modify the balance.
- The getBalance method provides read-only access to the value of balance.

It is also possible to use method definitions to change how data is accessed or modified. By implementing methods such as setBalance which could include verification or constraints, impactful changes to an object's state can be controlled scrupulously.

```
\\ Adding a setBalance method with constraints
procedure setBalance(newBalance); real newBalance;
begin
```

```
    if newBalance >= 0 then
        balance := newBalance
    else
        outtext("Balance cannot be negative."); outimage;
end;

\\ Usage Scenarios
procedure main;
begin
    ref(BankAccount) myAccount;
    myAccount :- new BankAccount;
    myAccount.deposit(100.0);
    myAccount.withdraw(50.0);

    \\ Direct access to balance is not possible, e.g., myAccount.balance := 200 is an
        error.
    myAccount.setBalance(-10.0); // Will print an error message about negative
        balance.
end;
```

The practice of accessing object data strictly through interfaces (methods) enforces encapsulation, providing benefits such as:

- **Security**: Data hiding ensures sensitive data is not exposed to unintended parts of the program.
- **Modularity**: Breaking the program into distinct classes enhances modularity, improves maintainability, and allows for easier updates.
- **Change Management**: Since the internal structure can be modified without affecting the external interface, the impact of changes can be reduced significantly.
- **Code Reusability**: Encapsulated classes with well-defined interfaces can be reused in different parts of the program or in different projects without worrying about internal details.

These principles are integral to designing robust, maintainable, and secure software. Properly encapsulated classes with hidden data and exposed operations allow developers to build complex systems with clearly defined boundaries and interactions, facilitating collaboration and code maintenance.

Encapsulation and data hiding contribute significantly to software engineering practices by promoting disciplined coding standards, reducing dependencies, and enhancing the robustness of the software design.

5.7 Object Lifetime and Memory Management

In Simula, understanding object lifetime and memory management is crucial for effective programming. This section provides an in-depth look into how objects are created, used, and destroyed, and how memory is allocated and freed. This knowledge enables the programmer to manage resources efficiently and avoid common pitfalls such as memory leaks and dangling references.

Object lifetime refers to the duration an object exists in memory from its creation to its destruction. In Simula, objects are created via constructors—special member functions that initialize new objects. Memory management pertains to how the programming language allocates and deallocates memory for objects.

Simula supports dynamic memory allocation for objects, meaning objects are typically created on the heap. The heap is a region of memory used for dynamic allocation. This is in contrast to stack allocation, which is used for local variables and has more rigid lifetime rules.

To illustrate object creation and memory allocation, consider the following Simula class definition and object instantiation:

```
Class Vehicle;
   Begin
      Integer speed;
      Real fuel;
      Vehicle();
      Begin
         speed := 0;
         fuel := 100.0;
      End;
   End;

Begin
   Vehicle MyCar;
   MyCar :- New Vehicle;
End;
```

In this example, Vehicle is a class with two fields, speed and fuel. The constructor Vehicle() initializes speed to 0 and fuel to 100. The object MyCar is dynamically instantiated using the New keyword.

When an object is no longer needed, it should be properly deallocated to free up memory. Simula uses garbage collection to manage memory for objects, which automatically deallocates memory that is no longer in use. However, explicit deallocation can be performed using the Detach procedure.

Consider the following scenario where objects are deallocated explicitly:

```
Begin
   Vehicle *MyCar, *YourCar;
   MyCar :- New Vehicle;
   YourCar :- New Vehicle;

   ! Finished using MyCar, deallocate the memory:
   Detach(MyCar);
   ! MyCar now points to null

   ! Finished using YourCar:
   Detach(YourCar);
End;
```

Here, Detach(MyCar) deallocates the memory associated with MyCar, and Detach(YourCar) does the same for YourCar. After calling Detach, the pointers MyCar and YourCar are set to null, ensuring they do not point to invalid memory locations.

Understanding how memory is allocated and deallocated is key to preventing memory leaks. A memory leak occurs when memory that is no longer needed is not released, causing a program to consume more memory over time and potentially leading to performance degradation or crashes.

Consider the following example where a memory leak can occur:

```
Begin
   Ref(Vehicle) MyCar;
   Integer i;

   For i := 1 Step 1 Until 100000 Do
   Begin
      MyCar :- New Vehicle;
   End;
End;
```

In this loop, each iteration allocates memory for MyCar without freeing the previous allocation. This results in a memory leak, as the previously allocated Vehicle objects remain in memory. To prevent such leaks, Detach should be used within the loop:

```
Begin
   Ref(Vehicle) MyCar;
   Integer i;

   For i := 1 Step 1 Until 100000 Do
   Begin
      If MyCar /= Null Then Detach(MyCar);
      MyCar :- New Vehicle;
   End;
```

```
End;
```

Incorporating Detach(MyCar) ensures that each old instance of MyCar is deallocated before a new instance is allocated, thus preventing memory leaks.

In summary, the lifetime of an object in Simula starts with its creation using a constructor and ends when its memory is deallocated, either automatically through garbage collection or explicitly using Detach. Effective management of object lifetime and memory ensures efficient use of resources and promotes robust, reliable program execution.

5.8 Access Specifiers: Public, Private, Protected

In object-oriented programming with Simula, access specifiers play a crucial role in controlling the visibility and accessibility of class members. These specifiers are essential to implement encapsulation, which is a fundamental concept of object-oriented design that allows the internal representation of an object to be hidden from the outside. Simula offers three primary access specifiers—public, private, and protected—each providing different levels of access control.

Public Access Specifier

Members declared as public are accessible from any other part of the program. This means that both internal methods and external functions can directly access these members. Public members are useful when an interface to an object's behavior or data needs to be exposed.

```
class SampleClass;
public integer x, y; ! x and y are accessible from outside the class.
begin
  x := 10;
  y := 20;
  procedure DisplayValues;
  begin
    outreal(x, 5, 3); newline;
    outreal(y, 5, 3); newline;
  end DisplayValues;
end SampleClass;

begin
  SampleClass obj;
  obj :- new SampleClass;
  obj.DisplayValues;
  outreal(obj.x, 5, 3); newline; ! Accessing public member x
  outreal(obj.y, 5, 3); newline; ! Accessing public member y
```

```
end;
```

In the above example, x and y are declared as public members of SampleClass, making them accessible from outside the class.

Private Access Specifier

Members declared as private are only accessible within the class in which they are declared. This ensures that the internal representation of the object remains hidden from other objects and functions. By using the private access specifier, we can safeguard data from unintended modifications.

```
class SampleClass;
private integer x, y; ! x and y are not accessible from outside the class.
begin
  x := 10;
  y := 20;
  procedure SetValues(a, b); ! Method to set the values of x and y
  integer a, b;
  begin
    x := a;
    y := b;
  end SetValues;

  procedure DisplayValues;
  begin
    outreal(x, 5, 3); newline;
    outreal(y, 5, 3); newline;
  end DisplayValues;
end SampleClass;

begin
  SampleClass obj;
  obj :- new SampleClass;
  obj.SetValues(100, 200);
  obj.DisplayValues;
  ! obj.x := 300; ! This would result in a compilation error
end;
```

In this example, x and y are declared as private, meaning that they are not accessible from outside SampleClass. Any attempt to access obj.x or obj.y outside the class scope will result in a compilation error, thus preserving the encapsulation.

Protected Access Specifier

Members declared as protected are similar to private members but with one crucial difference: they can be accessed by derived classes. This is particularly useful in inheritance scenarios where derived classes need access to certain members from the base class.

```
class BaseClass;
protected integer x; ! x is not accessible from outside the class but accessible by derived
    classes.
```

```
begin
  x := 10;
  procedure DisplayBase;
  begin
    outreal(x, 5, 3); newline;
  end DisplayBase;
end BaseClass;

class DerivedClass;
begin
  integer y;
  procedure SetValues(a); ! Method to set the value of y and base class x
  integer a;
  begin
    x := a; ! Accessing protected member from base class
    y := a + 10;
  end SetValues;

  procedure DisplayDerived;
  begin
    outreal(x, 5, 3); newline; ! Accessing protected member x
    outreal(y, 5, 3); newline;
  end DisplayDerived;
end DerivedClass;

begin
  DerivedClass obj2;
  obj2 :- new DerivedClass;
  obj2.SetValues(100);
  obj2.DisplayDerived;
end;
```

In this illustration, x is declared as protected in BaseClass, making it accessible to DerivedClass. This allows derived classes to interact with certain members of the base class, facilitating an appropriate level of access control.

Understanding and appropriately using access specifiers—public, private, and protected—in Simula is fundamental for robust and maintainable object-oriented design. Effective utilization of these access levels enhances data encapsulation, promoting better control over how data is accessed and modified within a program.

5.9 Static Members and Methods

In Simula, as in many other object-oriented programming languages, static members and methods are a critical feature that allows for defining class-level data and functions rather than instance-level. This means that static members are shared among all instances of a class, rather than belonging to a particular instance. Understanding static members and methods is essential for scenarios where shared data or utility functions are needed.

Static members are declared with the keyword static. These members can be accessed without creating an instance of the class. Let's consider a practical example of static members and methods.

```
CLASS BankAccount;
    BEGIN
        TEXT name;
        REAL balance;
        REAL INTEREST_RATE;

        ! Static member
        REAL LOGIN_COUNT;

        PROCEDURE init(n, b);
        TEXT n;
        REAL b;
        BEGIN
            name := n;
            balance := b;
        END;

        ! Static method
        PROCEDURE incrementLoginCount;
        BEGIN
            LOGIN_COUNT := LOGIN_COUNT + 1;
        END;

        PROCEDURE printDetails;
        BEGIN
            OutText(name); OutImage;
            OutReal(balance); OutImage;
            OutReal(LOGIN_COUNT); OutImage;
        END;

    END;
```

In the above example, LOGIN_COUNT is a static member shared by all instances of the BankAccount class.

To access or modify the static member LOGIN_COUNT from outside the class, you can directly use the class name, as demonstrated below:

```
BEGIN
    BankAccount.LOGIN_COUNT := 0; ! Initialize the static member
    REF(BankAccount) acc1, acc2;

    acc1 :- NEW BankAccount;
    acc1.init("Alice", 1000.0);
    acc1.incrementLoginCount;

    acc2 :- NEW BankAccount;
    acc2.init("Bob", 2000.0);
    acc2.incrementLoginCount;

    OutText("After Logins:"); OutImage;
    acc1.printDetails;
    acc2.printDetails;
```

```
END;
```

The output of the above code will show that the static member LOGIN_-COUNT is incremented across all instances of BankAccount, reflecting its shared nature.

```
After Logins:
Alice
1000.00000
2.00000

Bob
2000.00000
2.00000
```

When a static member is modified through one instance, the change is reflected across all instances. This characteristic makes static members particularly useful for implementing counters, configuration parameters, or singleton instances.

To declare static methods, you use the same static keyword. Static methods can only access other static members and cannot access instance members directly because there is no instance-specific context. Considering the above example, the method incrementLoginCount is static and can be called directly using the class name.

```
BankAccount.incrementLoginCount;
```

Some key points about static members and methods include:

- Static members are shared among all instances of a class.
- Static methods can be called without creating an instance of the class.
- Static members and methods can only interact with other static members and methods.
- Static members can be used for configurations, counters, or any data that needs a singular form across all instances.

Static methods can also be employed for utility functions which do not depend on instance-specific data. For example:

```
CLASS MathUtils;
   BEGIN
      ! Static method
      PROCEDURE addNumbers(a, b);
      REAL a, b;
      BEGIN
         RETURN a + b;
```

```
        END;
    END;

BEGIN
    REAL result;
    result := MathUtils.addNumbers(5.0, 7.3);
    OutReal(result); OutImage;
END;
```

The output will be:

```
12.30000
```

By using static members and static methods effectively, you can improve the efficiency and clarity of your Simula programs, especially in scenarios requiring shared data and common utility functions across various parts of an application.

5.10 Object Relationships: Association, Aggregation, Composition

In object-oriented programming (OOP), understanding the relationships between objects is crucial. These relationships define how objects interact with one another within a system. There are three primary types of object relationships in Simula: Association, Aggregation, and Composition. Each relationship type has distinct properties and implications for object management and lifetime.

Association is the most general form of relationship. It signifies that one object (the source object) interacts with another object (the target object). The association does not entail any lifecycle dependency between the associated objects. For instance, a Customer object might be associated with a BankAccount object. The customer's lifetime is independent of the bank account and vice versa.

The following is an example of Customer and BankAccount in Simula:

```
CLASS Customer;
    TEXT name;
    INTEGER id;
    REF(BankAccount) account;
    PROCEDURE addAccount(acc); REF(BankAccount) acc;
    BEGIN
        account := acc;
    END;
END;

CLASS BankAccount;
    INTEGER accountNumber;
```

```
    REAL balance;
    PROCEDURE deposit(amount); REAL amount;
    BEGIN
        balance := balance + amount;
    END;
END;

REF(Customer) c1;
c1:- NEW Customer;
c1.name:= "Alice";
c1.id:= 101;

REF(BankAccount) ba1;
ba1:- NEW BankAccount;
ba1.accountNumber:= 123456789;
ba1.balance:= 1000.0;

CALL c1.addAccount(ba1);
```

The Customer class has an association with the BankAccount class via the account field. However, they can exist independently of each other.

Aggregation represents a whole-part relationship between two objects. In this relationship, the part object (the aggregate) can exist independently of the whole object. For example, a Library object may aggregate Book objects. While books are part of the library, they can also exist independently as individual books are not bound by the library's lifecycle.

An implementation of aggregation between Library and Book in Simula could look like this:

```
CLASS Library;
    TEXT name;
    REF(LIST(Book)) books;
    PROCEDURE addBook(b); REF(Book) b;
    BEGIN
        IF books == NOTEXT() THEN
            books:- NEW LIST(Book);
        END;
        books.ADD_LAST(b);
    END;
END;

CLASS Book;
    TEXT title;
    TEXT author;
END;

REF(Library) lib := NEW Library;
lib.name := "City Library";

REF(Book) book1 := NEW Book;
book1.title := "Simula Programming";
book1.author := "Kristen Nygaard";

CALL lib.addBook(book1);
```

Here, the Library class aggregates multiple Book objects using a list. Each Book object can exist independently of the Library.

Composition is a stronger type of aggregation, where the lifecycle of the part object is strongly linked to the lifecycle of the whole object. If the whole object is destroyed, the part objects are also destroyed. For example, a Computer object might have a Processor object. The Processor exists only as long as the Computer exists.

An example in Simula for Computer and Processor might be:

```
CLASS Computer;
   TEXT model;
   REF(Processor) cpu;
   PROCEDURE initializeProcessor(specs); TEXT specs;
   BEGIN
      cpu:- NEW Processor(specs);
   END;
END;

CLASS Processor;
   TEXT specifications;
   PROCEDURE ProcessorConstructor(specs); TEXT specs;
   BEGIN
      specifications := specs;
   END ProcessorConstructor(specifications);
END;

REF(Computer) myComputer := NEW Computer;
myComputer.model := "Model X";
CALL myComputer.initializeProcessor("3.5 GHz, Quad-Core");
```

In this example, the Processor instance is initialized and tied to the Computer instance via the initializeProcessor procedure. If the myComputer object is destroyed, its component Processor will be destroyed as well, exemplifying composition.

Understanding the distinctions between association, aggregation, and composition is integral to designing robust object-oriented systems in Simula. These relationships influence object dependencies, lifetimes, and the overall architecture of the system. Proper use of these relationships leads to better modularity, maintainability, and clarity in the codebase.

5.11 Cloning and Copying Objects

In object-oriented programming, the ability to create copies of objects is a fundamental aspect that ensures flexibility and control over data manipulation. Simula, like many object-oriented languages, provides mechanisms to clone and copy objects. Understanding these mechanisms is crucial for avoiding unintended side effects and ensuring data integrity.

Cloning and copying, though often used interchangeably, have distinct meanings and implications. Cloning refers to creating a duplicate of an object with a new memory address, whereas copying can involve either shallow or deep copying, depending on whether the copy involves duplicating nested objects and lists or just the top-level structure.

Shallow vs. Deep Copy in Simula

A shallow copy of an object copies the object's top-level structure but not the objects that are referenced by it. Thus, both the original and the copy share references to the same nested objects. On the other hand, a deep copy duplicates not just the object, but also all objects referenced by it, recursively.

```
BEGIN
   CLASS Person;
      TEXT name;
      INTEGER age;
   BEGIN
      name := "";
      age := 0;
   END;

   REF(Person) original, shallowCopy;

   original :- NEW Person;
   original.name := 'Alice';
   original.age := 30;

   shallowCopy :- NEW Person;
   shallowCopy.name := original.name;
   shallowCopy.age := original.age;

   ! both original and shallowCopy share the same name reference
   shallowCopy.name.SetText('Bob');
END;
```

In the above example, modifying shallowCopy.name will affect original.name since both references point to the same TEXT object.

output: original.name and shallowCopy.name both display 'Bob'

Deep Copy Example

To achieve deep copying, we need to recursively duplicate all referenced objects.

```
BEGIN
   CLASS Person;
      TEXT name;
      INTEGER age;
```

```
    BEGIN
        name := '';
        age := 0;

        PROCEDURE Clone;
        REF(Person) p;
        BEGIN
            p :- NEW Person;
            p.name := COPY name;
            p.age := age;
            Clone := p;
        END;
    END;

    REF(Person) original, deepCopy;

    original :- NEW Person;
    original.name := 'Alice';
    original.age := 30;

    deepCopy :- original.Clone;

    ! modifying deepCopy will not affect the original
    deepCopy.name.SetText('Bob');
END;
```

Here, COPY name creates a new TEXT object, ensuring deepCopy.name and original.name are independent.

output: original.name is 'Alice', deepCopy.name is 'Bob'

Implementing Cloning in Custom Classes

For complex objects composed of several nested objects, a custom Clone method must be implemented in each class. This method should create a new instance and recursively clone every nested object.

Algorithm 1: Deep Cloning Algorithm

```
Function Clone(obj):
    Create a new instance of the class
    foreach field in obj do
        if field is a primitive then
            copy field value directly
        else
            call Clone on field and assign result to copied
              object's field
    return the copied object
```

Case Study: Employee Class

Consider an Employee class with nested objects representing address and project details.

```
CLASS Address;
   TEXT street, city;
BEGIN
   street := ''; city := ''; '
END;

CLASS Project;
   TEXT projectName;
BEGIN
   projectName := '';
END;

CLASS Employee;
   TEXT name;
   INTEGER id;
   REF(Address) address;
   REF(Project) project;
BEGIN
   name := ''; id := 0;
   address :- NEW Address;
   project :- NEW Project;

   PROCEDURE Clone;
   REF(Employee) e;
   BEGIN
      e :- NEW Employee;
      e.name := COPY name;
      e.id := id;
      e.address.street := COPY address.street;
      e.address.city := COPY address.city;
      e.project.projectName := COPY project.projectName;
      Clone := e;
   END;
END;
```

```
BEGIN
   REF(Employee) empl, emp2;

   empl :- NEW Employee;
   empl.name := 'John Doe';
   empl.id := 1234;
   empl.address.street := '123 Elm Street';
   empl.address.city := 'Wonderland';
   empl.project.projectName := 'Project X';

   emp2 :- empl.Clone;

   ! modifying emp2 will not affect empl
   emp2.name.SetText('Jane Doe');
   emp2.address.street.SetText('456 Oak Street');
   emp2.project.projectName.SetText('Project Y');
END;
```

By employing a deep cloning method, we ensure that changes to emp2 do not affect empl. This prevents unintended side effects, thereby maintaining data integrity and isolation between object instances.

Understanding and implementing cloning properly is essential for effective object-oriented programming, especially when managing complex objects with multiple levels of nested references. This skill helps in tasks such as implementing undo mechanisms, safely manipulating data copies, or whenever independent object instances are required.

Chapter 6

Inheritance and Polymorphism

This chapter investigates the concepts of inheritance and polymorphism in Simula. It discusses defining subclasses, the use of the 'super' keyword, and various types of inheritance such as single, multiple, and multilevel. Additionally, it covers method overriding, compile-time and run-time polymorphism, abstract classes, interfaces, the 'instanceof' keyword, and object casting, providing a comprehensive understanding of these advanced object-oriented features.

6.1 Introduction to Inheritance

Inheritance is a core concept in object-oriented programming (OOP) and is pivotal to understanding how classes and objects interact in Simula. Inheritance allows a class, known as a subclass, to inherit properties and methods from another class called a superclass. This mechanism promotes reusability, modularity, and the logical structuring of code by allowing shared attributes and behaviors to be defined once in the superclass and then used by the subclass.

The primary goal of inheritance is to enable new classes to receive, or inherit, the features of existing classes. This relationship is often described as an "is-a" relationship, meaning that the subclass is a specialized form of the superclass. For instance, if we have a superclass called Animal, we can create subclasses like Dog and Cat, which inherit from Animal.

In Simula, the syntax for creating a subclass that inherits from a superclass is straightforward. The subclass declaration includes the name of the superclass in its header. Consider the following example to illustrate this:

```
class Animal;
begin
    integer age;
    text name;

    procedure Speak;
    begin
        OutText("The animal makes a sound.");
    end Speak;
end Animal;

class Dog class Animal;
begin
    procedure Speak; ! Overriding the Speak method;
    begin
        OutText("The dog barks.");
    end Speak;
end Dog;
```

In this example, Dog is a subclass of Animal. The subclass inherits the properties age and name from Animal and also the method Speak. However, in the Dog class, the Speak method is overridden to provide a specific implementation for dogs.

Another fundamental aspect of inheritance is the use of the super keyword, allowing the subclass to access properties and methods of its superclass. This is particularly useful when the subclass wants to extend the functionality of an inherited method without completely overriding it. Here is an example demonstrating the use of the super keyword:

```
class Animal;
begin
    integer age;
    text name;

    procedure Speak;
    begin
        OutText("The animal makes a sound.");
    end Speak;
end Animal;

class Dog class Animal;
begin
    procedure Speak; ! Extending the Speak method;
    begin
        call Animal.Speak; ! Call the superclass's Speak method;
```

```
        OutText(" The dog barks.");
    end Speak;
end Dog;
```

In this example, the Dog class extends the Speak method from the Animal class by first calling the superclass's Speak method using the super keyword (in Simula, referenced via the class name Animal) and then adding its specific behavior.

Understanding inheritance requires familiarity with the following terms:

- Superclass: The class whose properties and behaviors are inherited by another class. In the examples above, Animal is the superclass.
- Subclass: The class that inherits properties and behaviors from the superclass. In the examples, Dog is the subclass of Animal.
- Overriding: The process through which a subclass provides a specific implementation of a method that is already defined in its superclass.
- super Keyword: A mechanism that allows the subclass to refer to the superclass, useful for calling the superclass's method or accessing its properties.

Simula supports various types of inheritance, enabling different class hierarchies. These include single inheritance, where a class inherits from one superclass; multiple inheritance, where a class can inherit from more than one superclass; and multilevel inheritance, where a class can be derived from another derived class.

By effectively utilizing inheritance, developers can create more modular, reusable, and maintainable code. It reduces redundancy, as common functionality can be defined once in a superclass and then inherited by multiple subclasses, each potentially adding their specific features or behaviors.

Let's examine a practical example to illustrate the application of inheritance in a more extensive context. Consider a set of classes representing different types of vehicles:

```
class Vehicle;
begin
    integer speed;

    procedure Move;
    begin
```

```
        OutText("The vehicle is moving.");
    end Move;
end Vehicle;

class Car class Vehicle;
begin
    integer numDoors;

    procedure Move; ! Overriding the Move method;
    begin
        call Vehicle.Move;
        OutText(" The car is driving.");
    end Move;
end Car;

class Bicycle class Vehicle;
begin
    boolean hasBell;

    procedure Move; ! Overriding the Move method;
    begin
        call Vehicle.Move;
        OutText(" The bicycle is pedaling.");
    end Move;
end Bicycle;
```

In this example, Vehicle is the superclass with a Move method, and both Car and Bicycle are subclasses that provide specific implementations of the Move method. Each subclass extends the Move method of Vehicle to include behavior specific to Car and Bicycle.

Executing the Move method on instances of Car and Bicycle will produce the following output:

```
The vehicle is moving. The car is driving.
The vehicle is moving. The bicycle is pedaling.
```

This illustrates how subclasses can inherit and extend the functionality of their superclass, allowing for more flexible and organized code.

6.2 Defining a Subclass

In Simula, creating a subclass allows a new class to inherit the properties and methods of an existing class, known as the superclass. This facilitates code reuse, enhances maintainability, and promotes a hierarchical organization of classes. To define a subclass, one must follow a specific syntax and understand the principles governing inheritance in Simula.

A subclass is defined using the class keyword, followed by the name of the subclass, a colon, and the name of the superclass. Optionally, the subclass can declare its own fields and methods in addition to those inherited from the superclass.

```
class SuperClass;
    begin
        integer x;
        x := 0;
        procedure display;
            begin
                OutInt(x, 5);
                OutImage;
            end;
    end;

class SubClass : SuperClass;
    begin
        integer y;
        y := 0;
        procedure show;
            begin
                OutInt(y, 5);
                OutImage;
            end;
    end;
```

In this example, SuperClass defines an integer field x and a procedure display. SubClass, which inherits from SuperClass, defines an additional integer field y and a procedure show. By inheriting from SuperClass, SubClass also gains access to the x field and the display method.

When an instance of SubClass is created, it contains the properties and methods of both SuperClass and SubClass.

```
ref(SubClass) obj;
obj:- new SubClass;

obj.x := 10;
obj.y := 20;
obj.display;
obj.show;
```

The output of this program would be:

```
10
20
```

It is significant to note that the fields and methods defined in the superclass are inherited directly and, unless overridden, become part of the subclass without any extra declaration. This example showcases the default behavior of field and method inheritance.

Moreover, subclass constructors and initializations follow a hierarchical execution. When a subclass is instantiated, the initialization code of the superclass is executed first. This ensures that the inherited fields and methods have their proper initial values before any subclass-specific initializations take place.

```
class SuperClass;
    begin
        integer x;
        x := 5;
        procedure display;
            begin
                OutInt(x, 5);
                OutImage;
            end;
    end;

class SubClass : SuperClass;
    begin
        integer y;
        y := 10; // This gets initialized after x
        procedure show;
            begin
                OutInt(y, 5);
                OutImage;
            end;
    end;

ref(SubClass) obj;
obj :- new SubClass;

obj.display; // Output: 5
obj.show; // Output: 10
```

When designing a system of classes, it is essential to consider which properties and methods should be common across multiple classes and define those in a superclass. Subclasses can then be used to extend or specialize the behavior as required.

Field visibility plays a crucial role in inheritance. Fields and methods declared as public in the superclass are accessible by the subclass directly. If access restrictions are necessary, fields and methods can be declared as private or protected to control their visibility.

Simula also supports method overriding, where a subclass provides its own implementation of a method defined in the superclass. The overriding method must have the same signature as the method in the superclass.

```
class SuperClass;
    begin
        integer x;
        x := 5;
        procedure display;
            begin
                OutText("SuperClass display: ");
                OutInt(x, 5);
                OutImage;
            end;
    end;
```

```
class SubClass : SuperClass;
    begin
        integer y;
        y := 10;
        procedure display; // Overridden method
            begin
                OutText("SubClass display: ");
                OutInt(x, 5);
                OutImage;
            end;
        procedure show;
            begin
                OutInt(y, 5);
                OutImage;
            end;
    end;

ref(SubClass) obj;
obj :- new SubClass;

obj.display; // Output: SubClass display: 5
obj.show; // Output: 10
```

In this instance, SubClass overrides the display method of SuperClass. During the execution of obj.display, the overridden method in SubClass is called rather than the method in SuperClass.

By defining subclasses properly and leveraging inheritance, it is possible to create a more dynamic and modular codebase in Simula. This approach not only reduces redundancy but also ensures a clear and maintainable code structure.

6.3 The 'super' Keyword

The super keyword in Simula is used to access members (variables and methods) of the superclass. This keyword serves as a bridge to invoke the more general aspects of an object's hierarchy, allowing developers to effectively reuse code and leverage the full power of inherited class frameworks. The super keyword finds extensive application in two primary contexts: invoking superclass methods and accessing superclass constructors.

Invoking Superclass Methods When a method in a subclass overrides a method from its superclass, it is sometimes necessary to execute the superclass's version of that method within the overridden method. This can be accomplished using the super keyword. Below is an example illustrating how this is done:

```
class A;
begin
   procedure Display;
   begin
      OutText("Class A Display");
   end;
end;

class B(A);
begin
   procedure Display;
   begin
      OutText("Class B Display");
      super.Display; // Calls 'Display' method of class A
   end;
end;

begin
   B objectB;
   objectB:- new B;
   objectB.Display; // Output: Class B DisplayClass A Display
end;
```

In this example, the class B is a subclass of class A. Both classes have a Display procedure. Within the Display procedure of class B, the super.Display; call invokes the Display procedure of class A after the print statement of class B. The output demonstrates how both methods are executed in sequence due to the use of super.

Accessing Superclass Constructors The super keyword also plays a crucial role during the instantiation of subclass objects. When a subclass constructor needs to invoke the constructor of its superclass, the super keyword facilitates this operation. This is particularly useful when the superclass requires parameters to initialize its state. Consider the following example:

```
class Person(name, age);
begin
   text name;
   integer age;

   procedure Init(pName, pAge);
   begin
      name := pName;
      age := pAge;
   end;

   Init(name, age); // Constructor
end;

class Employee(Person)(name, age, employeeId);
begin
   integer employeeId;

   procedure Init(pName, pAge, pEmployeeId);
```

```
    begin
        super.Init(pName, pAge); // Calls superclass constructor
        employeeId := pEmployeeId;
    end;

    procedure Display;
    begin
        OutText(name & " aged " & AgeText(age) & " has employee ID: " & Image(
            employeeId));
    end;

    Init(name, age, employeeId); // Constructor
end;

begin
    Employee employee1;
    employee1:- new Employee("John", 30, 12345);
    employee1.Display; // Output: John aged 30 has employee ID: 12345
end;
```

In this code snippet, the class Employee inherits from the class Person. The constructor of Employee calls the constructor of Person using super.Init(pName, pAge); to initialize the name and age fields. Subsequently, the employeeId is initialized within the same Init procedure of Employee. This ensures that shared attributes between subclasses and superclasses are appropriately initialized in hierarchical order. The final output exhibits the inherited and sub-class specific attributes seamlessly integrated.

In summary, the functionality provided by the super keyword is vital in advanced inheritance scenarios, promoting clean and maintainable code through effective superclass method calls and constructor invocations. Utilizing super renders a more structured and natural methodology for building upon existing, well-defined class properties and behaviors.

6.4 Types of Inheritance: Single, Multiple, Multilevel

Inheritance in Simula allows for code reusability and establishes a hierarchical relationship between classes. This section will delve into the different types of inheritance, namely Single Inheritance, Multiple Inheritance, and Multilevel Inheritance, explaining their respective characteristics, benefits, and implementation in Simula.

Single inheritance is the simplest and most common form of inheritance. It occurs when a class (referred to as a subclass or derived class) inherits from one and only one superclass (also known as a base class). Here's how it's realized in Simula:

```
Class A;
Begin
    Integer x;
    Procedure display();
    Begin
        OutText("Value of x: "); OutInt(x,5); OutImage();
    End display;
End A;

Class B(A);
Begin
    Integer y;
    Procedure show();
    Begin
        OutText("Value of y: "); OutInt(y,5); OutImage();
    End show;
End B;

Begin
    B objB;
    objB.x := 10;
    objB.y := 20;
    objB.display();
    objB.show();
End;
```

In the code example, Class B inherits from Class A. This allows objB, an instance of Class B, to access the members of Class A, providing code reuse and a clear hierarchical relationship.

Multiple Inheritance is more complex and involves a class inheriting from more than one superclass. Unlike some object-oriented languages like Java which do not support multiple inheritance directly due to the "Diamond Problem," Simula allows it. The Diamond Problem occurs when a single class inherits from two classes that both inherit from a common base class. Here's an example of multiple inheritance in Simula:

```
Class C;
Begin
    Integer a;
    Procedure showA();
    Begin
        OutText("Value of a: "); OutInt(a,5); OutImage();
    End showA;
End C;

Class D;
Begin
    Integer b;
    Procedure showB();
    Begin
        OutText("Value of b: "); OutInt(b,5); OutImage();
    End showB;
```

```
End D;

Class E(C, D);
Begin
    Integer c;
    Procedure showC();
    Begin
        OutText("Value of c: "); OutInt(c,5); OutImage();
    End showC;
End E;

Begin
    E objE;
    objE.a := 1;
    objE.b := 2;
    objE.c := 3;
    objE.showA();
    objE.showB();
    objE.showC();
End;
```

In this example, Class E inherits from both Class C and Class D, allowing objE to access members of both parent classes.

Multilevel inheritance occurs when a class is derived from another class, which in turn is derived from another class, creating a multi-tiered hierarchy. This type of inheritance helps build a layered structure of base classes and derived classes. Consider the following Simula program which demonstrates multilevel inheritance:

```
Class Base;
Begin
    Integer num;
    Procedure showNum();
    Begin
        OutText("Number: "); OutInt(num,5); OutImage();
    End showNum;
End Base;

Class Derived1(Base);
Begin
    Integer square;
    Procedure showSquare();
    Begin
        square := num * num;
        OutText("Square: "); OutInt(square,5); OutImage();
    End showSquare;
End Derived1;

Class Derived2(Derived1);
Begin
    Integer cube;
    Procedure showCube();
    Begin
        cube := num * num * num;
        OutText("Cube: "); OutInt(cube,5); OutImage();
    End showCube;
End Derived2;
```

```
Begin
    Derived2 objD2;
    objD2.num := 3;
    objD2.showNum();
    objD2.showSquare();
    objD2.showCube();
End;
```

In this implementation, Class Derived1 is derived from Class Base, while Class Derived2 is derived from Class Derived1. As a result, objD2, an instance of Class Derived2, has access to the members of all classes in the hierarchy.

By understanding the nuances of Single, Multiple, and Multilevel Inheritance, programmers can leverage these features to create robust and maintainable Simula programs.

6.5 Method Overriding

Method overriding is a critical concept in object-oriented programming that allows a subclass to provide a specific implementation of a method that is already defined in its superclass. This technique is pivotal for achieving run-time polymorphism, enabling objects to react differently to the same method call.

In Simula, method overriding occurs when a subclass declares a method with the same name, return type, and parameters as a method in its superclass. The overridden method in the subclass replaces the method implementation in the superclass for instances of that subclass. To comprehensively understand method overriding in Simula, let's walk through the rules, usage, and a practical example.

- Same Method Signature: The subclass method must have the same name, return type, and parameter list as the method in the superclass.

- Access Control: The access level (public, protected, private) of the overriding method should not be more restrictive than the overridden method.

- Use of super Keyword: To call the superclass version of the method within the subclass's overridden method, use the super keyword.

Consider the following Simula code illustrating method overriding. We have a superclass Animal and a subclass Dog. The Animal class has a method speak, which is overridden in the Dog class.

```
CLASS Animal;
BEGIN
  PROCEDURE speak;
  BEGIN
     OutText("Animal speaks");
  END speak;
END Animal;

CLASS Dog;
BEGIN
  INLINE Animal;

  PROCEDURE speak;
  BEGIN
     OutText("Dog barks");
  END speak;
END Dog;

BEGIN
  REF(Animal) a;
  a :- NEW Animal;
  a.speak; -- Outputs "Animal speaks"

  a :- NEW Dog;
  a.speak; -- Outputs "Dog barks"
END;
```

In this example: - The Animal class defines a method speak that outputs "Animal speaks." - The Dog class overrides the speak method to provide a different implementation that outputs "Dog barks." - When an Animal object calls the speak method, the output is "Animal speaks." - When a Dog object calls the speak method, the output is "Dog barks," demonstrating method overriding.

super Keyword: Using the super keyword allows accessing the superclass's method that has been overridden. Here's how to use super in the Dog class to call the speak method of the Animal class:

```
CLASS Dog;
BEGIN
  INLINE Animal;

  PROCEDURE speak;
  BEGIN
     super.speak;
     OutText(" followed by Dog barks");
  END speak;
END Dog;

BEGIN
  REF(Animal) a;
  a :- NEW Dog;
  a.speak; -- Outputs "Animal speaks followed by Dog barks"
```

```
END;
```

In this scenario: - The speak method in the Dog class first calls super.speak, invoking the Animal class's speak method. - After calling the superclass method, it appends " followed by Dog barks" to the output.

Protected Methods: When dealing with protected methods, the overridden method in the subclass retains access to the superclass's protected members, enabling more intricate interactions between superclass and subclass methods.

Consider a more intricate example that incorporates the protected access specifier:

```
CLASS Shape;
PROTECTED
   PROCEDURE area : REAL;
   BEGIN
      area := 0;
   END area;
END Shape;

CLASS Circle(REAL radius);
BEGIN
   INLINE Shape;

   PROCEDURE area : REAL;
   BEGIN
      area := 3.14 * radius * radius;
   END area;
END Circle;

BEGIN
   REF(Shape) s;
   s :- NEW Circle(5.0);
   OutReal(s.area); -- Outputs the area of the circle with radius 5.0
END;
```

In this example: - The Shape class has a protected method area. - The Circle class, which inherits from Shape, overrides the area method to provide an implementation specific to a circle's area calculation. - When the area method is called on an instance of Circle, the overridden method in Circle executes, providing the correct area calculation for a circle.

Method overriding is fundamental to runtime polymorphism in Simula, facilitating the dynamic determination of method calls during execution time. This flexibility enhances code reuse and maintainability, making object-oriented programs more robust and adaptable.

6.6 Polymorphism: Compile-Time vs Run-Time

Polymorphism in object-oriented programming allows objects to be treated as instances of their parent class rather than their actual class, enabling a unified interface while maintaining specific behavior. This concept is a cornerstone of Simula programming and is broadly categorized into compile-time polymorphism (also known as static polymorphism) and run-time polymorphism (dynamic polymorphism).

Compile-time polymorphism is achieved through method overloading and operator overloading. Method overloading allows multiple methods in the same class to have the same name but different parameters. Consider the following example illustrating method overloading:

```
CLASS ExampleOverload;
 PUBLIC PROCEDURE Add(a, b);
  BEGIN
   OutInt(a + b, 5); ! Print the sum of two integers;
  END;

 PUBLIC PROCEDURE Add(a, b, c);
  BEGIN
   OutInt(a + b + c, 5); ! Print the sum of three integers;
  END;

 PUBLIC PROCEDURE Executable;
  BEGIN
   ! Testing the overloaded Add methods;
   Add(2, 3); ! Calls the version with 2 arguments;
   Add(1, 2, 3); ! Calls the version with 3 arguments;
  END;
END;
```

In this example, both Add procedures are defined within the ExampleOverload class, but they differ in the number and types of their parameters. The decision as to which method will be executed is determined at compile-time, hence the term compile-time polymorphism.

Run-time polymorphism, on the other hand, is achieved via method overriding, where a method defined in a parent class is redefined in its subclass with the same signature. The decision as to which method will be executed is made at run-time. Consider the scenario below:

```
CLASS BaseClass;
 PUBLIC PROCEDURE Display;
  BEGIN
   OutText('Display from BaseClass');
  END;
END;
```

```
CLASS DerivedClass; INHERIT BaseClass;
  PUBLIC PROCEDURE Display;
    BEGIN
      OutText('Display from DerivedClass');
    END;
END;

Begin
  BaseClass obj1;
  DerivedClass obj2;

  ! Demonstrating run-time polymorphism;
  obj1 :- New BaseClass;
  obj2 :- New DerivedClass;

  obj1.Display; ! Outputs "Display from BaseClass";
  obj1 :- obj2;
  obj1.Display; ! Outputs "Display from DerivedClass";
END;
```

Here, the Display method is defined in both the BaseClass and the DerivedClass. When obj1 is assigned an instance of DerivedClass (using object casting), calling Display on obj1 results in Display from DerivedClass being executed, showcasing run-time polymorphism.

The key difference between compile-time and run-time polymorphism lies in the nature of their execution timing:

- **Compile-time Polymorphism:**
  - Achieved by method overloading or operator overloading.
  - Decision made during compilation.
  - Promotes method signature differentiation within the same class.
- **Run-time Polymorphism:**
  - Achieved by method overriding.
  - Decision made during runtime.
  - Enables method differentiation through inheritance hierarchy.

Understanding both forms of polymorphism enables developers to design flexible and scalable systems. Compile-time polymorphism enhances code readability through concise method signatures, while run-time polymorphism enhances interactivity among different object instances within an inheritance hierarchy.

To further elaborate, let's consider a more complex example where both forms of polymorphism are utilized in a single program. This example will demonstrate how these polymorphism concepts can coexist and operate in tandem:

```
CLASS BaseShape;
  PUBLIC PROCEDURE Area;
  OUTTEXT('Area method of BaseShape');
  PUBLIC PROCEDURE Draw(a, b);
    BEGIN
      OutText('Drawing shape with two parameters');
    END;
  PUBLIC PROCEDURE Draw(a, b, c);
    BEGIN
      OutText('Drawing shape with three parameters');
    END;
END;

CLASS Circle; INHERIT BaseShape;
  PUBLIC PROCEDURE Area;
    BEGIN
      OutText('Area method of Circle');
    END;
END;

CLASS Rectangle; INHERIT BaseShape;
  PUBLIC PROCEDURE Area;
    BEGIN
      OutText('Area method of Rectangle');
    END;
END;

BEGIN
  BaseShape baseObj;
  BaseShape ref;
  Circle circleObj;
  Rectangle rectObj;

  ! Demonstrating compile-time polymorphism with Draw method overloading;
  baseObj :- New BaseShape;
  baseObj.Draw(5, 10);
  baseObj.Draw(3, 4, 5);

  ! Demonstrating run-time polymorphism with Area method;
  circleObj :- New Circle;
  rectObj :- New Rectangle;
  ref :- circleObj;
  ref.Area; ! Outputs "Area method of Circle";
  ref :- rectObj;
  ref.Area; ! Outputs "Area method of Rectangle";
END;
```

This demonstrates the interplay of compile-time and run-time polymorphism. The Draw method in the BaseShape class overloads based on parameter count, showing compile-time polymorphism. Meanwhile, the Area method can be overridden in the Circle and Rectangle classes, exhibiting run-time polymorphism when instances of these classes are referred to by a BaseShape reference.

6.7 Abstract Classes and Methods

In object-oriented programming, abstract classes and methods provide a way to define common behaviors that must be implemented by derived classes, ensuring a consistent interface across different implementations. In Simula, abstract classes and methods enable the creation of a partially defined class that cannot be instantiated directly but can only be used as a base class for other classes.

An abstract class in Simula is declared using the keyword ABSTRACT. This keyword signifies that the class contains abstract methods, which are methods declared without an implementation. The concrete subclasses of an abstract class must provide implementations for these abstract methods, thereby enforcing a specific behavior.

```
ABSTRACT CLASS Shape;
    ABSTRACT PROCEDURE Real Area;
    ABSTRACT PROCEDURE Real Perimeter;
END CLASS;
```

In the above code snippet, the class Shape is an abstract class with two abstract procedures: Area and Perimeter. These methods do not have implementations in the Shape class, which means Shape cannot be instantiated directly. Subclasses of Shape must implement these procedures to compute the area and perimeter specific to the shape they represent.

Concrete subclasses that extend an abstract class must use the CLASS keyword followed by the keyword INHERITS. The inherited class must provide concrete implementations of all the abstract methods declared in the base abstract class.

```
CLASS Circle(IN REAL radius) INHERITS Shape;
   BEGIN
      PROCEDURE Real Area;
      BEGIN
         Area := 3.14 * radius * radius;
      END Area;

      PROCEDURE Real Perimeter;
      BEGIN
         Perimeter := 2 * 3.14 * radius;
      END Perimeter;
   END Circle;
```

In the example, Circle is a concrete subclass of Shape that provides implementations for the Area and Perimeter methods. By defining these procedures, the Circle class meets the contract specified by the Shape abstract class, allowing it to be instantiated.

Similarly, we can define another subclass such as Rectangle, which also inherits from the Shape abstract class and provides the necessary implementations for the abstract methods:

```
CLASS Rectangle(IN REAL width, IN REAL height) INHERITS Shape;
  BEGIN
    PROCEDURE Real Area;
    BEGIN
      Area := width * height;
    END Area;

    PROCEDURE Real Perimeter;
    BEGIN
      Perimeter := 2 * (width + height);
    END Perimeter;
  END Rectangle;
```

The Rectangle class calculates the area and perimeter specific to rectangles, implementing the abstract methods defined in Shape.

Abstract classes are essential in designing systems that require a common interface for a group of related objects. They allow the creation of a skeletal structure for future classes, promoting code reuse and reducing redundancy. This coding technique adheres to the principle of abstraction, one of the four fundamental principles of object-oriented programming, along with encapsulation, inheritance, and polymorphism.

By using abstract classes and methods, programmers can define templates for other classes, ensuring that derived classes fulfill the specified contracts. This provides both flexibility and robustness in designing complex systems, as it enforces a predetermined structure while allowing diverse implementations.

The significance of abstract classes becomes particularly evident when dealing with large software systems, where maintaining a consistent interface is crucial for effective code management and collaboration. Developers can rely on these abstract definitions to develop different parts of an application independently while ensuring they can seamlessly integrate later.

The use of abstract classes and methods forms the basis for implementing design patterns such as Factory Method, Template Method, and Strategy, which extend the utility of these concepts beyond basic class hierarchies. Understanding and implementing abstract classes effectively is a key step towards mastering object-oriented programming in Simula and other related languages.

Finally, consider the following simulation to elucidate the conception of using abstract classes:

```
BEGIN
  REF(Shape) s;
  s :- NEW Circle(5.0);
  OutText("Circle Area: "); OutFix(s.Area, 2); OutImage;
  OutText("Circle Perimeter: "); OutFix(s.Perimeter, 2); OutImage;

  s :- NEW Rectangle(4.0, 6.0);
  OutText("Rectangle Area: "); OutFix(s.Area, 2); OutImage;
  OutText("Rectangle Perimeter: "); OutFix(s.Perimeter, 2); OutImage;
END;
```

In this example, a reference s of type REF(Shape) can refer to objects of any subclass of Shape, demonstrating polymorphism. The type Shape acts as an interface that declares what methods must be available, while the concrete subclasses (Circle and Rectangle) provide the implementations.

The output confirms the calculations of areas and perimeters for different shapes:

```
Circle Area: 78.50
Circle Perimeter: 31.40
Rectangle Area: 24.00
Rectangle Perimeter: 20.00
```

Such implementations illustrate the power and flexibility of abstract classes and methods, reinforcing their role in building scalable and maintainable object-oriented systems in Simula.

6.8 Interfaces and Their Implementation

Interfaces in Simula serve as a blueprint for classes, defining a set of abstract methods that the implementing classes must provide. They enable a form of multiple inheritance, allowing a class to implement multiple interfaces and thereby integrate varied functionalities. This section explores the syntax and semantics of defining and implementing interfaces within the Simula language.

An interface in Simula is declared using the interface keyword. Unlike classes, interfaces cannot contain any concrete method implementations or instance variables. They only contain method signatures—that is, the method name, return type, and parameter list without any body. This is exemplified in the following interface definition:

```
interface Drivable {
    void startEngine();
    void stopEngine();
```

```
    void accelerate(int speed);
    void brake();
}
```

In this example, the Drivable interface includes four methods: startEngine, stopEngine, accelerate, and brake. Any class implementing this interface must provide concrete implementations for these methods.

To implement an interface, a class uses the implements keyword followed by the interface name. The implementing class must override all the abstract methods declared in the interface. The following illustrates the implementation of the Drivable interface by a Car class:

```
class Car implements Drivable {
    bool engineRunning;

    // Constructor
    Car() {
        this.engineRunning = false;
    }

    void startEngine() {
        if (!engineRunning) {
            engineRunning = true;
            writeln("Engine started.");
        }
    }

    void stopEngine() {
        if (engineRunning) {
            engineRunning = false;
            writeln("Engine stopped.");
        }
    }

    void accelerate(int speed) {
        if (engineRunning) {
            writeln("Accelerating to " + speed + " km/h.");
        } else {
            writeln("Engine is not running. Can't accelerate.");
        }
    }

    void brake() {
        writeln("Brake applied.");
    }
}
```

In this Car class, all four methods defined in the Drivable interface are implemented. The class maintains an instance variable engineRunning to keep track of the engine state. Notice that the constructor initializes engineRunning to false, indicating that the engine is off when a Car object is instantiated.

Similarly, we can implement multiple interfaces in a single class. This provides the flexibility to design classes that adhere to multiple contracts specified by different interfaces.

```
interface Electric {
    void chargeBattery();
}

class ElectricCar implements Drivable, Electric {
    bool engineRunning;
    int batteryLevel;

    // Constructor
    ElectricCar() {
        this.engineRunning = false;
        this.batteryLevel = 100; // Assume fully charged
    }

    void startEngine() {
        if (!engineRunning) {
            engineRunning = true;
            writeln("Electric engine started.");
        }
    }

    void stopEngine() {
        if (engineRunning) {
            engineRunning = false;
            writeln("Electric engine stopped.");
        }
    }

    void accelerate(int speed) {
        if (engineRunning) {
            writeln("Accelerating to " + speed + " km/h.");
        } else {
            writeln("Electric engine is not running. Can't accelerate.");
        }
    }

    void brake() {
        writeln("Brake applied.");
    }

    void chargeBattery() {
        batteryLevel = 100;
        writeln("Battery fully charged.");
    }
}
```

In this implementation, the class ElectricCar simultaneously implements both the Drivable and Electric interfaces. This demonstrates the flexibility and modularity provided by interfaces, enabling the ElectricCar to inherit the functionalities specified by multiple interfaces.

The following is the output demonstrating the use of the ElectricCar class:

```
ElectricCar myElectricCar = new ElectricCar();
myElectricCar.startEngine();
myElectricCar.accelerate(50);
myElectricCar.brake();
myElectricCar.stopEngine();
myElectricCar.chargeBattery();
```

Here is the expected output:

```
Electric engine started.
Accelerating to 50 km/h.
Brake applied.
Electric engine stopped.
Battery fully charged.
```

Interfaces promote a form of multiple inheritance, supporting the design of robust, modular, and maintainable code. The design enforces adherence to a specific contract, ensuring that any class implementing the interface will provide the necessary functionalities defined by the interface. This enables developers to design flexible and extensible applications, leveraging polymorphism and ensuring that the implementations can evolve without the need for alterations in client code.

6.9 The 'instanceof' Keyword

The instanceof keyword in Simula is a critical operator used to determine whether an object is an instance of a specific class or subclass. This capability is indispensable in object-oriented programming since it allows for dynamic type checking, enabling developers to confirm the type of an object at runtime. Understanding and utilizing instanceof efficiently can prevent runtime errors and facilitate safer type conversions.

When deploying instanceof, it is vital to adhere to the following syntax:

```
object instanceof ClassName
```

Here, object represents the reference to an instance of a class, and ClassName denotes the name of the class against which the type check is performed. If the object is an instance of ClassName or any of its subclasses, the instanceof operator returns true; otherwise, it returns false.

Consider the following example to elucidate the usage of instanceof:

```
Class Animal;
Class Dog: Animal;
Class Cat: Animal;

begin
    Animal a1;
```

```
    Dog d1;
    Cat c1;

    a1 :- Dog.New;
    writeln(a1 instanceof Dog); /* Outputs: true */
    writeln(a1 instanceof Animal); /* Outputs: true */
    writeln(a1 instanceof Cat); /* Outputs: false */

    a1 :- Cat.New;
    writeln(a1 instanceof Cat); /* Outputs: true */
    writeln(a1 instanceof Animal); /* Outputs: true */
    writeln(a1 instanceof Dog); /* Outputs: false */
end;
```

The snippet above demonstrates various instanceof checks. Initially, a1 is assigned an instance of Dog. The subsequent instanceof checks confirm that a1 is indeed an instance of Dog and its superclass Animal, but not Cat. Reassigning a1 to a Cat instance reverses the outcome accordingly.

The instanceof operator is particularly beneficial when managing polymorphic objects. It can help enforce contextually appropriate behavior by allowing type-specific logic execution, illustrated as follows:

```
begin
    Animal animalArray[2];
    animalArray[1] :- Dog.New;
    animalArray[2] :- Cat.New;

    for i :- 1 step 1 until 2 do
    begin
        if (animalArray[i] instanceof Dog) then
            writeln("Dog detected");
        else if(animalArray[i] instanceof Cat) then
            writeln("Cat detected");
        else
            writeln("Unknown animal");
    end;
end;
```

In this context, the animal array accommodates different animal subclasses. The instanceof checks within the loop ensure the correct subclass is identified, resulting in distinct output:

```
Dog detected
Cat detected
```

Moreover, instanceof plays a vital role in secure casting. Attempting to cast an object to an incompatible type triggers a runtime error. Preceding the cast with instanceof ensures the cast will succeed. Consider the subsequent code demonstrating safe casting:

```
begin
    Animal genericAnimal;
    Dog specificDog;
```

```
    genericAnimal :- Dog.New;

    if (genericAnimal instanceof Dog) then
        specificDog :- (Dog) genericAnimal;
end;
```

Without employing instanceof, the cast could potentially fail, resulting in unstable code. The instanceof check guarantees that genericAnimal is indeed an instance of Dog before casting.

When cascading through class hierarchies, it's crucial to remember that instanceof verifies against the entire inheritance tree. Here is a more complex example with multilevel inheritance:

```
Class Animal;
Class Mammal: Animal;
Class Reptile: Animal;
Class Dog: Mammal;

begin
    Animal a2;
    Mammal m2;
    Reptile r2;
    Dog d2;

    a2 :- Dog.New;
    writeln(a2 instanceof Dog); /* Outputs: true */
    writeln(a2 instanceof Mammal); /* Outputs: true */
    writeln(a2 instanceof Animal); /* Outputs: true */
    writeln(a2 instanceof Reptile); /* Outputs: false */
end;
```

Handling classes like Dog, which are deep in the inheritance hierarchy, instanceof efficiently navigates through layers, providing accurate results reflecting the true nature of the object.

In practical scenarios, instanceof contributes to robust and adaptable code structures, addressing dynamic type identification needs across diverse applications and systems. Through rigorous application, it enhances code reliability, ensuring type integrity and preventing classifications errors that could lead to system vulnerabilities.

6.10 Casting Objects

In object-oriented programming and Simula specifically, casting is a crucial technique that allows for treating instances of different classes as instances of a parent class, or vice versa. This technique is especially useful when dealing with polymorphism, as it enables dynamic method binding. Understanding both implicit and explicit casting can enhance your ability to manipulate objects effectively in Simula.

In Simula, casting is necessary when you want to convert an object of one type into another type, typically up or down an inheritance hierarchy. There are two main categories of casting: upcasting and downcasting.

Upcasting refers to casting an object to a type higher up in the inheritance hierarchy. This process is generally safe and often implicit, meaning that the compiler will automatically perform the casting without any specific syntax.

```
// Example of upcasting
Class A;
Begin
   Procedure display;
   Begin
      OutText("A display");
   End;
End;

Class B(A);
Begin
   Procedure display;
   Begin
      OutText("B display");
   End;
End;

Ref(B) bObj;
Ref(A) aObj;

bObj:- New B;
aObj:- bObj; // Implicit upcasting
aObj.display; // Outputs: "B display"
```

In the example above, the object bObj of class B is assigned to the reference variable aObj of class A. Since B is a subclass of A, this upcasting is implicit and requires no additional syntax. The method display belonging to B is still invoked, demonstrating polymorphic behavior.

Downcasting is the reverse process and involves casting an object to a type lower down in the inheritance hierarchy. This process is not implicit because it can introduce runtime errors if not handled carefully. In Simula, explicit casting is achieved using type conversion functions or checks such as instanceof.

```
// Example of downcasting
Class A;
Begin
   Procedure display;
   Begin
      OutText("A display");
   End;
End;
```

```
Class B(A);
Begin
   Procedure display;
   Begin
      OutText("B display");
   End;
   Procedure bSpecific;
   Begin
      OutText("B specific method");
   End;
End;

Ref(A) aObj;
Ref(B) bObj;

aObj:- New B;
If aObj IsInstance B Then
   Begin
      bObj :- Ref(B)A(aObj); // Explicit downcasting
      bObj.bSpecific; // Outputs: "B specific method"
   End
Else
   OutText("Downcasting failed");
```

In the example above, the object aObj of class A is checked to be an instance of class B using the instanceof keyword. If the check is true, explicit casting is performed with Ref(B)A(aObj). This notation tells Simula that aObj should now be treated as an object of type B. Following the cast, the bSpecific method is accessible, producing the expected output.

Casting Pitfalls

While casting is a powerful tool, misuse or overuse can lead to several pitfalls:

- **Runtime Errors:** Casting without proper checks can lead to runtime errors. Always ensure that the object type matches the target type before casting.
- **Loss of Specificity:** Through upcasting, you might lose access to the specific attributes and methods of the child class.
- **Performance Overheads:** Excessive casting can introduce performance overhead, especially in critical sections of code.

Consider another example to illustrate the misuse of downcasting:

```
// Misuse of downcasting leading to runtime error
Class A;
Begin
   Procedure display;
   Begin
```

```
        OutText("A display");
    End;
End;

Class B(A);
Begin
    Procedure display;
    Begin
        OutText("B display");
    End;
End;

Class C(A);
Begin
    Procedure display;
    Begin
        OutText("C display");
    End;
End;

Ref(A) aObj;
Ref(B) bObj;

aObj:- New C;

// Incorrect downcasting
bObj:- Ref(B)A(aObj);
bObj.display; // Runtime error
```

In this example, aObj actually references an object of class C. Downcasting aObj to class B results in an invalid cast, leading to potential runtime errors. This underscores the importance of using instanceof or equivalent checks before performing downcasting.

Understanding and applying casting correctly ensures that your Simula programs handle inheritance and polymorphism with precision and elegance, avoiding common pitfalls and runtime errors.

6.11 Real-world Examples of Inheritance and Polymorphism

Examining real-world examples facilitates a deeper understanding of inheritance and polymorphism in Simula. These concepts are pivotal in designing flexible, scalable, and maintainable systems. By implementing inheritance, a class can inherit fields and methods from another class, reducing redundancy. Polymorphism enhances the ability of objects to be processed in different ways depending on their data type or class. Below, several practical examples are explored to illustrate these principles thoroughly.

First, consider a simplified case in the context of a banking system. We define a superclass Account and create subclasses SavingsAccount and CheckingAccount. Each subclass will inherit properties and behaviors from the Account class and may also override methods to provide specific implementations.

Defining the Superclass Account

```
Class Account;
Begin
    Real balance;
    Procedure Deposit(amount);
    Begin
        balance := balance + amount;
    End;

    Procedure Withdraw(amount);
    Begin
        balance := balance - amount;
    End;
End;
```

The Account class includes the balance field and methods for depositing and withdrawing funds. Next, we define the SavingsAccount and CheckingAccount subclasses.

Defining the SavingsAccount and CheckingAccount Subclasses

```
Class SavingsAccount : Account;
Begin
    Real interestRate;

    Procedure ApplyInterest;
    Begin
        balance := balance * (1 + interestRate);
    End;
End;

Class CheckingAccount : Account;
Begin
    Real overdraftLimit;

    Procedure Withdraw(amount);
    Begin
        If balance - amount < -overdraftLimit Then
            OutText("Overdraft limit exceeded");
        Else
            balance := balance - amount;
    End;
End;
```

SavingsAccount introduces an additional field interestRate and the ApplyInterest method to apply interest to the balance. CheckingAccount includes an overdraftLimit field and overrides the Withdraw method to account for the overdraft limit. This demonstrates method overriding, an essential aspect of polymorphism.

To further explore polymorphism, examining the use of a function designed to handle an array of Account objects, which could be instances of either SavingsAccount or CheckingAccount, is useful.

Polymorphism in Action

```
Procedure ProcessEndOfMonth(accounts, Integer n);
Begin
    For i := 1 Step 1 Until n Do
    Begin
        accounts[i].Withdraw(10);
        If accounts[i] Is SavingsAccount Then
            accounts[i]$SavingsAccount.ApplyInterest;
    End;
End;
```

The ProcessEndOfMonth procedure iterates over an array of Account objects, withdrawing a fixed fee from each. For instances of SavingsAccount, the interest is applied. This leverages polymorphism to handle different Account types through a common interface, illustrating the power of runtime polymorphism.

Another Real-world Scenario: Shape Hierarchy

Consider a graphical application requiring various shapes, such as circles, rectangles, and triangles. Define a base class Shape and specific subclasses like Circle, Rectangle, and Triangle.

```
Class Shape;
Begin
    Procedure Draw;
    Begin
        OutText("Default draw method");
    End;
End;

Class Circle : Shape;
Begin
    Real radius;

    Procedure Draw;
    Begin
        OutText("Drawing a Circle");
    End;
```

```
End;

Class Rectangle : Shape;
Begin
    Real width, height;

    Procedure Draw;
    Begin
        OutText("Drawing a Rectangle");
    End;
End;

Class Triangle : Shape;
Begin
    Real base, height;

    Procedure Draw;
    Begin
        OutText("Drawing a Triangle");
    End;
End;
```

Each subclass Circle, Rectangle, and Triangle overrides the Draw method to provide specific implementations. This ensures that the correct method is called based on the object's runtime type.

Utilizing Polymorphism

```
Procedure RenderShapes(shapes, Integer n);
Begin
    For i := 1 Step 1 Until n Do
        shapes[i].Draw;
End;
```

The RenderShapes procedure calls the Draw method for each shape in the array, leveraging polymorphism to execute the appropriate method based on the actual object's type. This approach simplifies the code and makes it more maintainable by adhering to the open/closed principle, where classes are open for extension but closed for modification.

Chapter 7

Modules and Libraries

This chapter covers the creation and usage of modules and libraries in Simula. It explains how to import and export modules, use standard libraries, and create custom libraries. The chapter also addresses managing dependencies, documenting libraries, version control, packaging, and distribution, offering a practical guide to modular programming and efficient code organization.

7.1 Introduction to Modules and Libraries

Modules and libraries play a crucial role in Simula programming by providing a structured way to organize code. They enable code reusability, maintainability, and modularity. A module is a collection of related functions and procedures, while a library is an organized collection of modules that can be shared across different programs.

A module in Simula typically encompasses a namespace that contains definitions for variables, functions, classes, and other constructs. This namespace prevents naming conflicts and assists in maintaining the scope of variables and functions. Libraries, on the other hand, are compilations of these modules, made available for broader usage across various projects.

```
MODULE ExampleModule;
   BEGIN
      INTEGER x;
      PROCEDURE add(a, b); INTEGER a, b;
         BEGIN
```

```
        add := a + b;
    END add;
END ExampleModule;
```

In this example, ExampleModule is a module containing an integer variable x and a procedure add that takes two integers as arguments and returns their sum.

Importing and exporting modules involves making the contents of one module available to another. This is achieved through specific syntax within Simula:

```
MODULE Main;
    EXTERNAL ExampleModule;
    BEGIN
        INTEGER result;
        result := ExampleModule.add(3, 4);
    END Main;
```

Here, the Main module imports ExampleModule and uses its add procedure to compute the sum of 3 and 4.

Standard libraries in Simula are pre-existing collections of modules provided to perform common tasks such as mathematical computations, file handling, and data manipulation. These libraries enhance productivity by offering tested and optimized functions, reducing the need for duplicating code.

```
LIBRARY StandardLib;
    USE MathLib, StringUtils;
    BEGIN
        PRINT('This is a standard library example.');
    END StandardLib;
```

Above, StandardLib uses MathLib and StringUtils, which could contain various mathematical functions and string manipulation utilities respectively.

Creating custom libraries involves grouping user-defined modules to establish reusable code components tailored to specific needs. These custom libraries promote code reuse and simplify project management by separating concerns into distinct modules.

```
LIBRARY CustomLib;
    MODULE Utility;
        BEGIN
            PROCEDURE showMessage(msg); TEXT msg;
                BEGIN
                    PRINT(msg);
                END showMessage;
        END Utility;
    USE Utility;
```

```
BEGIN
    Utility.showMessage('Hello from CustomLib!');
END CustomLib;
```

In this custom library example, CustomLib includes a module Utility with a showMessage procedure. This demonstrates how custom libraries encapsulate functionality for extensive reuse.

Dependency management is an essential part of working with modules and libraries. Dependencies are external modules or libraries required by a project. Proper management ensures that all parts of a program have access to the dependencies they need. Tools and practices for dependency management include using version control systems and package managers to handle library versions and their dependencies.

Documenting libraries involves creating comprehensive and accurate documentation that describes the purpose, usage, functions, and classes contained within a library. Proper documentation is critical for both users and developers, as it aids in understanding and using the library effectively.

```
! CustomLib Documentation.
! This library provides utility functions for various tasks.
!
! MODULE Utility:
! - showMessage(msg): Displays a message.
```

Version control helps in tracking changes to code over time, coordinating work among multiple developers, and managing releases of libraries. Using systems such as Git, changes can be committed, branched, and merged, providing a comprehensive history of modifications.

Packaging and distribution of libraries make the custom libraries available for use by others. This involves bundling the code into a distributable format and sharing it through appropriate channels such as repositories or distribution networks.

Best practices for modular programming include keeping modules focused, minimizing dependencies, adhering to consistent naming conventions, and emphasizing readability and documentation. A well-structured module aids understanding and reduces the complexity of the overall system.

By using modules and libraries effectively, programmers can build robust, maintainable, and scalable programs in Simula.

7.2 Creating and Using Modules

Modules serve as a fundamental aspect of Simula programming, providing structure and reusability to code. This section elaborates on the techniques for creating and utilizing modules within Simula programs, emphasizing syntax, best practices, and practical examples.

To start, consider the syntax for defining a module in Simula. Modules are encapsulated within the MODULE keyword. Let's examine a basic example:

```
MODULE ExampleModule;
BEGIN
    INTEGER x;
    TEXT message;

    PROCEDURE Initialize;
    BEGIN
        x := 0;
        message :- 'Initialized';
    END Initialize;

    PROCEDURE Increment;
    BEGIN
        x := x + 1;
    END Increment;

    PROCEDURE GetMessage;
    BEGIN
        MESSAGE :- message;
    END GetMessage;
END ExampleModule;
```

This simple module, ExampleModule, contains variables x and message, along with procedures Initialize, Increment, and GetMessage. The procedures help manage the state of the module's variables.

To utilize this module in another Simula program, the module must be imported using the EXTERNAL keyword. Here's how one could import and use the ExampleModule:

```
EXTERNAL ExampleModule;

BEGIN
    ExampleModule.Initialize;
    ExampleModule.Increment;
    ExampleModule.Increment;

    TEXT result;
    result :- ExampleModule.GetMessage;
    OutText(result);
END;
```

This code block demonstrates calling the procedures of the Example-

Module from an external file. After importing, the Initialize procedure sets up the initial state, and subsequent calls to Increment modify the state. Finally, the GetMessage procedure retrieves a message, iterated to the console using OutText(result).

It's important to structure modules effectively to ensure clarity and maintainability. This involves grouping related procedures and variables, using meaningful names, and encapsulating functionality to avoid unintended interactions.

Let's consider a more advanced example that includes nested modules. Nested modules allow for further encapsulation and structured modularity.

```
MODULE OuterModule;

MODULE InnerModule;
BEGIN
   INTEGER y;
   PROCEDURE SetValue(v); INTEGER v;
   BEGIN
      y := v;
   END SetValue;

   PROCEDURE GetValue; INTEGER;
   BEGIN
      RETURN y;
   END GetValue;
END InnerModule;

BEGIN
   INTEGER x;
   PROCEDURE Initialize;
   BEGIN
      x := 0;
      InnerModule.SetValue(0);
   END Initialize;

   PROCEDURE Increment;
   BEGIN
      x := x + 1;
      InnerModule.SetValue(InnerModule.GetValue + 1);
   END Increment;

   PROCEDURE GetStatus; TEXT;
   BEGIN
      RETURN 'Outer: ' & x & ', Inner: ' & InnerModule.GetValue;
   END GetStatus;
END OuterModule;
```

In this example, OuterModule encapsulates another module, InnerModule. This nested structure allows OuterModule to manage its internal state while also manipulating the state of InnerModule.

To use this nested module structure in another Simula program:

```
EXTERNAL OuterModule;

BEGIN
    OuterModule.Initialize;
    OuterModule.Increment;
    OuterModule.Increment;

    TEXT status;
    status :- OuterModule.GetStatus;
    OutText(status);
END;
```

When executed, this code will output the state information of both the outer and inner modules, evidencing the encapsulation and interaction between nested modules.

Effective usage of modules can also involve exporting specific procedures and variables while keeping others private. This selective exposure is crucial for maintaining abstraction and protecting internal states from unintended modifications.

Consider this example where only certain procedures are exposed:

```
MODULE SelectiveExportModule;
    INTEGER privateData;

    EXPORT Initialize, GetStatus;

    PROCEDURE Initialize;
    BEGIN
        privateData := 0;
    END Initialize;

    PROCEDURE Increment;
    BEGIN
        privateData := privateData + 1;
    END Increment;

    PROCEDURE GetStatus; TEXT;
    BEGIN
        RETURN 'Data: ' & privateData;
    END GetStatus;
END SelectiveExportModule;
```

Here, privateData and Increment are internal to the module and not accessible externally, providing a controlled interface for interaction.

When employing such selective export mechanisms, the external file will have limited access, ensuring encapsulation. Here's how you might import and use the SelectiveExportModule:

```
EXTERNAL SelectiveExportModule;

BEGIN
    SelectiveExportModule.Initialize;
```

```
    TEXT status;
    status :- SelectiveExportModule.GetStatus;
    OutText(status);
END;
```

By following these practices, programmers can create robust, maintainable, and scalable Simula applications employing modular programming principles.

7.3 Importing and Exporting Modules

The concept of importing and exporting modules in Simula plays a critical role in modular programming. Modules encapsulate related functions, types, and variables, enabling better organization, reuse, and maintainability of code. This section describes the syntax and usage patterns for importing and exporting modules, with examples to illustrate these operations.

To start with, it is essential to understand the syntax for importing a module. In Simula, the import statement is used to include a module's content into the current namespace. This allows access to functions, types, and variables defined in the imported module.

```
import ModuleName;
```

For example, consider a module named MathFunctions that contains several mathematical functions. We can import this module as follows:

```
import MathFunctions;

procedure Main;
    begin
    Integer x, y;
    x := 10;
    y := 20;
    writeReal(Product(x, y)); ! Assuming Product is a function in MathFunctions
    end;
```

It is also possible to import specific elements from a module, such as individual functions or variables, to avoid potential name conflicts and to make the code clearer regarding which elements are being used.

```
import MathFunctions.Product, MathFunctions.Sum;

procedure Main;
    begin
    Integer a, b;
    a := 5;
    b := 15;
```

```
    writeReal(Product(a, b));
    writeReal(Sum(a, b));
    end;
```

When it becomes necessary to use a module with a very lengthy or generic name, an alias can be employed for brevity and clarity. The usage of the as keyword assigns a new name to the imported module.

```
import LongModuleName as LMN;

procedure Main;
    begin
    Integer m, n;
    m := 3;
    n := 4;
    writeInt(LMN.Add(m, n)); ! Using the alias LMN for LongModuleName
    end;
```

Next, we will explore how to export modules. Creating a module involves defining a set of logically related functions, variables, and types within a module file. To make these definitions available to other parts of a program or other programs, use the export keyword.

```
module MathFunctions;

export Product, Sum;

procedure Product(Integer a, Integer b) Real;
    begin
    Product := a * b;
    end;

procedure Sum(Integer a, Integer b) Real;
    begin
    Sum := a + b;
    end;
end module;
```

In this example, the Product and Sum procedures are exported from the MathFunctions module, making them accessible to any other code that imports this module.

Often, modules include internal functions or variables that are not intended for external use. These elements should be omitted from the export list, ensuring they remain encapsulated within the module. This encapsulation protects the internal implementation details from external dependency and maintains code integrity.

The following example demonstrates a module that includes both public and private elements:

```
module ComplexOperations;
```

```
export AddComplex, MultiplyComplex;

type Complex = record
    RealPart, ImaginaryPart: Real;
end record;

procedure AddComplex(Complex c1, Complex c2) Complex;
    begin
    AddComplex.RealPart := c1.RealPart + c2.RealPart;
    AddComplex.ImaginaryPart := c1.ImaginaryPart + c2.ImaginaryPart;
    end;

procedure MultiplyComplex(Complex c1, Complex c2) Complex;
    begin
    MultiplyComplex.RealPart := (c1.RealPart * c2.RealPart) - (c1.ImaginaryPart * c2.
          ImaginaryPart);
    MultiplyComplex.ImaginaryPart := (c1.RealPart * c2.ImaginaryPart) + (c1.
          ImaginaryPart * c2.RealPart);
    end;

! Private function not exported
procedure Conjugate(Complex c) Complex;
    begin
    Conjugate.RealPart := c.RealPart;
    Conjugate.ImaginaryPart := -c.ImaginaryPart;
    end;
end module;
```

Here, the AddComplex and MultiplyComplex procedures are exported, while Conjugate remains private within the ComplexOperations module.

Using modules also enhances maintainability and code organization. When modification of a module is necessary, changes can be made in the module file itself without affecting other parts of the program, provided the interface remains consistent.

Finally, Simula modules can include documentation comments that describe the purpose and usage of the module or its elements. Proper documentation is essential for understanding and maintaining modules, especially in larger projects or when the module is intended for distribution.

```
module Statistics;

export Mean, Median, Mode;

! Calculates the mean of a list of numbers
procedure Mean(Real list[]);

! Calculates the median of a list of numbers
procedure Median(Real list[]);

! Calculates the mode of a list of numbers
procedure Mode(Real list[]);
    begin
    ! Implementation goes here.
    end;
```

```
end module;
```

By following these guidelines and practices for importing and exporting modules, developers can create well-structured, reusable, and maintainable Simula programs.

7.4 Standard Libraries in Simula

Standard libraries in Simula provide a wealth of pre-written code that allows developers to perform a wide range of common tasks efficiently and reliably. These libraries cover various domains, including input/output operations, mathematical computations, data structures, and utility functions. Understanding and effectively using these libraries is a vital skill for any Simula programmer.

Input and Output Libraries

Simula includes robust input and output libraries that facilitate interaction with users, files, and other systems. The most commonly used I/O functions are encapsulated in the simio library. Here is a typical example of how to use the standard I/O library:

```
BEGIN
  INTEGER i;
  REAL x;
  TEXT line;
  i := 10;
  x := 3.14;
  line := "Example Line";
  OutInt(i, 3); -- Outputs: 010
  OutReal(x, 8, 4); -- Outputs: 3.1400
  OutText(line);
  OutImage;
END;
```

The functions OutInt, OutReal, and OutText are used to print an integer, real number, and text line, respectively. The OutImage function ensures that the output is flushed and properly displayed.

Mathematical Libraries

Mathematical computations are indispensable in many Simula programs. The mathlib library provides a suite of mathematical functions, including trigonometric, logarithmic, and exponential functions. Examples of these functions include:

```
BEGIN
```

```
  REAL angle, value, result;
  angle := 1.5708; -- angle in radians (approximately 90 degrees)
  value := 2.0;
  result := Sin(angle); -- result = 1.0
  result := Cos(angle); -- result = 0.0
  result := Exp(value); -- result = 7.3891
  result := Log(value); -- result = 0.6931
END;
```

The functions Sin, Cos, Exp, and Log compute the sine, cosine, exponential, and natural logarithm of their arguments, respectively.

Data Structure Libraries

Effective data manipulation often requires the use of complex data structures. The standard libraries in Simula offer a variety of ready-made data structures such as stacks, queues, and lists. For instance, the simlist library provides an implementation of linked lists. Here is an example of using a list to store and retrieve integers:

```
REF(LIST) l;
REF(LIST) node;
BEGIN
  l := NewList;
  node := NewListNode;
  node.val := 10;
  l.Insert(node);

  node := l.First;
  WHILE node /= None DO
  BEGIN
    OutInt(node.val, 3);
    node := node.Suc;
  END;
  OutImage;
END;
```

The NewList function creates a new list, while NewListNode creates a new node in the list. The Insert method adds a node to the list, and the First field retrieves the first element. The traversal through the list is conducted using the Suc (successor) method.

Utility Libraries

Simula includes various utility libraries that provide functions for string manipulation, random number generation, and more. For random number generation, the randomlib is often used:

```
BEGIN
  REAL randVal;
  randVal := Random; -- Generates a random number between 0 and 1
  OutReal(randVal, 8, 4);
  OutImage;
END;
```

Here, the Random function generates a random number between 0 and 1, and the OutReal function is used to print it.

Practical Considerations

When using standard libraries in Simula, it is essential to include the relevant library at the beginning of your program using the EXTERNAL keyword. This ensures that all functions and types from the library are available for use.

For example:

```
EXTERNAL CLASS simio;
EXTERNAL CLASS mathlib;
EXTERNAL CLASS simlist;
EXTERNAL CLASS randomlib;
```

By incorporating these standard libraries, Simula programmers can significantly enhance the functionality and efficiency of their code, making it easier to focus on solving specific problems rather than reinventing common solutions.

Understanding and effectively utilizing these libraries is a crucial competency that facilitates the development of robust and reliable programs.

7.5 Custom Libraries

Custom libraries in Simula are instrumental in modularizing and reusing code, thereby improving maintainability and reducing redundancy. This section delves into the creation, organization, and usage of custom libraries. It addresses the critical aspects of defining a library, structuring it effectively, and integrating it with existing projects.

To create a custom library, you define a set of related functions, classes, and variables within a module. The primary goal is to encapsulate functionality that can be reused across different programs.

Consider a scenario where you need a library for mathematical operations beyond the standard functions provided by Simula. Begin by designing the library's structure. Assume the library will include operations like factorial calculation, prime number checking, and permutation generation.

```
MODULE MathLib;

-- Factorial calculation
```

```
CLASS Factorial;

  PUBLIC:
    REF INTEGER PROCEDURE Compute(n);

  PROCEDURE Compute(n INTEGER);
    INTEGER i, result;
  BEGIN
    result := 1;
    FOR i := 2 STEP 1 UNTIL n DO
      result := result * i;
    Compute := result;
  END Compute;

END Factorial;

-- Prime number checking
CLASS PrimeChecker;

  PUBLIC:
    BOOLEAN PROCEDURE IsPrime(n);

  PROCEDURE IsPrime(n INTEGER);
    INTEGER i;
  BEGIN
    IF n <= 1 THEN
      IsPrime := FALSE;
    ELSE
      FOR i := 2 STEP 1 UNTIL n-1 DO
        IF (n MOD i) = 0 THEN
          IsPrime := FALSE;
          RETURN;
        ELSE
          IsPrime := TRUE;
  END IsPrime;

END PrimeChecker;

-- Permutation generation
CLASS PermutationGenerator;

  PUBLIC:
    REF (ARRAY INTEGER) PROCEDURE GeneratePermutations(arr);

  PROCEDURE GeneratePermutations(arr REF (ARRAY INTEGER));
    BEGIN
      -- Permutation generation logic
    END GeneratePermutations;

END PermutationGenerator;

END MathLib;
```

A custom library like MathLib has defined classes Factorial, PrimeChecker, and PermutationGenerator. Each class contains public procedures that provide the library's functionality. Organizing the library in this manner promotes clarity and ease of access.

To use this library, it needs to be imported into your Simula programs.

Importing is achieved using the IMPORT statement:

```
BEGIN
  IMPORT MathLib;

  REF (Factorial) fac;
  REF (PrimeChecker) primeChk;

  fac :- NEW Factorial;
  primeChk :- NEW PrimeChecker;

  INTEGER result;
  BOOLEAN isPrime;
  result := fac.Compute(5);
  isPrime := primeChk.IsPrime(17);

  OutText("Factorial of 5: "); OutInt(result, 0); OutImage;
  OutText("Is 17 prime?: "); OutBool(isPrime); OutImage;
END;
```

When using MathLib, instances of its classes are created using the NEW keyword. The library's methods can be called on these instances to perform the desired operations.

Documentation is crucial for any custom library. Document each class, procedure, and variable comprehensively to ensure ease of use. Typically, the following information should be included:

- Description of the library's purpose
- Detailed explanation of each class and its methods
- Usage examples
- Notes on any dependencies or special considerations

Adhering to these practices facilitates the effective usage and maintenance of the library.

```
MODULE MathLib;

-- MathLib: A library for advanced mathematical operations
--
-- Classes and Methods:
-- 1. Factorial
-- - Compute(n): Calculates factorial of n
-- Usage: fac := NEW Factorial; result := fac.Compute(5);
--
-- 2. PrimeChecker
-- - IsPrime(n): Checks if n is a prime number
-- Usage: primeChk := NEW PrimeChecker; isPrime := primeChk.IsPrime(17);
--
-- 3. PermutationGenerator
-- - GeneratePermutations(arr): Generates permutations of the input array
-- Usage: permGen := NEW PermutationGenerator; perms := permGen.
     GeneratePermutations(Array);
```

```
--
-- Factorial calculation
CLASS Factorial;
...

END Factorial;

-- Prime number checking
CLASS PrimeChecker;
...

END PrimeChecker;

-- Permutation generation
CLASS PermutationGenerator;
...

END PermutationGenerator;

END MathLib;
```

Version control is also an essential practice when dealing with libraries. It allows tracking of changes over time, reversion to previous versions if issues arise, and helps in collaborative environments. Using systems like Git, each significant modification can be committed with a message detailing the changes.

```
$ git init
$ git add MathLib.sim
$ git commit -m "Initial commit of MathLib with basic functions"
$ git push origin main
```

Properly organizing files and adhering to naming conventions further enhance the library's usability. Ensure that the library files are stored in a directory structure that mirrors the logical organization of functionality.

```
MathLib/
    Factorial.sim
    PrimeChecker.sim
    PermutationGenerator.sim
    MathLib.sim
```

By meticulously organizing and documenting custom libraries, Simula programmers can greatly enhance their code's modularity, readability, and maintainability.

7.6 Managing Dependencies

In developing software, managing dependencies is crucial for ensuring efficient and reliable code execution. Dependencies refer to external modules, libraries, or packages that a project relies upon to function correctly. Properly managing these dependencies in Simula is vital for maintaining the integrity of your codebase, facilitating collaboration, and simplifying updates and maintenance.

The typical workflow in dependency management involves specifying, resolving, installing, and updating the required dependencies. Let us delve into each stage and understand the best practices specific to Simula programming.

Specification of Dependencies: Dependencies should be explicitly defined in a manifest file, which details the modules and libraries your project requires. This file is often named dependencies.sim or similar. Here is an example of how to define dependencies:

```
dependencies {
  module1 = "1.2.3"
  library2 = ">= 4.0.0"
}
```

Each entry specifies the module or library name and the version or version range. It is recommended to pin versions explicitly to avoid unexpected behavior due to updates in dependencies.

Resolution of Dependencies: Dependency resolution involves determining the exact versions that satisfy the specified requirements. This step is crucial in avoiding version conflicts and ensuring compatibility. Simula provides tools to facilitate dependency resolution, which can be invoked through command-line interfaces or integrated development environments (IDEs). A typical command-line instruction might look like:

```
simula resolve dependencies.sim
```

The resolution process outputs a detailed report of the satisfied dependencies, indicating any conflicts or issues that need manual intervention.

Installation of Dependencies: Once resolved, installing dependencies is the next step. This process often involves downloading the required modules or libraries from a repository and making them available within your project. In Simula, this could be accomplished using:

```
simula install dependencies.sim
```

This command ensures that all the specified dependencies are ready for use, stored in a designated directory structure. It is essential to ensure that the installation process is repeatable and consistent across different environments.

Updating Dependencies: Maintaining up-to-date dependencies is crucial for benefiting from the latest features, improvements, and security patches. Updating can be managed by revising the version specifications in the manifest file and re-running the resolution and installation processes. To automate this:

```
simula update dependencies.sim
```

It is advisable to review and test updates thoroughly to avoid introducing unexpected behavior into the system.

Best Practices and Tools: Effective dependency management is supported by several best practices and tools:

- **Version Pinning:** Specify exact versions for critical dependencies to safeguard against incompatibilities.
- **Lock Files:** Use lock files (e.g., dependencies.lock) generated after resolution to ensure consistency across different environments.
- **Automated Tools:** Employ automated tools for handling dependencies to reduce manual errors. Simula's built-in tools and third-party package managers can streamline this process.
- **Environment Isolation:** Use virtual environments or containers to isolate dependencies and avoid conflicts between different projects.
- **Documentation:** Document the purpose and nature of dependencies in your project to enhance maintainability and team collaboration.

Understanding and adhering to these practices will optimize your workflow and ensure the robustness of your Simula projects. Automated tools and a disciplined approach to managing dependencies will mitigate risks and streamline the development process, facilitating scalable and maintainable codebases.

Ensure that changes in the dependencies are subjected to rigorous version control, allowing traceability and rollback to previous states if necessary. This practice is especially critical in collaborative environments where multiple developers must synchronize their workflows efficiently.

Consider the following example to illustrate the process of managing dependencies using a comprehensive approach:

```
project.sim
  dependencies.sim
src
    main.sim
    utils.sim
tests
    test_main.sim
```

In dependencies.sim, we might define:

```
dependencies {
  json_parser = "2.1.0"
  logging = "~3.5.0"
}
```

Resolution and installation commands executed sequentially:

```
simula resolve dependencies.sim
simula install dependencies.sim
```

Upon resolution, a lock file (e.g., dependencies.lock) is created to ensure consistency:

```
json_parser = "2.1.0"
logging = "3.5.0"
```

Updating dependencies periodically or as required involves:

```
simula update dependencies.sim
```

Effective dependency management thus involves meticulous specification, resolution, installation, and updating, supported by automated tools, adherence to best practices, and rigorous documentation. These methods enhance collaboration, maintainability, and robustness in Simula-based development projects.

7.7 Library Documentation

Effective documentation is essential for the usability and maintainability of libraries. In Simula, comprehensive documentation ensures that other developers can understand the library's purpose, functionality, and usage. This section details the strategies and tools available for documenting Simula libraries to facilitate their integration and effective use.

Importance of Documentation: Documentation provides several benefits:

- Facilitates ease of use for other developers by explaining the functionalities of the library.
- Enhances maintainability by providing detailed information about the library's structure and design.
- Encourages contributions from the community by lowering the learning curve for new developers.
- Helps in debugging and updating the library by having a clear reference of its components.

Key Components of Library Documentation: For robust documentation, several key components should be included:

- *Name and Purpose:* Clearly state the library's name and describe its intended purpose.
- *Installation Instructions:* Provide detailed steps for installing the library, including any dependencies.
- *Usage Examples:* Include code snippets demonstrating how to utilize various functionalities of the library.
- *API Reference:* Document each class, method, and attribute, specifying their parameters, return values, and potential exceptions.
- *Changelog:* Maintain a version history detailing the changes, enhancements, and bug fixes in each release.
- *Contributing Guide:* Outline requirements and procedures for contributing to the library.

Creating Documentation in Simula: Simula does not have inherently built-in tools for generating documentation. However, adopting standardized formats and external documentation generators can be effective. Below are steps and guidelines to document a Simula library.

1. Code Comments and Docstrings: Begin by writing descriptive comments and docstrings within the code. Ensure every function and class is annotated with a docstring explaining its purpose, parameters, and return values.

```
class MyLibrary
begin
    ! Function to add two numbers:
    integer procedure add(a, b);
    integer a, b;
    begin
        add := a + b;
    end add;
end MyLibrary;
```

2. *Inline and External Documentation:* Provide inline documentation for quick reference and detailed external documentation to elaborate on the library's usage. Inline documentation should be concise, while external documentation could be more comprehensive, possibly hosted on platforms such as GitHub or a custom web page.

3. *Documentation Generators:* Utilize documentation generators like Doxygen or Natural Docs to convert comments and annotations into structured documentation. To operate such tools, follow these steps:

- **Install Doxygen:** sudo apt-get install doxygen
- **Create a Configuration File:** doxygen -g
- **Annotate Code:** Ensure the Simula code has proper comments (as shown above).
- **Run Doxygen:** doxygen Doxyfile

4. *Maintaining Documentation:* Documentation should be updated concurrently with the codebase. Establishing a practice of updating documentation with every code change helps keep the documentation relevant and useful.

5. *Hosting and Distribution:* Host the documentation in an easily accessible location. Popular options include GitHub Pages, Read the Docs, or even within a wiki associated with the code repository. A consistent and navigable structure is crucial for usability.

Example Documentation Structure:

```
MyLibrary/
    README.md
    INSTALL.md
    CHANGELOG.md
    CONTRIBUTING.md

  docs/
      index.html
      usage_guide.html
      api_reference.html
      examples.html
```

Automating Documentation Processes: Automate the generation and deployment of documentation to streamline the workflow using Continuous Integration (CI) tools. For example, by using GitHub Actions or Travis CI, set up a workflow that generates documentation and deploys it upon committing changes to the master branch.

```
name: Generate Documentation

on:
  push:
    branches:
      - master

jobs:
  build:
    runs-on: ubuntu-latest

    steps:
      - name: Checkout code
        uses: actions/checkout@v2

      - name: Setup Doxygen
        run: sudo apt-get install doxygen

      - name: Generate Documentation
        run: doxygen Doxyfile

      - name: Deploy to GitHub Pages
        uses: peaceiris/actions-gh-pages@v3
        with:
          github_token: ${{ secrets.GITHUB_TOKEN }}
          publish_dir: ./docs
```

This thorough approach to documentation not only facilitates easier adoption and contribution but also ensures the long-term sustainability and quality of the library.

7.8 Version Control for Libraries

Version control is critical in managing the development and evolution of libraries within Simula projects. By employing version control, you can maintain multiple versions of your libraries, track changes, collaborate with other developers, and revert to previous states when necessary. This section will delve into the essentials of version control systems (VCS), using Git as the primary example, and how to effectively apply these systems to manage Simula libraries.

Version Control Systems (VCS): These systems allow developers to keep track of changes in the source code over time. There are various VCS options available, but Git is one of the most widely used due to its distributed nature, robustness, and extensive community support.

Basic Concepts of Git:

Repository: A repository, or 'repo', is a storage location for software packages and contains all project files, along with the history of their changes.

Commit: A commit records changes to one or more files in the repository. Each commit has a unique identifier (SHA) and typically includes a message describing the changes.

Branch: A branch is a separate line of development created to work on different features or fixes independently. The default branch in Git is usually named master or main.

Merge: Merging is the process of combining changes from different branches into a single branch.

Remote: A remote is a version of the repository hosted on the internet or network. A typical remote repository platform is GitHub.

To begin using version control for Simula libraries, follow these steps:

Initializing a Repository: Start by initializing a new Git repository in your Simula library directory.

```
$ git init
```

This command creates a hidden .git directory that contains all the necessary files for the repository.

Adding Files to the Repository: Next, add your library files to the repository. Typically, you start by adding all files:

```
$ git add .
```

This command stages all the files in the current directory (and subdirectories) for the next commit.

Committing Changes: Commit the added files to the repository with a descriptive message.

```
$ git commit -m "Initial commit with Simula library files"
```

Creating and Using Branches: To develop new features or fix bugs without affecting the main branch, create a new branch:

```
$ git checkout -b feature-new-algorithm
```

Switch back to the main branch using:

```
$ git checkout main
```

Merge the feature branch back into the main branch once development is complete and tested:

```
$ git merge feature-new-algorithm
```

Working with Remote Repositories: To collaborate with others or maintain a backup, push your local repository to a remote server like GitHub. First, add the remote repository:

```
$ git remote add origin https://github.com/username/simula-library.git
```

Push the main branch to the remote repository:

```
$ git push -u origin main
```

Tagging Versions: Tags in Git mark specific commits as important, often used to denote release versions. Create a tag for a new release:

```
$ git tag -a v1.0 -m "Initial release version 1.0"
```

Push tags to the remote repository:

```
$ git push origin --tags
```

Managing Dependencies with Tags and Branches: When other projects depend on your Simula library, using tags ensures they reference specific, stable versions. If the library undergoes significant changes, use branches to allow developers to choose between different feature sets or versions.

Documenting Changes with Commit Messages: Well-documented commit messages are crucial. Each message should succinctly describe what changed and why. Follow a conventional format:

```
FILENAME: Short summary of changes

- Detailed explanation of changes
- Additional information as necessary
```

Using .gitignore: To prevent unnecessary files (e.g., compiled binaries, temporary files) from being included in the repository, create a .gitignore file:

```
*.o
*.tmp
*.log
```

Add and commit the .gitignore file to the repository:

```
$ git add .gitignore
$ git commit -m "Add .gitignore file"
```

Collaborative Development: Git's branch and merge features support collaborative development by allowing multiple developers to work on different parts of the library simultaneously. Use pull requests on platforms like GitHub to review and discuss code changes before merging them into the main branch.

Maintaining a Clean History: Keep the history clean and understandable. Rebase commits instead of merging for a linear history and use interactive rebase to combine or edit commits:

```
$ git rebase -i HEAD~3
```

The strategic application of a version control system like Git in managing Simula libraries ensures a disciplined and organized approach to software development, facilitating effective collaboration and robust version management.

7.9 Packaging and Distribution

Packaging and distribution refer to the processes of bundling your Simula projects into a format that can easily be shared, installed, and utilized by others. These processes ensure that the code is accessible, maintainable, and reproducible, allowing other developers to efficiently include your modules and libraries into their own applications.

Packaging: This involves organizing your code and its associated resources into a standardized format. Typically, this includes not only the code itself but also metadata such as version information, dependencies, and installation instructions.

Distribution: This is the method by which the packaged software is shared with other users. This can be done through version control systems, direct downloads, or package repositories.

Creating a Package in Simula: To create a package, you must follow a structured format. This typically involves setting up a directory structure that includes your source code, binaries, documentation, and metadata files.

- **Source Code**: The actual Simula source files (.sim) for your library or module.

- **Binaries**: If your library has compiled components, they should be included in an appropriate subdirectory.
- **Documentation**: This should include explanatory text files, such as a README.md file, and detailed API documentation.
- **Metadata Files**: These files specify additional information about the package, such as version, author, license, and dependencies. Typically, a file like package.yml or manifest.json is used.

Example: Directory Structure:

```
my_simula_library/
  src/
    my_module1.sim
    my_module2.sim
  bin/
    my_module1.o
    my_module2.o
  docs/
    README.md
    API.md
  package.yml
```

Metadata Files: Metadata is crucial for package management systems to understand the contents, compatibility, and dependencies of your package. Below is an example of what a package.yml file might look like for a Simula library.

```
name: my_simula_library
version: 1.0.0
author: Dr. John Doe
license: MIT
description: A comprehensive library for advanced Simula programming
dependencies:
  - stdlib: ">= 1.5.0"
  - utils_lib: ">= 2.2.0"
```

Distributing the Package: Once the package is prepared, it needs to be distributed. There are several ways to do this, each with its own benefits and drawbacks:

- **Direct Download**: Upload your package to a server and provide a download link. Users can download and manually install the package.
- **Package Repositories**: Register your package with public or private repositories where users can easily search for and install it using package management tools.

- **Version Control Systems (VCS)**: Host your package in a repository (e.g., GitHub, GitLab) from which users can clone and build it.

Example: Distribution via VCS: Below is a git command that demonstrates how to clone a package repository:

```
$ git clone https://github.com/username/my_simula_library.git
```

Installing the Package: Installation procedures will differ based on the distribution method. Commonly, for direct downloads and VCS, you can use make or cmake scripts included in the package.

```
$ cd my_simula_library
$ make install
```

If using package repositories, your installation command might look like this:

```
$ pkg_manager install my_simula_library
```

Package Management Tools: Using package management tools simplifies the process of handling dependencies, versioning, and installation. For Simula, there might be specific tools available or general-purpose tools like cmake or make can be used. It is essential to specify clear instructions for building and installing your package.

Algorithm 2: Package Installation Algorithm

Data: Package directory with metadata file
Result: Installed package

```
for each dependency listed in metadata do
    Check if dependency is already installed
    if not installed then
        Download and install dependency
Build the package
Copy the resulting binaries to the appropriate system directory
Update system's package registry (if applicable)
```

By adhering to structured packaging and clear distribution methods, Simula developers can create reusable, maintainable code that enhances collaborative development and efficient code management. Proper versioning and dependency management further ensure the longevity and compatibility of code across different environments and use cases.

7.10 Best Practices for Modular Programming

Modular programming is a powerful technique that enhances code organization, readability, maintainability, and reusability by dividing code into separate modules. These modules can be independently developed and tested, making it easier to manage complex software systems. To fully leverage the benefits of modular programming in Simula, consider the following best practices:

- **Cohesion and Coupling**: Aim for high cohesion within modules and low coupling between them. A module should represent a single concept or functionality, encapsulating all related data and behavior. This focus on cohesion promotes clear and focused modules. Conversely, minimize dependencies between modules to achieve low coupling, making each module resilient to changes in others.

- **Clear Interfaces**: Define clear and minimal public interfaces for your modules. Only expose what is necessary for other modules to interact with, keeping the internal implementation details private. This practice, known as encapsulation, helps in mitigating the ripple effect of changes and reduces the risk of introducing bugs.

```
MODULE ExampleModule;
EXTERNAL PROCEDURE ExampleProc;
BEGIN
  INTERNAL PROCEDURE InternalProc;
  INTEGER PublicVar;

  EXTERNAL PROCEDURE ExampleProc;
  InternalProc := PROCEDURE;
  BEGIN
    (* Implementation *)
  END InternalProc;

  PublicVar := 42;
END ExampleModule;
```

- **Consistent Naming Conventions**: Use meaningful and consistent names for modules, procedures, variables, and parameters to enhance readability and maintainability. Adopting a naming convention helps in understanding the purpose and scope of each element and prevents naming conflicts.

- **Documenting Modules**: Provide comprehensive documentation for each module. Document the purpose, public interfaces, and any assumptions or dependencies. Well-documented modules are easier to understand, use, and maintain.

```
MODULE MathLibrary;
/* This module provides various mathematical procedures and constants. */
EXTERNAL REAL PROCEDURE CalculateSquareRoot(REAL number); /*
    Calculates the square root of a given number. */
EXTERNAL REAL Pi; /* Value of Pi constant */
BEGIN
  Pi := 3.141592653589793;

  CalculateSquareRoot := PROCEDURE(number);
  BEGIN
    CalculateSquareRoot := SQRT(number); /* Use built-in sqrt function */
  END CalculateSquareRoot;
END MathLibrary;
```

- **Version Control**: Use a version control system (VCS) to track changes and manage different versions of your modules. This practice ensures that you can revert to previous versions if necessary and collaborate effectively with other developers.

- **Testing and Validation**: Develop and maintain a suite of tests for each module. Unit tests should cover the public interfaces, ensuring they perform as expected under various conditions. Regular testing helps in early detection of bugs and ensures module reliability.

```
MODULE MathLibraryTests;
BEGIN
  INTEGER TEST_NUMBER;

  OUTTEXT("Testing CalculateSquareRoot procedure:"); OUTIMAGE;
  TEST_NUMBER := 16;
  IF MathLibrary::CalculateSquareRoot(TEST_NUMBER) = 4 THEN
    OUTTEXT("Test passed!"); OUTIMAGE;
  ELSE
    OUTTEXT("Test failed!"); OUTIMAGE;
  END IF;
END MathLibraryTests;
```

- **Refactoring**: Periodically review and refactor modules to improve their structure without changing their external behavior. Refactoring can help in removing redundancy, simplifying code, and ensuring consistent style across the codebase.

- **Avoiding Global State**: Minimize the use of global variables and state. Instead, use module-specific state or parameters passed between procedures. Global state can lead to unpredictable behavior and makes debugging difficult.

- **Dependency Management**: Carefully manage dependencies between modules. Use dependency injection where applicable to enhance flexibility and testability. Ensure that modules depend on abstractions (e.g., interfaces) rather than concrete implementations.

- **Packaging and Distribution**: Organize modules into cohesive packages for distribution. Use a standard directory structure and conventional package management tools. Include metadata, such as version numbers and dependency information, to facilitate module integration into larger systems.

- **Performance Considerations**: Optimize the performance of your modules by identifying and mitigating bottlenecks. Consider algorithmic improvements, efficient data structures, and concurrency mechanisms where appropriate.

By adhering to these best practices, you will create Simula modules that are well-organized, robust, and maintainable, contributing positively to the overall quality of the software system.

Chapter 8

Input and Output Handling

This chapter examines input and output handling in Simula. It discusses standard input and output streams, reading from and writing to the console, and the basics of file handling. The chapter also covers formatted I/O operations, binary data handling, and error management in I/O operations, providing a comprehensive guide to managing input and output effectively in Simula programs.

8.1 Overview of Input and Output in Simula

Input and output (I/O) operations are fundamental aspects of programming in Simula, a language designed for discrete event simulation but also capable of general-purpose programming. This section delves into the mechanisms by which data can be read from external sources and written to outputs, be it the console or files. Understanding these operations is critical to developing programs that interact with users or other systems.

Simula provides comprehensive facilities for handling various forms of input and output. Central to Simula's I/O operations are the concepts of files and streams, which abstract the complexities of hardware-level data handling, presenting a more programmer-friendly interface. These abstractions enable a uniform approach to different I/O sources and destinations.

Standard Input and Output Streams are the primary means through which data is read from the keyboard and written to the screen. The standard input stream is usually associated with the keyboard, while the standard output stream is linked to the console. Simula encapsulates these streams in a way that simplifies the process of reading from and writing to the console.

To perform console input, the inimage statement and the sysin standard text file are employed. Similarly, console output typically utilizes the outimage statement and the sysout standard text file. Each read or write operation processes a line of text at a time, which is a useful abstraction for command-line applications.

Here is an example of reading from the console in Simula:

```
begin
  integer num;
  text line;
  line := sysin.inimage; ! Reads a line from the console
  scan(line, (cardinal num)); ! Converts and stores the input
end;
```

In this snippet, sysin.inimage reads a line of input from the console, which is then converted to an integer and stored in the num variable using the scan function.

Writing to the console is equally straightforward. For example, consider the following Simula code snippet:

```
begin
  integer num;
  num := 42;
  outtext("The answer is: ");
  outint(num, 0);
  outimage; ! Sends the text buffer to the console
end;
```

In this case, the program prints "The answer is: 42" to the console. The outtext, outint, and outimage functions are used to write text and integer values to the standard output stream.

Simula also supports file handling operations, allowing data to be read from and written to files. Files are typically interconnected with streams in Simula, enabling file data to be processed using the same operations that are used for console I/O. This unification simplifies the learning curve for new programmers, as they do not need to learn disparate sets of operations for console and file I/O.

To create or open a file for reading or writing, the open statement is used. Here is an illustrative example:

```
begin
  ref (infile) myFile;
  myFile :- new infile("data.txt");
  if not myFile.open then error("cannot open file");
  while not myFile.endfile do
     begin
        text line;
        line := myFile.inimage;
        outtext(line);
        outimage;
     end;
  myFile.close;
end;
```

In this example, the infile class is instantiated to read from a file named "data.txt". The program checks if the file opens successfully and reads each line from the file until the end is reached, printing each line to the console.

Conversely, writing to a file requires an instance of the outfile class:

```
begin
  ref (outfile) myFile;
  myFile :- new outfile("output.txt");
  if not myFile.open then error("cannot open file");
  myFile.outtext("Hello, Simula!");
  myFile.outimage; ! Writes the buffered text to the file
  myFile.close;
end;
```

This code opens a file named "output.txt" and writes the string "Hello, Simula!" to it. The buffer is flushed to the file using outimage, and the file is then closed.

Understanding the basics of input and output in Simula is essential for effective programming. The constructs provided by Simula facilitate seamless and efficient data handling, enabling programmers to focus on the core logic of their applications without getting bogged down by I/O intricacies.

8.2 Standard Input and Output Streams

Understanding standard input and output streams is integral to mastering input and output handling in Simula. These streams facilitate communication between the program and the external environment, enabling it to receive input from users and display output. In Simula, standard input and output are managed through predefined stream objects.

Standard input (stdin) refers to the default stream from which a Simula program reads its input data. Typically, this corresponds to the keyboard input during console interactions. Standard output (stdout), on the other hand, is the default stream where a Simula program writes its output data, usually displayed on the monitor.

To read from the standard input, Simula utilizes the inimage stream, while writing to standard output employs the outimage stream. Below is an example of using these streams:

```
begin
    integer x;
    outtext("Enter a number: "); outimage;
    inint(x);
    outtext("You entered: "); outint(x, 0); outimage;
end;
```

In this example, outtext writes the string "Enter a number: " to the standard output stream, prompting the user to input a number. Subsequent usage of inint reads an integer value from the standard input and stores it in the variable x. Finally, outtext and outint display the entered number using standard output.

Simula provides several I/O procedures, including:

- inchar: Reads a single character from standard input.
- inint: Reads an integer value from standard input.
- inreal: Reads a real (floating-point) number from standard input.
- inimage: Reads a line of text from standard input.
- outchar: Writes a single character to standard output.
- outint: Writes an integer value to standard output.
- outreal: Writes a real (floating-point) number to standard output.
- outtext: Writes a string of text to standard output.
- outimage: Writes a newline character to standard output, effectively flushing the output buffer.

Correct usage of these procedures ensures efficient interaction with the user through the console. Additionally, it is essential to properly handle the output buffer. The outimage command, for instance, not only outputs a newline but also ensures that all previously buffered output is displayed immediately.

Consider the following sequence demonstrating these procedures:

```
begin
   character c;
   integer i;
   real r;

   outtext("Reading inputs from the user: "); outimage;

   outtext("Enter a character: "); outimage;
   inchar(c);
   outtext("You entered character: "); outchar(c); outimage;

   outtext("Enter an integer: "); outimage;
   inint(i);
   outtext("You entered integer: "); outint(i, 0); outimage;

   outtext("Enter a real number: "); outimage;
   inreal(r);
   outtext("You entered real number: "); outreal(r, 0); outimage;
end;
```

In this expanded example, the program reads a character, an integer, and a real number from the user, and subsequently displays each one. Each input is read using inchar, inint, and inreal respectively, highlighting the flexibility of Simula's input handling functions.

Furthermore, Simula supports formatted output operations which allow for more control over the display format of data. For instance, the outint and outreal procedures can take additional parameters to specify field width and precision:

- outint(i, w): Writes integer i to standard output with a field width of w characters.
- outreal(r, d): Writes real number r to standard output with d decimal places.

An illustration of formatted output:

```
begin
   integer num;
   real pi;
   pi := 3.141592653589793;

   num := 1234;
   outtext("Formatted integer: "); outint(num, 10); outimage;

   outtext("Formatted real number: "); outreal(pi, 4); outimage;
end;
```

The outint(num, 10) call in this example outputs the integer num right-justified in a field of 10 characters, while outreal(pi, 4) displays the real number pi with 4 decimal places. Proper utilization of field widths and precision is crucial for creating readable and visually appealing output, especially in tabular data presentation or aligning multiple columns.

Finally, it is important to handle end-of-file (EOF) conditions gracefully during input operations. EOF occurs when no more data is available for reading from a stream. Simula provides the endfile function to check for EOF:

```
if endfile then
    outtext("No more data available"); outimage
else
    outtext("Data available for reading"); outimage;
```

The endfile function returns a boolean value indicating whether the end of the file (or input stream) has been reached. This function is critical when processing input in loops, as it helps avoid reading errors and allows for the implementation of clean exit conditions.

Understanding and effectively utilizing Simula's standard input and output streams serves as the foundation for more advanced I/O operations, such as file handling and binary data processing, which will be elaborated in subsequent sections.

8.3 Reading from the Console

In Simula, reading from the console is an essential operation that enables interaction between the user and the program. It involves capturing input data typed by the user at runtime and utilizing that data within the program. Console input in Simula is straightforward, leveraging predefined procedures that facilitate this interaction.

To begin with, Simula uses the inchar procedure for reading individual characters from the console. This procedure captures the next character from the input stream and returns it, thereby allowing the program to react to each keystroke. Consider the following example where a single character is read from the console and printed out:

```
BEGIN
    INTEGER CHARACTER;
    CHARACTER := inchar;
    OutText('You entered: ');
    OutChar(CHARACTER);
    OutImage;
END;
```

When the code above is executed, it waits for the user to input a character, which is then stored in the variable CHARACTER. The entered character is subsequently displayed using OutChar followed by OutImage to ensure the output is displayed on the console.

For reading strings from the console, Simula provides the intextf and intexti procedures. The procedure intextf reads a fixed-length string from the console, while intexti reads an input line terminated by the carriage return. Using intexti ensures that the entire line of input is captured, which is advantageous for processing commands or sentences typed by the user. Below is an example demonstrating intexti:

```
BEGIN
    TEXT UserInput;
    UserInput := BlankText(80);
    intexti(UserInput);

    OutText('You entered: ');
    OutText(UserInput);
    OutImage;
END;
```

In this program, a TEXT variable UserInput with the capacity of 80 characters is created and initialized using BlankText. The intexti procedure then reads the input from the console until a carriage return is encountered and stores it in UserInput. The entered text is printed back to the console using OutText.

Console input can be managed more effectively by validating the input data before processing it. This ensures robustness and prevents errors due to invalid user inputs. Consider the task of reading an integer from the console:

```
BEGIN
    INTEGER UserNumber;
    TEXT InputLine;
    BOOLEAN ValidInput;

    InputLine := BlankText(20);
    ValidInput := FALSE;

    WHILE NOT ValidInput DO
    BEGIN
        OutText('Please enter an integer: ');
        OutImage;
        intexti(InputLine);

        IF ScanText(InputLine, UserNumber) THEN
            ValidInput := TRUE;
        ELSE
            OutText('Invalid input. Try again.');
```

```
        OutImage;
    END;

    OutText('You entered the integer: ');
    OutInt(UserNumber, 0);
    OutImage;
END;
```

In this scenario, the program prompts the user to enter an integer. The input is validated using the ScanText function, which attempts to parse the string into an integer. The while loop continues until valid input is provided. This technique enhances error handling by ensuring that only valid integers are passed to UserNumber.

Reading from the console in Simula can also involve handling more complex input scenarios such as capturing a sequence of inputs or reading multiple data types within a single line. This requires a combination of the aforementioned procedures along with additional string manipulation and validation functions.

Overall, mastering console input in Simula is fundamental for creating interactive applications and improving user experience. The combination of inchar, intextf, intexti, and error validation techniques creates a robust framework for user data entry and processing in Simula programs. Properly handling and validating this input is crucial for developing resilient and user-friendly software.

8.4 Writing to the Console

In Simula, writing to the console is accomplished using the outtext, outfix, or outreal procedures, each suited for writing different types of data. Console output is primarily used for displaying results, debugging, or providing information to the user during program execution. This section details the usage of these procedures and their various parameters.

The outtext procedure is used for outputting text strings to the console. The basic syntax for outtext is as follows:

```
outtext("Your text here");
```

If one wishes to include escape sequences like new lines (\n) or tabs (\t), they would be embedded within the string. An example demonstrating their use is:

```
outtext("Hello, World!\nThis is a new line.\tAnd this is a tabbed space.");
```

The outfix procedure is used to print fixed-point numbers to the console. This procedure permits specifying the number of digits to print after the decimal point. The syntax for outfix is:

```
outfix(number, numDigits);
```

The number parameter is the numeric value to be printed, and numDigits is the integer specifying the number of decimal places. For instance:

```
outfix(123.456789, 4);
```

This would output:

```
123.4568
```

The outreal procedure is similar to outfix, but it prints real numbers in a floating-point format. It also accepts an optional parameter to control the number of significant digits. Its syntax is:

```
outreal(number, numDigits);
```

For example:

```
outreal(123.456789, 6);
```

This would output:

```
123.457
```

Chainable statements in Simula allow for more succinct code when multiple console outputs are desired. For instance:

```
outtext("The value of pi: "); outreal(3.14159, 5); outtext("\nCalculation complete.");
```

When executed, the output would be:

```
The value of pi: 3.14159
Calculation complete.
```

For aligning outputted text or numbers, Simula provides the outint procedure which is used for printing integers with specified width. This aids in aligning columns of numbers or text uniformly.

```
outint(12345, 10);
```

The second parameter specifies the total width. The above example would right-align the integer within 10 spaces. Similarly, left alignment or zero-padding can be achieved using other formatting options such as text justification or width specifiers.

In practical applications, combining these procedures allows for constructing more readable and well-formatted console outputs. Below is an example program that demonstrates writing various data types to the console:

```
Begin
  outtext("Temperature Readings for the Week:\n");
  outtext("Day\tMorning\tAfternoon\tEvening\n");
  outtext("Mon\t" ); outfix(19.2, 1 ); outtext("\t"); outfix(23.5, 1 ); outtext("\t");
       outfix(20.1, 1 ); outtext("\n");
  outtext("Tue\t" ); outfix(18.6, 1 ); outtext("\t"); outfix(24.8, 1 ); outtext("\t");
       outfix(22.5, 1 ); outtext("\n");
  outtext("Wed\t" ); outfix(20.8, 1 ); outtext("\t"); outfix(25.5, 1 ); outtext("\t");
       outfix(21.0, 1 ); outtext("\n");
  outtext("Thu\t" ); outfix(17.5, 1 ); outtext("\t"); outfix(22.2, 1 ); outtext("\t");
       outfix(19.1, 1 ); outtext("\n");
  outtext("Fri\t" ); outfix(16.4, 1 ); outtext("\t"); outfix(21.5, 1 ); outtext("\t"); outfix
       (18.0, 1 ); outtext("\n");
  outtext("Sat\t" ); outfix(15.0, 1 ); outtext("\t"); outfix(20.0, 1 ); outtext("\t");
       outfix(17.5, 1 ); outtext("\n");
  outtext("Sun\t" ); outfix(14.5, 1 ); outtext("\t"); outfix(19.5, 1 ); outtext("\t");
       outfix(16.8, 1 ); outtext("\n");
End;
```

Upon execution, the output will be neatly formatted as:

```
Temperature Readings for the Week:
Day   Morning Afternoon Evening
Mon   19.2    23.5      20.1
Tue   18.6    24.8      22.5
Wed   20.8    25.5      21.0
Thu   17.5    22.2      19.1
Fri   16.4    21.5      18.0
Sat   15.0    20.0      17.5
Sun   14.5    19.5      16.8
```

Overall, these procedures provide robust mechanisms for outputting formatted data to the console in Simula, making the program's interface more user-friendly and informative.

8.5 File Handling Basics

Simula provides robust mechanisms for file handling, crucial for many applications. Files allow programs to store data persistently and interact with vast amounts of data efficiently. This section explores the fundamental concepts and operations related to file handling in Simula, including opening and closing files, reading from and writing to files, and understanding file modes.

Opening and Closing Files

In Simula, file operations start with opening a file. This associates a file with the program, enabling various input and output operations. The Open statement is used to open a file. The syntax is as follows:

```
Open(file_variable, file_mode, file_name)
```

file_variable is the identifier for the file. file_mode specifies the mode in which the file is opened and can be one of the following:

- inmode - Open the file for reading.
- outmode - Open the file for writing. If the file already exists, it will be overwritten.
- appendmode - Open the file for writing. If the file already exists, data is appended to the end of the file.
- updmode - Open the file for reading and writing.

file_name is the name of the file and should be enclosed in quotation marks. Here is an example of opening a file for reading:

```
Open(inpfile, inmode, "data.txt");
```

Once operations on the file are complete, it is essential to close the file using the Close statement to free resources:

```
Close(inpfile);
```

Reading from a File

To read data from a file, the InInt, InReal, InChar, or InText procedures are used, depending on the type of data:

```
integer v;
real r;
character c;
text t;

InInt(inpfile, v);
InReal(inpfile, r);
InChar(inpfile, c);
InText(inpfile, t);
```

These procedures read the next available data item from the file and store it in the corresponding variable v, r, c, or t.

Writing to a File

To write data to a file, the OutInt, OutReal, OutChar, or OutText procedures are utilized:

```
integer v = 10;
real r = 3.14;
character c = 'A';
text t = "Hello, Simula";

OutInt(outfile, v);
OutReal(outfile, r);
OutChar(outfile, c);
OutText(outfile, t);
```

The above example writes an integer, a real number, a character, and a string to the file associated with outfile.

File Modes

The mode in which a file is opened is critical, as it dictates the operations that can be performed on the file.

- inmode - Only read operations are permitted. Any attempt to write to the file will raise an error.
- outmode - Only write operations are allowed. The file's existing content is truncated.
- appendmode - Similar to outmode, but data is appended rather than overwriting existing content.
- updmode - Both read and write operations are supported. This mode is useful for modifying specific parts of a file.

Proper understanding and management of file modes ensure that file operations are performed safely and correctly. When handling files, ensure that errors are managed, for example, by checking if a file was successfully opened:

```
if Not Open(inpfile, inmode, "data.txt") then
    OutText(Out, "Error: File could not be opened");
else
    ! Proceed with file operations
endif;
```

This construct prevents runtime errors that may occur if file operations are attempted on an unopened file.

8.6 Reading from Files

Reading from files in Simula requires understanding the essential steps and functions provided by the language to handle file operations. This section delves into the mechanisms and syntax used in Simula to read data from files, ensuring that the processes are both efficient and error-free.

Simula provides a robust set of functionalities for file handling, encapsulated within the InFile class. The InFile class offers methods to open files, read various data types, and manage file pointers.

To begin reading from a file, one must first instantiate the InFile object and then open the desired file using the appropriate method. Below is an example demonstrating the steps involved in reading from a file:

```
REF (InFile) inputFile;
inputFile :- New InFile("example.txt");

inputFile.Open();
```

In the instantiation process, example.txt is the name of the file we wish to read. The Open method opens the specified file and readies it for reading operations. If the file does not exist or cannot be opened, the Open method would typically manage the exception accordingly or return an appropriate error status.

Once the file is open, various methods can be employed to read data. Commonly used methods are GetChar, GetInt, GetReal, and GetLine.

```
CHAR c;
INTEGER i;
REAL r;
TEXT line;

c :- inputFile.GetChar();
write(c);
```

The GetChar method reads the next character from the file. If the end of the file is reached, it commonly returns a special end-of-file indicator or raises an end-of-file exception.

For reading integers, GetInt is utilized as follows:

```
i :- inputFile.GetInt();
write(i);
```

Similarly, for real numbers, GetReal is used:

```
r :- inputFile.GetReal();
write(r);
```

To read an entire line of text from the file, the GetLine method is employed:

```
line :- inputFile.GetLine();
write(line);
```

The GetLine method reads characters from the current file position until a newline character is found, then constructs a TEXT object from them.

Error handling is crucial in file operations to ensure that the program behaves correctly under all conditions. Simula provides mechanisms to check the file status continuously. Below is an example demonstrating checking the file status after opening:

```
IF ~inputFile.Open() THEN
  OutText("Error: Could not open file.");
```

Simula offers built-in members to handle the file's state, often including methods to determine if the end of the file is reached or if an error has occurred during reading operations. The end-of-file condition can typically be checked using a direct method call or a property.

To properly conclude file operations and release resources, the file should always be closed once all reading is done:

```
inputFile.Close();
```

Properly closing the file ensures that all associated resources are freed and that any buffered operations are finalized. Failure to close the file could lead to resource leaks and undefined behavior in the program.

With the basics of reading from files covered, it is possible to handle more complex scenarios, such as reading structured data or processing files in binary mode. However, the fundamental concepts demonstrated offer a solid foundation to build upon as one progresses to more advanced file handling in Simula. The next section will address various use cases, enriching the reader's ability to handle specific I/O requirements effectively.

8.7 Writing to Files

Writing data to files is an essential aspect of many Simula programs. This section will delve into the procedure for writing data to files using Simula, covering file creation, opening files for writing, writing text and binary data, and closing files properly. By understanding these components, one is able to manage persistent data storage effectively.

To initiate file writing operations in Simula, it is crucial to first understand how to handle file objects. Simula uses the outintf class and related subclasses for managing output files. The following example demonstrates the steps for writing text data to a file:

```
BEGIN
    INTEGER i;
    TEXT file_name;
    REF(outfile) file;

    ! Define the name of the file ;
    file_name :- "output.txt";

    ! Create the file object ;
    file :- NEW outfile(file_name);

    IF NOT file THEN
        OutText("Cannot create file: "); OutText(file_name); OutImage;
    ELSE
        ! Write integer values from 1 to 10 into the file ;
        FOR i := 1 STEP 1 UNTIL 10 DO
            file.OutInt(i, 5);
            file.OutImage;
        OD;

        ! Close the file ;
        file.Close;
    ENDIF;
END;
```

In this example, the outfile class is used to create and manage the output file. The NEW outfile(file_name) expression constructs a new file on the disk with the specified name. The program checks if the file object was successfully created before proceeding to writing operations.

OutInt and OutImage methods are employed to write formatted text to the file. OutInt(i, 5) writes the integer variable i to the file with a field width of 5 characters, ensuring proper alignment. OutImage method is used to output a newline sequence in the file, similar to \n in other programming languages.

When writing binary data, the approach involves encoding information into a binary format before writing. Simula's OutRecord method can be employed for this purpose, along with the previously defined outfile class. The following augmented example demonstrates writing binary records:

```
BEGIN
    INTEGER i, record_length;
    TEXT file_name;
    REF(outfile) file;
    REF(RecordClass) bin_record;

    ! Define the name of the file ;
    file_name :- "binary_output.dat";
    record_length := 10;
```

```
    ! Create the file object ;
    file :- NEW outfile(file_name);

    IF NOT file THEN
        OutText("Cannot create file: "); OutText(file_name); OutImage;
    ELSE
        ! Write integer values as binary records into the file ;
        FOR i := 1 STEP 1 UNTIL 10 DO
            bin_record :- NEW RecordClass(record_length);
            bin_record.SetInt1(i); ! Assuming SetInt1 is a method to set first integer ;
            file.OutRecord(bin_record);
        OD;

        ! Close the file ;
        file.Close;
    ENDIF;
END;
```

RecordClass is a hypothetical class designed to encapsulate records with methods like SetInt1 for setting integer values. OutRecord writes the binary content represented by the record into the file sequentially.

Properly closing the file using the Close method is essential to ensure data integrity and release system resources. Failure to close the file can result in data loss or file corruption.

When handling file writing operations, it is critical to be aware of common errors and implement error handling mechanisms. Errors such as “file not found” or “permission denied” can prevent successful file creation or writing. While the sample code above includes a basic error message output using OutText, more sophisticated error handling strategies should be implemented for robust programs.

```
Cannot create file: output.txt
```

By adhering to these practices for writing to files in Simula, one can create programs that effectively manage persistent data storage and ensure data accuracy and safety.

8.8 Formatted Input and Output

Formatted input and output are crucial for creating programs that interact with users or other systems in a clear and readable manner. This section explores various techniques and functions in Simula for managing formatted I/O operations, which enable the formatting of data to meet specific requirements, such as aligning text, controlling the number of decimal places, and ensuring consistent data representation.

Formatted Output:

In Simula, formatted output can be achieved using the outimage statement or by manipulating the outstream class. These mechanisms allow precise control over how the data is represented when printed to the console or a file.

To print formatted text, you can use the built-in outimage statement, which manages the formatting of the data before it is output. The following example demonstrates how to use outimage to format numerical output to a fixed number of decimal places:

```
! Simula code for formatted output using outimage;
Begin
   Real x;
   x := 123.456789;
   outimage(x,-10,3);
End;
```

In this example, the outimage statement formats the real number x to fit within a field width of 10 characters and display 3 decimal places. If the number is smaller than the field width, it will be right-aligned, and leading spaces will be added to fill the field.

Formatted Input:

Formatted input is handled through the use of the inimage statement, allowing the user to specify the format of the incoming data. This is particularly useful for parsing strings or numbers that adhere to specific formats.

Consider the following example, which demonstrates reading a real number from the console with a precise format:

```
! Simula code for formatted input using inimage;
Begin
   Real y;
   inimage(y,12,4);
   Inspect y Do OutReal(y,0,4);
End;
```

In this example, the inimage statement reads a real number, expecting a field width of 12 characters and 4 decimal places. The OutReal function then prints the number to verify the input was correctly parsed. The Inspect construct is used here to ensure that the OutReal function operates on the variable y directly.

Formatting Strings:

Textual data often requires formatting to ensure proper alignment and presentation. Simula provides mechanisms to manipulate strings, aligning them to the left, right, or center.

To align a string to the right within a specified field width, the following example can be utilized:

```
! Simula code for right-aligning a string;
Begin
   Text str;
   str := 'Simula Programming';
   outimage(str,20);
End;
```

In this example, the string 'Simula Programming' is formatted to fit within a field width of 20 characters, and it will be right-aligned by default.

For left alignment, Simula does not provide a direct statement like outimage, but one can manipulate the string with padding spaces manually before output. Here's an example illustrating this manual method:

```
! Simula code for left-aligning a string;
Begin
   Text str;
   str := 'Simula Programming';
   str := str & ' '; ! Add padding for left alignment
   OutText(str Sub 1, 20 Outlength);
End;
```

In this case, the additional space character is concatenated to ensure that str fits within 20 characters when output through OutText.

Handling Numbers with Different Bases:

Simula also supports formatted output for numbers in various bases (binary, octal, hexadecimal). The following example demonstrates formatting an integer in hexadecimal format:

```
! Simula code for outputting an integer in hexadecimal format;
Begin
   Integer number;
   number := 255;
   OutInt(number, 0, '16r');
End;
```

In this case, OutInt is used to print the integer 255 in hexadecimal format by specifying the base '16r', which is the Simula notation for radix 16.

Custom Format Specifiers:

Simula's flexibility allows for custom formatting functions to be defined when predefined methods do not meet the specific needs. For instance, creating a custom function to format a date string in the YYYY-MM-DD format can be beneficial.

```
! Simula code for custom date formatting function;
Begin
   Procedure FormatDate(Year, Month, Day); Integer Year, Month, Day;
   Begin
      Text dateStr;
      dateStr := Copy(InText(IntegerToText(Year,4)) & '-' & IntegerToText(Month,2)
            & '-' & IntegerToText(Day,2));
      OutText(dateStr);
   End;

   ! Usage of the custom date formatting function;
   FormatDate(2023, 10, 5);
End;
```

This example illustrates a custom procedure FormatDate that takes year, month, and day integers and combines them into a properly formatted date string.

These techniques enable the Simula programmer to create clear, precise, and user-friendly outputs. Accurate formatting helps ensure the data is easily understood and correctly interpreted, which is essential in professional software development and data analysis tasks.

8.9 Binary Data Handling

Handling binary data is an essential aspect of many applications in Simula programming, particularly when dealing with file I/O operations that require efficient storage and retrieval of data. Binary files store data in a format that is not human-readable, but they are compact and faster to process compared to text files. In this section, we will explore how to manage binary data in Simula, including reading, writing, and manipulating binary files.

Binary data operations typically involve reading and writing raw bytes rather than formatted text. To perform these operations, it is crucial to understand file access modes and the appropriate functions to handle binary data.

Accessing Binary Files:

To work with binary files in Simula, you need to open the files in binary mode. Simula provides specific modes for this purpose, such as rb for reading binary files and wb for writing binary files. The rb+ and wb+ modes can be used for reading and writing, respectively, while allowing both operations.

Reading Binary Data:

Reading binary data involves reading raw bytes from a file. In Simula, the fread function is used to read binary data from a file. The function requires specifying the pointer to a block of memory where the data will be stored, the size of each element to be read, and the number of elements to read. Here is an example illustrating how to read binary data from a file:

```
FILE \*file;
char buffer[256];
size_t bytesRead;

file = fopen("data.bin", "rb");
if (file != NULL) {
    bytesRead = fread(buffer, sizeof(char), 256, file);
    if (bytesRead < 256) {
        if (feof(file)) {
            printf("End of file reached.\n");
        } else if (ferror(file)) {
            printf("Error reading from file.\n");
        }
    }
    fclose(file);
} else {
    printf("Failed to open the file.\n");
}
```

In this example, fopen is used to open the file data.bin in binary read mode (rb). The fread function reads up to 256 bytes into buffer. The actual number of bytes read is stored in bytesRead. The code also checks for the end of the file and reading errors using feof and ferror, respectively, before closing the file.

Writing Binary Data:

Writing binary data to a file in Simula is performed using the fwrite function, which writes raw bytes from a specified memory block to the file. The following example demonstrates writing binary data to a file:

```
FILE \*file;
char data[] = "Binary data example";
size_t bytesWritten;

file = fopen("output.bin", "wb");
if (file != NULL) {
    bytesWritten = fwrite(data, sizeof(char), sizeof(data), file);
    if (bytesWritten < sizeof(data)) {
        printf("Error writing to file.\n");
    }
    fclose(file);
} else {
    printf("Failed to open the file.\n");
}
```

Here, the file output.bin is opened in binary write mode (wb), and the fwrite function writes the contents of data to the file. The number of bytes successfully written is stored in bytesWritten and compared to the size of data to check for potential errors.

Manipulating Binary Data:

Manipulating binary data often involves working with structures and arrays, which need to be properly handled when writing to or reading from files. Care must be taken to ensure that data is correctly aligned and that any padding bytes are managed appropriately.

Consider the following structure:

```
struct Record {
    int id;
    double value;
    char name[50];
};
```

To write an array of Record structures to a file, you could use the following code:

```
struct Record records[10];
FILE \*file;
size_t recordsWritten;

file = fopen("records.bin", "wb");
if (file != NULL) {
    recordsWritten = fwrite(records, sizeof(struct Record), 10, file);
    if (recordsWritten < 10) {
        printf("Error writing records to file.\n");
    }
    fclose(file);
} else {
    printf("Failed to open the file.\n");
}
```

This code initializes an array of Record structures and writes it to the file records.bin. The fwrite function writes 10 records, and the number of records successfully written is compared to 10 to check for errors.

Endianness:

Binary data handling must take endianness into account, which refers to the byte order used to represent multi-byte data types. Different systems may use different endianness, such as little-endian or big-endian. When writing binary files intended for use across different systems, it is crucial to ensure that the data is interpreted correctly.

To handle endianness, you can use functions to convert data to a common byte order before writing and after reading. Here is an example of converting an integer to network byte order (big-endian) before writing:

```
#include <arpa/inet.h>

int value = 12345;
int convertedValue = htonl(value);

fwrite(&convertedValue, sizeof(int), 1, file);
```

The htonl function converts the integer value to network byte order, ensuring consistent data representation regardless of the platform.

Overall, handling binary data in Simula requires careful attention to detail, particularly regarding file access modes, data alignment, and endianness. Proper management of these aspects ensures efficient and reliable binary data operations.

8.10 Error Handling in I/O Operations

Error handling in I/O operations is a crucial aspect of ensuring the robustness and reliability of Simula programs. This section delves into the mechanisms provided by Simula to detect and manage errors during input and output (I/O) operations. Effective error handling can prevent a program from crashing unexpectedly and can provide useful feedback to the user.

Simula, like many programming languages, offers a series of constructs and predefined variables to handle errors encountered during I/O operations. These include checking the status of I/O operations, using built-in procedures to handle exceptions, and employing the InFile and OutFile class methods to manage file-related errors.

1. Checking I/O Operation Status

One of the fundamental methods to handle errors is to check the status of the I/O operations. In Simula, the status of an I/O operation can be checked using pre-defined functions and variables. For example, when reading from a file, you can verify if the end of the file has been reached using the More() function.

```
REF(InFile) inputFile;
BOOLEAN isMore;

inputFile :- New InFile("data.txt");
if inputFile.Open then
begin
  WHILE inputFile.More DO
  begin
```

```
    ... /* Read from file */
  end;
  inputFile.Close;
end else
begin
  OutText("Failed to open file.");
  OutImage;
end;
```

In the example above, inputFile is an instance of the InFile class. Before attempting to read from the file, the Open method is called to open the file. The More method is then used within a WHILE loop to read until the end of the file. If the file cannot be opened, the program handles this by outputting a failure message.

2. Handling File Opening Errors

Opening a file is a common operation that can fail due to various reasons, such as the file not existing or lacking the necessary permissions. Simula allows handling such errors gracefully by checking the return value of the Open method.

```
REF(InFile) inputFile;

inputFile :- New InFile("nonexistentfile.txt");
if NOT inputFile.Open then
begin
  OutText("Error: Unable to open the file.");
  OutImage;
end else
begin
  ... /* Proceed with file operations */
  inputFile.Close;
end;
```

In this snippet, if the file named "nonexistentfile.txt" cannot be opened, the program outputs an error message and does not proceed with any file operations, thus avoiding potential runtime errors.

3. Managing Input and Output Exceptions

Besides file operations, errors can occur during console I/O operations. Simula provides mechanisms to catch and handle these exceptions using built-in procedures and exception handling constructs.

```
TRY
  ... /* Code that might generate an error */
EXCEPTION
  WHEN IOLineTooLong DO
    OutText("Input line is too long.");
    OutImage;
  WHEN IOFormatError DO
    OutText("Formatting error in input.");
    OutImage;
END;
```

The TRY-EXCEPTION block in Simula allows handling specific exceptions that may occur during I/O operations. IOLineTooLong and IOFormatError are two common errors associated with input operations. The example demonstrates how to catch these exceptions and output corresponding error messages.

4. Using Predefined Variables for Detailed Error Info

Simula provides predefined variables like IOStatus and IOErrorCode which contain detailed information about the status and error codes of the last I/O operation. This can be beneficial for diagnosing and handling specific errors.

```
REF(OutFile) outputFile;

outputFile :- New OutFile("output.txt");
if outputFile.Open then
begin
  ... /* Write to the file */
  if IOStatus # 0 then
  begin
    OutText("Error: I/O operation failed.");
    OutInt(IOErrorCode, 1);
    OutImage;
  end;
  outputFile.Close;
end else
begin
  OutText("Error: Unable to open output file.");
  OutImage;
end;
```

Here, after an attempt to write to outputFile, the IOStatus is checked. If IOStatus is non-zero, indicating an error, the IOErrorCode is output to provide specific information about the error.

5. Best Practices for Error Handling

- Always check the return values of I/O operations such as Open(), Close(), Read(), and Write(). - Use TRY-EXCEPTION blocks to handle runtime I/O errors gracefully. - Utilize predefined variables like IOStatus and IOErrorCode for detailed error information. - Ensure that resources such as file handles are properly released even in case of errors.

Adhering to these practices not only makes your Simula programs more robust but also enhances their readability and maintainability, allowing for more comprehensive error handling and debugging processes.

8.11 Common I/O Use Cases

Input and output operations in Simula are foundational to interactive program behavior and data management. This section will explore prevalent use cases associated with I/O operations in Simula, including typical patterns and best practices. These use cases will cover scenarios such as reading user input, writing data to the console, reading from and writing to text and binary files, and managing errors effectively.

Reading User Input

User input is typically required for interactive programs. In Simula, you can use the inimage and intext statements to read input from the console. Here's an example of reading a string and an integer from the user:

```
BEGIN
  TEXT name;
  INTEGER age;
  OutText("Enter your name: ");
  name :- Inimage;
  OutText("Enter your age: ");
  Inint(age);
  OutText("Hello, ");
  OutText(name);
  OutText(", you are ");
  Outint(age, 1);
  OutText(" years old!");
  OutImage;
END;
```

This program snippet prompts the user for their name and age, then prints a greeting message with the provided details.

Writing Data to the Console

To display data to the console, you often use the OutText, OutInt, and OutImage procedures. Here is a typical example:

```
BEGIN
  INTEGER value;
  value := 123;
  OutText("The value is: ");
  OutInt(value, 1);
  OutImage;
END;
```

This code outputs the string "The value is: 123" to the console.

Reading from Files

Reading from text files involves opening a file for input, then reading its contents. Here is an example:

```
BEGIN
  INFILE inputFile;
  TEXT line;
  inputFile.Open("myfile.txt");
  WHILE NOT inputFile.EndOfFile DO
  BEGIN
    inputFile.Intext(line);
    OutText(line); OutImage;
  END;
  inputFile.Close;
END;
```

This code opens myfile.txt for reading, prints each line to the console, and then closes the file.

Writing to Files

Writing data to a file in Simula involves opening a file for output and then writing the necessary content. Here's an example:

```
BEGIN
  OUTFILE outputFile;
  outputFile.Open("output.txt");
  outputFile.OutText("This is a line of text.");
  outputFile.OutImage;
  outputFile.Close;
END;
```

This program will write "This is a line of text." to output.txt and close the file.

Formatted Input and Output

Simula provides formatted I/O operations through procedures like OutFix, OutReal, etc. For example, to output a floating-point number in a formatted manner:

```
BEGIN
  REAL r;
  r := 3.14159;
  OutText("Pi is approximately: ");
  OutFix(r, 1, 5, 2); ! Width 5, 2 decimal places
  OutImage;
END;
```

This code outputs the string "Pi is approximately: 3.14".

Binary File Handling

Handling binary data requires treating files as streams of bytes. Here's an example involving reading binary data:

```
BEGIN
  INFILEBIN binaryFile;
```

```
  INTEGER value;
  binaryFile.Open("data.bin");
  binaryFile.InInt(value);
  OutText("Read value: "); OutInt(value, 1); OutImage;
  binaryFile.Close;
END;
```

This code snippet reads an integer from a binary file data.bin and outputs it.

Error Handling in I/O Operations

Error handling is crucial for robust programs. Simula allows you to detect and respond to I/O errors using appropriate checks. Here's a pattern to handle possible errors:

```
BEGIN
  OUTFILE fileOut;
  BOOLEAN fileStatus;
  fileStatus := fileOut.Open("nonexistent_directory/output.txt");
  IF NOT fileStatus THEN
  BEGIN
    OutText("Error: Unable to open the file."); OutImage;
  END
  ELSE
  BEGIN
    fileOut.OutText("Successfully opened the file.");
    fileOut.OutImage;
    fileOut.Close;
  END;
END;
```

This code attempts to open a file for writing and handles the case where the file cannot be opened by providing an appropriate error message.

Understanding these common I/O use cases equips you with the knowledge required to handle typical scenarios encountered during Simula programming. Each example demonstrates precise reading and writing patterns, enhancing your ability to manage input and output operations effectively.

Chapter 9

Exception Handling

This chapter addresses exception handling in Simula. It explores the fundamentals of exceptions, including the 'try' and 'catch' blocks, creating custom exceptions, and throwing exceptions. Additionally, it covers exception propagation, the 'finally' block, nested 'try' statements, handling multiple exceptions, and best practices for debugging and logging exceptions, providing a comprehensive approach to robust error management.

9.1 Introduction to Exception Handling

Exception handling is a critical aspect of robust and reliable software development. In Simula, as in many contemporary programming languages, exception handling mechanisms enable developers to manage and resolve errors or exceptional circumstances that arise during program execution. This section provides an in-depth introduction to exception handling, elucidating its purpose, the fundamental concepts involved, and the specific constructs provided by Simula for effective error management.

An exception is an event that disrupts the normal flow of the program. It often represents an error or anomalous condition that must be addressed to maintain the program's stability and reliability. Common examples of conditions that may raise exceptions include division by zero, file I/O errors, and invalid user input.

Simula's approach to exception handling revolves around the use of try and catch blocks, which allow for structured and predictable error management. Within a try block, code is executed that might cause an exception, while the catch block is responsible for handling the exception if one arises. This separation of normal execution flow and error handling facilitates better organization and readability of code.

To implement a basic exception handling scenario in Simula, consider the following example:

```
begin
    try
        begin
            ! Code that might raise an exception;
        end
    catch any
        begin
            ! Code to handle the exception;
        end
end;
```

In this example, try encloses a code section that potentially raises an exception. If an exception occurs, the control is transferred to the catch block, which contains the code to handle the exception. The keyword any here signifies that any type of exception will be caught and processed.

Beyond addressing common errors, exception handling is also used to signal and recover from unforeseen scenarios. By raising and catching exceptions, a program can maintain control flow even when unexpected events occur, thereby preventing crashes and ensuring a more graceful degradation of functionality.

Creating custom exceptions is another significant feature of Simula's exception handling capabilities. Developers can define their own exception types to represent specific error conditions pertinent to their application logic. This adds a layer of semantic meaning to error handling, making it easier to understand and maintain.

Exception propagation is the process whereby an exception, if not caught in the current scope, is passed up the call stack to parent scopes. This allows higher levels of the program to handle exceptions appropriately when lower levels cannot. Here's a simple illustration showing exception propagation:

```
begin
    procedure A;
    begin
        call B; ! Calling procedure B which might raise an exception;
    end A;
```

```
    procedure B;
    begin
        ! Code that raises an exception;
        raise Error;
    end B;

    try
        call A; ! Calling the top-level procedure A;
    catch Error
        begin
            outtext("An error occurred in procedure B");
        end
end;
```

In this code, procedure B raises an Error exception, which propagates to the caller procedure A. Since procedure A does not handle the exception, it continues to propagate until it reaches the try block in the main program, where it is caught and processed.

The finally block provides a mechanism to execute code regardless of whether an exception was raised. This is particularly useful for resource cleanup and ensuring that certain critical code sections are always executed. Contrasted with the catch block, the finally block is optional but highly recommended for robust error handling and resource management.

Another essential aspect of exception handling is the ability to nest try statements. It is not uncommon to encounter situations where multiple layers of exception handling are necessary to gracefully recover from complex error scenarios. In such cases, nesting try blocks can help localize error handling and improve modularity.

Multiple exceptions can also be handled using consecutive catch clauses, each targeting a specific type of exception. This pattern allows for more granular and precise error management:

```
begin
    try
        begin
            ! Code that might raise multiple types of exceptions;
        end
    catch Error1
        begin
            ! Handle Error1;
        end
    catch Error2
        begin
            ! Handle Error2;
        end
end;
```

In this example, if the code inside the try block raises an Error1, the specific catch Error1 block is executed. Similarly, Error2 exceptions are handled by catch Error2.

Effective exception handling is not only about catching and managing errors but also about implementing best practices for debugging and logging. Detailed logging of exceptions can provide invaluable insights during the development and maintenance phases, allowing for easier identification and resolution of underlying issues. Reviewing complete error logs helps avoid redundancy and aids in institutionalizing a more defensive programming approach, thereby ensuring the production of robust and resilient software.

9.2 Understanding Exceptions

Exceptions in Simula are integral to robust error management. They provide a mechanism for responding to runtime errors, allowing a program to continue or terminate gracefully. Understanding exceptions involves grasping several core concepts such as what exceptions are, how they are signaled, and the mechanisms involved in their handling.

An exception in Simula is a runtime event that interrupts normal execution flow. This interruption typically occurs due to an abnormal condition or an unexpected event, such as divide-by-zero, accessing an out-of-bounds array element, or any other scenario that deviates from normal operations. Recognizing such anomalies through exceptions is essential for developing resilient and error-tolerant software.

```
BEGIN
  INTEGER DIVIDEND, DIVISOR;
  REAL QUOTIENT;
  DIVIDEND := 100;
  DIVISOR := 0;
  QUOTIENT := DIVIDEND / DIVISOR;
END;
```

In the above example, dividing a number by zero will prompt an exception as division by zero is undefined and results in an error.

When an exception occurs, it is signaled, meaning the control flow of the program is interrupted, and the search for an appropriate handler begins. The handler is a block of code designed to manage the exception. This search proceeds up the call stack from the point where the exception was signaled. If no encompassing context provides a handling mechanism, the program may terminate or invoke a default exception handler provided by the runtime environment.

Consider when an exception is signaled from a procedure within nested procedure calls. The search for a handler starts at the procedure where the exception occurred and propagates outward, following the calling chain.

```
PROCEDURE LevelOne;
  BEGIN
    PROCEDURE LevelTwo;
      BEGIN
        INTEGER E;
        E := 0;
        E := 1 / E; ! Causes a divide-by-zero exception to be signaled
      END;

    LevelTwo;
  END;

LevelOne;
```

An exception handler in Simula is typically associated with the try construct, which encapsulates code that can potentially signal an exception. The catch block follows the try block and contains the code to execute when an exception is encountered.

Simula's handling of exceptions fosters a structured approach to error management, allowing specific responses to different exception types without muddying the mainline code with error-checking logic. This separation enhances the readability and maintainability of programs.

```
BEGIN
  INTEGER DIVIDEND, DIVISOR;
  REAL QUOTIENT;
  DIVIDEND := 100;
  DIVISOR := 0;

  TRY
    QUOTIENT := DIVIDEND / DIVISOR
  CATCH
    WHEN ArithmeticError DO
      OutText("Arithmetic Error: Division by zero");
  END;
END;
```

In the example, the try block encapsulates the division operation, which risks signaling an ArithmeticError. The catch block provides the handler. The statement OutText("Arithmetic Error: Division by zero") within the catch block will be executed if the attempted division results in an error.

The flexibility of Simula's exception handling allows multiple catch blocks to manage various exception types declared within the same try block. This way, specific actions can be taken depending on the exact nature of the exception signaled.

```
BEGIN
  INTEGER INDEX, ARRAY_SIZE;
  REAL ARRAY[10];
  INDEX := 11;
  DIVIDEND := 100;
  DIVISOR := 0;

  TRY
    ARRAY[INDEX] := DIVIDEND / DIVISOR;
  CATCH
    WHEN ArithmeticError DO
      OutText("Caught an ArithmeticError.");
    WHEN IndexOutOfBoundsError DO
      OutText("Index is out of bounds.");
  END;
END;
```

In this illustration, there are two potential exceptions: ArithmeticError due to division by zero and IndexOutOfBoundsError caused by accessing an array element beyond its limits. Each exception type has a corresponding catch block to process it appropriately.

Understanding and leveraging exceptions in Simula effectively lead to developing more robust programs. By preemptively managing unexpected conditions, developers can ensure that their applications can recover gracefully from errors, maintain consistency, and deliver a seamless user experience.

9.3 The 'try' and 'catch' Blocks

Exception handling in Simula involves using try and catch blocks for managing errors that occur during program execution. The try block contains code that may throw an exception, while the catch block handles the exception to prevent the program from terminating abruptly.

Here is the basic structure of a try and catch block in Simula:

```
try {
    // Code that may cause an exception
} catch (exceptionType ex) {
    // Code to handle the exception
}
```

In this structure, exceptionType denotes the type of exception the catch block will handle. The parameter ex is a variable representing the caught exception, and it provides access to the exception's details.

The following example illustrates the use of try and catch blocks to handle a division by zero exception:

```
begin
    integer numerator, denominator, result;
    text exceptionText;

    numerator := 10;
    denominator := 0;

    try {
        result := numerator // denominator; // Potential division by zero
    } catch (ArithmeticException e) {
        exceptionText := "Error: Division by zero.";
        OutText(exceptionText);
    }
end;
```

In this snippet, a division by zero in the try block triggers an ArithmeticException handled by the catch block. The error message "Error: Division by zero." is printed using OutText.

Multiple catch blocks can be associated with a single try block to handle various exception types. Each catch block specifies a different exception type and includes code to handle it. For example:

```
begin
    integer numerator, denominator, result;
    text exceptionText;

    numerator := 10;
    denominator := 0;

    try {
        result := numerator // denominator;
    } catch (ArithmeticException e) {
        exceptionText := "Error: Division by zero.";
        OutText(exceptionText);
    } catch (NullPointerException np) {
        exceptionText := "Error: Null pointer encountered.";
        OutText(exceptionText);
    }
end;
```

Here, the try block may throw either an ArithmeticException or a NullPointerException. Each catch block handles a specific exception type and executes the relevant error-handling code.

It is critical to understand that the order of catch blocks matters. Simula checks the catch blocks sequentially from top to bottom to find a match for the thrown exception. If the first catch block matches the exception type, its code executes, and subsequent catch blocks are ignored. Therefore, more specific exceptions should appear before general exceptions.

Consider the following example:

```
begin
    integer numerator, denominator, result;
    numerator := 10;
    denominator := 0;

    try {
        result := numerator // denominator;
    } catch (Exception ex) {
        exceptionText := "General error occurred.";
        OutText(exceptionText);
    } catch (ArithmeticException e) {
        exceptionText := "Error: Division by zero.";
        OutText(exceptionText);
    }
end;
```

In this example, Exception is a general exception type that would also catch an ArithmeticException. As a result, the "Error: Division by zero." message would never appear because the first catch block always catches the exception. Therefore, ArithmeticException should precede Exception:

```
begin
    integer numerator, denominator, result;
    numerator := 10;
    denominator := 0;

    try {
        result := numerator // denominator;
    } catch (ArithmeticException e) {
        exceptionText := "Error: Division by zero.";
        OutText(exceptionText);
    } catch (Exception ex) {
        exceptionText := "General error occurred.";
        OutText(exceptionText);
    }
end;
```

This structure ensures exceptions are handled by the most specific catch block first, promoting more accurate error handling. Proper ordering and specificity in catch blocks are critical for writing reliable and maintainable Simula programs, allowing developers to identify and respond to various error conditions effectively.

9.4 Creating Custom Exceptions

Creating custom exceptions in Simula is a fundamental aspect of robust error handling, enabling programmers to define specific error conditions that are pertinent to their applications. This section will delve into the methodology for defining and employing custom exceptions, building upon the foundational concepts of the 'try' and 'catch' blocks examined earlier.

To create a custom exception in Simula, one typically defines a class that inherits from the built-in Exception class. This custom class can include additional information or methods to provide more context about the error. The following example illustrates the steps to create and use a custom exception class.

Firstly, we define a custom exception class named InvalidOperationException:

```
Class InvalidOperationException(Exception);
Begin
   Text ErrorMessage;

   Procedure Init(t Text errorMessage);
   Begin
      ErrorMessage := errorMessage;
   End;

   Procedure PrintMessage;
   Begin
      OutText("Invalid Operation: "); OutText(ErrorMessage); OutImage;
   End;
End;
```

In the above code, InvalidOperationException is derived from the Exception class. This custom exception includes a member variable ErrorMessage, a procedure Init for initialization, and a procedure PrintMessage to display the error message.

Next, we employ this custom exception in a program that demonstrates throwing and catching the exception:

```
Begin
   Ref(InvalidOperationException) invalidOpEx;

   Try
      ! Simulating an invalid operation
      If True Then
         invalidOpEx :- New InvalidOperationException;
         invalidOpEx.Init("Cannot divide by zero");
         Raise invalidOpEx;
      End If;
   Catch InvalidOperationException do
      Begin
         OutText("Caught Exception: "); OutImage;
         invalidOpEx.PrintMessage;
      End;
End;
```

In this program, an instance of InvalidOperationException is created and initialized with a specific error message. The Raise statement is used to throw the exception. The Catch block catches InvalidOperationException and calls the PrintMessage method to output the error details.

Using custom exceptions, developers can convey specific error states and handle them appropriately, which is not always possible with generic exceptions. This specificity enhances code readability and maintainability, as seen in the above example.

To ensure the utility of custom exceptions, it is essential to define them in a manner that encapsulates all relevant error information. This practice facilitates debugging and provides insight into the nature of the error and its context. Additionally, by structuring custom exceptions with meaningful names and clear messages, developers can easily deduce the cause and location of an error within the broader codebase.

When designing custom exceptions, consider the following best practices:

- **Use Descriptive Names**: Ensure that the exception class names clearly indicate the type of error. Names like InvalidOperationException or AuthenticationFailedException are self-explanatory.
- **Provide User-Friendly Messages**: Include error messages that are easy to understand and that offer insight into the cause of the error.
- **Avoid Overuse**: While custom exceptions are powerful, overuse can lead to a cluttered codebase. Use them judiciously for scenarios where built-in exceptions are insufficient.
- **Maintain Consistency**: Follow a consistent naming and structural convention across all custom exception classes to facilitate readability and maintenance.

The utility of custom exceptions is significantly enhanced when combined with diligent logging practices, which will be covered in the subsequent sections. Effective logging not only records the occurrence of exceptions but also captures the state of the application at the time of the error, providing invaluable context for troubleshooting.

As observed, creating and utilizing custom exceptions in Simula involves defining a new class derived from the Exception class and implementing relevant methods to handle the specific error condition. This approach ensures that the application can manage specialized error conditions gracefully and with precision, thereby contributing to more robust and maintainable code.

9.5 Throwing Exceptions

Throwing exceptions in Simula provides a mechanism for signaling the occurrence of an unexpected condition during the execution of a program. This condition is typically an error, and handling it appropriately is critical for developing robust and reliable software. In this section, we will meticulously examine how to throw exceptions using Simula syntax and semantics.

To throw an exception, the detach statement is used, which forces termination of the currently running procedure or class, passing control to the nearest enclosing catch block capable of handling the specified exception type. The general form of a throw statement in Simula looks like this:

```
if condition then
  detach new ExceptionType;
end if;
```

Here, ExceptionType is the exception being thrown, and condition specifies the situation under which the exception should be thrown. Let's delve deeper into an example for better clarity.

Consider a simple program that checks division by zero:

```
class DivisionByZero;
begin
end;

procedure divide(a, b); real a, b;
begin
  if b = 0 then
    detach new DivisionByZero;
  else
    outreal(a / b);
  end if;
end;

begin
  ! Test division;
  begin
    try
      divide(10, 0);
    catch DivisionByZero do
      outtext("Error: Division by zero!");
    end;
  end
end;
```

In this example: - A custom exception DivisionByZero is defined as a class. - The divide procedure attempts to divide two real numbers a and b. - If b equals 0, the detach statement is executed, throwing a DivisionByZero exception. - This exception is handled in the enclosing try block.

When the divide procedure is called with the second argument as 0, the output will be:

```
Error: Division by zero!
```

Throwing exceptions is not limited to error handling but also for signaling specific conditions or states within a program. It is important to capture these signals appropriately using the corresponding catch blocks to ensure that the program can recover gracefully from exceptional states.

It is also possible to pass additional information with the exception, which can be critical in diagnosing issues. This can be accomplished by extending the exception class. An example of this is provided below:

```
class DivisionByZero(dividend); real dividend;
begin
  this.dividend := dividend;
end;

procedure divide(a, b); real a, b;
  ref (DivisionByZero) ex;
begin
  if b = 0 then
    ex :- new DivisionByZero(a);
    detach ex;
  else
    outreal(a / b);
  end if;
end;

begin
  ! Test division;
  begin
    try
      divide(10, 0);
    catch DivisionByZero do
      outtext("Error: Division by zero! Dividend was: ");
      outreal(%.dividend%);
    end;
  end
end;
```

Here: - The DivisionByZero class is expanded to include the dividend attribute, which stores the numerator value that caused the division error. - When the exception is thrown, an instance of DivisionByZero is created with the dividend. - In the catch block, this additional information is accessed.

The output in this scenario will be:

```
Error: Division by zero! Dividend was: 10.0
```

Adopting a good strategy for throwing exceptions ensures that your program can both handle errors gracefully and provide informative diagnostic information to the developers or users.

Care must be taken to throw exceptions only under genuine exceptional conditions. Overuse of exceptions for regular control flow can lead to obfuscated code and performance overhead. Additionally, handling exceptions close to the point of their occurrence can simplify debugging and reduce the chances of exceptions propagating excessively through the call stack.

Understanding when and how to throw exceptions proficiently can significantly enhance the reliability and maintainability of your Simula programs. Integrating thoughtful exception handling in your codebase is a fundamental practice to adhere to software engineering principles, ensuring your applications behave predictably under various runtime conditions.

9.6 Exception Propagation

Exception propagation is a crucial concept in robust error management, allowing exceptions to traverse the call stack until they are appropriately handled. In Simula, exceptions propagate through the call hierarchy, providing flexibility in error handling. This section delves into how exceptions propagate, the involves mechanics, and practical code snippets that illustrate its implementation.

When an exception is thrown in Simula, the runtime environment begins searching for an appropriate catch block starting from the closest enclosing try block. If no such block is found, the exception propagates to the next outer try block, continuing this process up the call stack until a suitable handler is encountered. If no handler is found by the time the root of the call stack is reached, the program terminates and output an error message.

Consider the following example where an exception is thrown within a nested function call:

```
procedure A;
begin
  procedure B;
  begin
```

```
    procedure C;
    begin
      throw MyException;
    end C;
    C;
  end B;
  try
    B;
  catch MyException do
    OutText("MyException caught in procedure A")
  end catch;
end A;

A;
```

In this example, procedure C raises MyException, which is not handled within C or B. Consequently, the exception propagates back to procedure A, where it is caught and handled, outputting the message:

```
MyException caught in procedure A
```

Exception propagation affirms the importance of defining specific catch blocks at appropriate levels in the call stack hierarchy. This design strategy permits localized error handling while keeping higher-level contextual handling available for broader control.

For complex software systems, using a global exception handler can be beneficial, avoiding the redundancy of numerous specific handlers and thus centralizing error management. Let's illustrate this with a modified version of the previous example, implementing a global handler:

```
procedure GlobalExceptionHandler(exception);
begin
  OutText("Global handler caught: ", exception);
end GlobalExceptionHandler;

procedure A;
begin
  procedure B;
  begin
    procedure C;
    begin
      throw MyException;
    end C;
    C;
  end B;
  try
    B;
  catch MyException do
    throw; // Rethrow exception
  end catch;
end A;

try
  A;
catch any do
  GlobalExceptionHandler(exception)
```

```
end catch;
```

In this extended example, the catch block within procedure A rethrows the exception instead of handling it. The global catch any block then captures this rethrown exception, passing it to GlobalExceptionHandler, which outputs the message:

```
Global handler caught: MyException
```

This strategy ensures that all uncaught exceptions are handled uniformly, enhancing the maintainability of extensive codebases while centralizing debugging processes.

Lastly, having a thorough understanding of rethrowing exceptions is essential. Situations arise where exceptions should be partially handled and then passed on for further processing. The throw statement within a catch block facilitates this mechanism.

```
procedure A;
begin
  procedure B;
  begin
    procedure C;
    begin
      throw MyException;
    end C;
    C;
  end B;
  try
    B;
  catch MyException do
    OutText("MyException partially handled in procedure A");
    throw; // Rethrow to propagate further
  end catch;
end A;

try
  A;
catch MyException do
  OutText("MyException finally handled");
end catch;
```

In this example, MyException is partially handled within A, outputting a message, then rethrown to be fully handled by the outer catch block, producing the output:

```
MyException partially handled in procedure A
MyException finally handled
```

Mastering exception propagation equips developers to write more flexible and maintainable code, ensuring exceptions are handled at the appropriate level of the call stack. This practice not only enhances robustness but also contributes significantly to the clarity and predictiveness of the error management processes in Simula programs.

9.7 The 'finally' Block

The finally block is an important construct in Simula programming, providing a mechanism to ensure that specific code runs regardless of whether an exception occurs within a try block. This feature is particularly useful for resource management tasks such as closing files, releasing memory, or terminating database connections, which must be executed to maintain the system's integrity.

In Simula, the finally block follows the catch blocks (if any) of a try statement. Its syntax is as follows:

```
try {
    // code that might throw an exception
} catch (Exception1 e1) {
    // handling Exception1
} catch (Exception2 e2) {
    // handling Exception2
} finally {
    // code that is always executed
}
```

The finally block can be used even if no catch blocks are present. In such cases, it follows directly after the try block:

```
try {
    // code that might throw an exception
} finally {
    // code that is always executed
}
```

When an exception occurs within the try block, Simula first looks for an appropriate catch block to handle the exception. Regardless of whether an exception is thrown or handled, the code within the finally block is executed. This is guaranteed execution, which makes it an ideal location for cleanup code. Consider the following example:

```
try {
    computeOperation(); // method that could throw an exception
} catch (ArithmeticException ae) {
    write("Arithmetic Exception caught.");
} finally {
    cleanUp(); // method to clean up resources
}
```

In this scenario, cleanUp() is invoked regardless of whether computeOperation() completes successfully or throws an ArithmeticException.

This ensures the system remains in a stable state, freeing resources used during the try block.

The primary motivation for using the finally block is to avoid resource leakage, particularly in contexts involving streams, files, or other resources that require explicit deallocation. Omitting such cleanup can lead to situations where resources remain unavailable for other parts of the application or even cause the system to become unresponsive.

Consider another example where a file must be closed, whether an exception occurs or not:

```
File f = null;
Scanner s = null;
try {
    f = new File("data.txt");
    s = new Scanner(f);
    processFile(s); // method that processes the file content
} catch (FileNotFoundException fne) {
    write("File not found.");
} finally {
    if (s != null) {
        s.close(); // ensuring the file is always closed
    }
}
```

In this example, regardless of the exception status, the scanner s is closed, releasing the resource associated with the opened file.

It is important to note that while the finally block ensures that its code is executed, it does not handle exceptions. If an exception is thrown within the finally block itself, it propagates up the call stack, possibly bypassing any remaining code in the block. For this reason, exception handling within a finally block should be minimal, focusing primarily on resource cleanup.

```
try {
    databaseConnect();
} catch (SQLException se) {
    write("SQL Exception occurred.");
} finally {
    try {
        databaseDisconnect();
    } catch (SQLException se2) {
        write("An error occurred while disconnecting the database.");
    }
}
```

Here, the nested try-catch within the finally block ensures that exceptions occurring during the disconnection process are caught and logged, allowing for graceful error handling even within the cleanup phase.

The finally block is an essential element of robust error management in Simula, supporting reliable resource management by guaranteeing cleanup operations irrespective of how a try block terminates. This deterministic cleanup helps maintain the application's stability, which is crucial for developing resilient and maintainable software systems.

9.8 Nested 'try' Statements

In robust programming, it is often necessary to handle multiple levels of exceptions, especially in complex programs where various parts of code may fail independently. Simula allows for the use of nested try statements, enabling granular control over exception handling across different scopes of a program. A nested try statement means placing a try block within another try block, each with their associated catch and possibly finally blocks.

Consider the following example to illustrate the concept of nested try statements:

```
begin
  try
    begin
      ! Outer block code
      try
        begin
          ! Inner block code
        end
      catch
        when InnerException do
          ! Handle inner exception
      finally
        ! Cleanup for inner block
    end
  catch
    when OuterException do
      ! Handle outer exception
  finally
    ! Cleanup for outer block
end;
```

In this example, the outer try block contains code that may produce an OuterException, while the inner try block may produce an InnerException. The inner catch block handles InnerException, and the outer catch block handles OuterException. This approach ensures that you can handle exceptions specific to the inner block separately from those of the outer block.

An essential aspect of nested try statements is understanding how exception propagation works. If an InnerException is thrown within the inner try block and is not caught there, it can propagate upwards to the outer try block.

```
begin
  try
    begin
      ! Outer block code
      try
        begin
          ! Inner block code
          raise(InnerException)
        end
      catch
        when DifferentException do
          ! This does not catch InnerException
        ! The InnerException will propagate
    end
  catch
    when InnerException do
      ! Handle InnerException here
  finally
    ! Cleanup for outer block
end;
```

Here, the InnerException raised inside the inner try block is not caught by its corresponding catch block. Consequently, it propagates to the outer catch block where InnerException is finally handled. This behavior allows exceptions to be managed at appropriate levels of the program hierarchy, improving code organization and reliability.

When using nested try statements, it is crucial to avoid catching exceptions indiscriminately at higher levels, as this can obscure the actual source and context of errors. Instead, handle exceptions as locally as possible to the code that may fail, only allowing propagation when it's necessary for broader context.

```
begin
  procedure ComplexOperation;
  begin
    ! Perform some complex operation
    raise(InnerException)
  end;
  try
    begin
      try
        ComplexOperation;
      catch
        when InnerException do
          ! Log and handle InnerException locally
      finally
        ! Local cleanup
    end;
  catch
    when OuterException do
      ! Handle OuterException, not InnerException
  finally
    ! Global cleanup
```

```
end;
```

In this example, the ComplexOperation procedure deliberately raises an InnerException. The inner try block within the main try block specifically handles this exception, ensuring that the responsible code section can manage and log the error appropriately. This isolation of exception handling prevents higher-level code from becoming polluted with low-level error management details, making the program easier to debug and maintain.

By adhering to these principles, nested try statements in Simula become powerful tools for managing errors in a granular and structured manner, enhancing overall program reliability and clarity.

9.9 Handling Multiple Exceptions

In complex programs, multiple exceptions may arise from different segments of code or operations within a single try block. To ensure robust error handling, Simula provides mechanisms to catch and manage multiple exceptions using multiple catch clauses within a try block. Understanding how to effectively handle multiple exceptions is essential to creating resilient and error-tolerant applications.

When handling multiple exceptions, the syntax structure involves a try block followed by multiple catch clauses, each specifying different exception types. The Simula runtime environment will match the first encountered exception with the corresponding catch block based on the exception type.

```
try {
    // Code segment that might throw exceptions
} catch (ExceptionType1 e1) {
    // Handle ExceptionType1
} catch (ExceptionType2 e2) {
    // Handle ExceptionType2
} catch (ExceptionType3 e3) {
    // Handle ExceptionType3
}
```

The priority of matching is top-down, ensuring that the first catch clause whose type matches the thrown exception is executed. Therefore, it's crucial to order the catch blocks from the most specific to the most general exception types. This ensures that more specific exceptions are caught and handled appropriately before their more general superclasses can intercept them.

Consider an example:

```
try {
    // Code segment that might throw exceptions
    someFunctionThatMightThrow();
} catch (FileNotFoundException fnfe) {
    // Handle file not found error
    System.out.println("File not found: " + fnfe.getMessage());
} catch (IOException ioe) {
    // Handle general input/output errors
    System.out.println("Input/output error: " + ioe.getMessage());
} catch (Exception e) {
    // Handle any other exceptions
    System.out.println("An unexpected error occurred: " + e.getMessage());
}
```

In this example, the FileNotFoundException is a subclass of IOException. We place its catch block before the IOException block to give it priority. Any FileNotFoundException will be caught by the first block, while other IOExceptions will be handled by the second block. If an exception does not match any of the more specific types, it will be caught by the generalized Exception block.

Handling multiple exceptions also facilitates different corrective actions based on the exception type. For example, in a file processing application, one might retry the operation if an IOException occurs due to transient issues, whereas a FileNotFoundException might prompt the user to select a new file.

```
try {
    processFile(fileName);
} catch (FileNotFoundException fnfe) {
    System.out.println("The specified file does not exist: " + fileName);
    // Prompt user to choose another file
    promptForNewFile();
} catch (IOException ioe) {
    System.out.println("An I/O error occurred while processing the file: " + ioe.
        getMessage());
    // Retry operation
    retryOperation();
}
```

Additionally, when dealing with exceptions that have hierarchical relationships, consider the potential for code redundancy or inefficiency. For instance, if every catch block contains repeated logic such as logging, one could refactor the code using a helper function to avoid redundancy.

```
private void logExceptionDetails(Exception e) {
    System.out.println("Exception occurred: " + e.getMessage());
    // Additional logging logic
}

try {
```

```
    performRiskyOperation();
} catch (FileNotFoundException fnfe) {
    logExceptionDetails(fnfe);
    // Handle specific logic for file not found
} catch (IOException ioe) {
    logExceptionDetails(ioe);
    // Handle specific logic for I/O error
} catch (Exception e) {
    logExceptionDetails(e);
    // Handle any other exceptions
}
```

This approach ensures that common functionalities (like logging) are consolidated and maintained efficiently, thus adhering to the DRY principle (Don't Repeat Yourself).

Robust exception handling must also consider runtime performance. In scenarios where exceptions are very frequent, overheads from multiple catch clauses can affect performance. Adopting a strategic approach, such as logging the errors in the respective catch blocks and addressing them post-hoc if retry logic isn't essential, can mitigate these concerns.

Simula's treatment of multiple exceptions fosters fine-grained error management, allowing developers to handle clusters of errors in contextually appropriate manners. By harmonizing catch block ordering and shared functionality through helper methods, programs can achieve both functional robustness and maintainable, scalable codebases.

9.10 Best Practices for Exception Handling

Effective exception handling is crucial for writing robust and maintainable programs. Following best practices ensures that exceptions are managed gracefully, and the program remains functional and user-friendly even when errors occur. The key principles include preserving the program state, providing meaningful error messages, using exceptions for exceptional conditions only, avoiding overuse of try-catch blocks, and logging exceptions for future debugging and analysis.

First and foremost, it is essential to catch only those exceptions that you can handle meaningfully. Catching generic exceptions with actions that do not address the root cause of the issue can obscure problems and make debugging more complicated. Instead, it is advisable to catch specific exceptions and provide a concrete solution or notify the user accurately.

```
try {
    // Specific exception handling
} catch (FileNotFoundException e) {
    texttt{System.out.println}("File not found: " + e.getMessage());
} catch (IOException e) {
    texttt{System.out.println}("Input-output error: " + e.getMessage());
}
```

Preservation of program state guarantees that the system remains consistent even when an unexpected situation occurs. Ensure that the program reverts to a stable state or compensates for any partial updates to avoid data corruption.

Using informative error messages is equally critical. When an exception surfaces, the messages should thoroughly describe what went wrong and, if possible, how to correct it. This practice not only aids in debugging but also improves the user's comprehension of the issue.

Exceptions should not be used for controlling normal program flow. They are designed to handle unexpected or exceptional conditions. Overusing exceptions for regular conditions can lead to performance drawbacks and convoluted code, thereby reducing its readability.

Avoid nesting try-catch blocks unnecessarily. Deeply nested exception handling makes the code difficult to read and understand. Refactor and segregate code into smaller methods, each with its own exception handling mechanisms.

```
try {
    methodThatMayThrowException();
} catch (SpecificException e) {
    handleException(e);
}

public void methodThatMayThrowException() throws SpecificException {
    // Code that may throw SpecificException
}
```

In scenarios where a method throws multiple exceptions, handling these exceptions appropriately can avoid multiple catch blocks. This can be achieved using multi-catch statements to handle exceptions that need similar treatment, enhancing the code's brevity and clarity.

```
try {
    // Code that may throw multiple exceptions
} catch (IOException | NullPointerException e) {
    texttt{System.out.println}("An error occurred: " + e.getMessage());
}
```

Encapsulating exception handling logic in separate methods or classes may also be beneficial. This approach promotes code reuse and helps maintain the single responsibility principle, making the code more modular and maintainable.

```
public void processFile(String fileName) {
    try {
        readFile(fileName);
    } catch (Exception e) {
        handleException(e);
    }
}

private void readFile(String fileName) throws FileNotFoundException {
    // Code to read the file
}

private void handleException(Exception e) {
    // Centralized exception handling
}
```

Always ensure that resources like file handles, database connections, or network sockets are released appropriately. Utilizing the finally block or the try-with-resources statement guarantees that resources are released even if an exception occurs, preventing resource leaks.

```
try (BufferedReader reader = new BufferedReader(new FileReader("example.txt"))) {
    // Code to read from the file
} catch (IOException e) {
    texttt{System.out.println}("File reading error: " + e.getMessage());
}
```

Proper logging of exceptions is another fundamental practice. Logs provide valuable insights into the application's behavior and can be instrumental in identifying and resolving issues. Use a logging framework to capture essential details such as timestamps, stack traces, and contextual information about the error.

```
try {
    // Code that may throw an exception
} catch (Exception e) {
    Logger logger = Logger.getLogger(Main.class.getName());
    logger.log(Level.SEVERE, "An error occurred", e);
}
```

While handling exceptions, propagating the exception up the call stack may sometimes be the correct choice, especially when the current method cannot remedy the issue. Re-throwing exceptions allows higher-level methods to deal with them, maintaining a clear separation of concerns.

```
try {
    methodThatMayThrowException();
} catch (Exception e) {
    texttt{throw new RuntimeException}("Error in processing", e);
}
```

Lastly, avoid catching exceptions just to suppress them. Silencing exceptions without addressing them leads to hidden bugs. Every caught exception should result in some corrective action, be it logging, notifying the user, or a fallback mechanism.

Adhering to these practices enhances exception handling, making programs more resilient and easier to maintain.

9.11 Debugging and Logging Exceptions

Effective debugging and logging of exceptions are crucial components in managing errors and enhancing software reliability. This section delineates the techniques and practices essential for debugging exception-related issues and implementing comprehensive exception logging in Simula programs.

Debugging Exceptions

Debugging is the systematic process of identifying, isolating, and resolving defects or malfunctions within a program. When dealing with exceptions, debugging entails tracking down the root cause of an error that disrupts the normal flow of the program.

To debug exceptions in Simula, one must:

- Utilize print statements or logging within catch blocks to output information about the exception.
- Assess the stack trace to pinpoint the location and context where the exception occurred.
- Employ integrated development environment (IDE) tools or debuggers that support breakpoint setting and step-by-step execution.

Consider the following Simula code where an exception is intentionally triggered and caught:

```
BEGIN
   INTEGER RESULT, DIVISOR;
   DIVISOR := 0;
   TRY
      BEGIN
         RESULT := 10 DIV DIVISOR;
      END
   EXCEPT WHEN DivisionByZero DO
```

```
        BEGIN
            OutText("Division by zero exception caught.");
        END;
    OutImage;
END;
```

In this example, a division by zero exception is expected and caught. To debug this, you may include additional print statements or use the debugger within your IDE:

```
BEGIN
    INTEGER RESULT, DIVISOR;
    DIVISOR := 0;
    TRY
        BEGIN
            RESULT := 10 DIV DIVISOR;
        END
    EXCEPT WHEN DivisionByZero DO
        BEGIN
            OutText("Division by zero exception caught.");
            OutImage;
            OutText("Debug Info: Attempted to divide by zero.");
        END;
    OutImage;
END;
```

Logging Exceptions

Logging entails recording information about program execution to a file or other persistence mechanism. This is critical for post-mortem analysis, allowing developers to track historical data about exceptions, identify recurring issues, and gain insight into the application's behavior during runtime.

To implement logging in Simula, follow these steps:

1. **Initialize a Log File:** Establish a file for logging exception details. 2. **Augment Exception Handling Blocks:** Enhance catch blocks with logging functionality. 3. **Log Detailed Information:** Record the type of exception, stack trace, and any relevant data points.

Example of logging implementation in Simula:

```
PROCEDURE LogException(MSG); TEXT MSG;
! This procedure logs exception messages to a file.
BEGIN
    OPEN(OutFile, "exception_log.txt");
    WRITETEXT(OutFile, MSG);
    OutImage(OutFile);
    CLOSE(OutFile);
END;

BEGIN
    INTEGER RESULT, DIVISOR;
    DIVISOR := 0;
    TRY
```

```
        BEGIN
            RESULT := 10 DIV DIVISOR;
        END
    EXCEPT WHEN DivisionByZero DO
        BEGIN
            OutText("Division by zero exception caught.");
            LogException("Division by zero encountered. Stack trace: [...]");

@section{closure} ! Here, the stack trace is simplified.
        END;
    OutImage;
END;
```

This logging mechanism ensures that exceptions are recorded effectively, facilitating the debugging process and continuous improvement of application robustness.

Best Practices for Debugging and Logging Exceptions

Adhering to best practices enhances the efficacy of debugging and logging:

- Catch and Log Early: Capture and log exceptions as close to their origin as possible to preserve contextual information.
- Log Sufficient Detail: Include pertinent details such as timestamp, exception type, function names, and parameter values.
- Consistent Logging Format: Maintain a standardized format for log entries to streamline subsequent analysis.
- Non-intrusive Logging: Ensure logging does not significantly affect application performance, particularly in production environments.
- Error-Level Differentiation: Differentiate between error levels, e.g., info, warning, error, and critical, to prioritize responses.

Implementing these techniques fortifies the exception handling framework, making the Simula applications more reliable and maintainable. By integrating thorough debugging and logging practices, developers can preemptively address and resolve potential errors, thereby improving the overall quality of their software projects.

Chapter 10

Advanced Topics in Simula

This chapter delves into advanced topics in Simula, including complex data structures, generics, and concurrency. It covers memory management, garbage collection, design patterns, metaprogramming, networking, and graphical user interface development. Additionally, it examines interfacing with other languages, performance optimization techniques, and real-world case studies, equipping readers with sophisticated skills for advanced Simula programming and application development.

10.1 Advanced Data Structures

In this section, we explore advanced data structures in Simula, focusing on their implementation and application within complex programming contexts. Mastering these structures is essential for efficient data manipulation and effective problem-solving in advanced Simula programming. We will discuss trees, graphs, and hash tables, along with the operations and algorithms associated with each.

Binary Trees: A binary tree is a hierarchical data structure with nodes, each having at most two children, referred to as the left child and the right child. Binary trees are essential for various applications like expression parsing, searching, and sorting.

To define a binary tree in Simula, we must first define a node class:

```
class TreeNode;
  ref(TreeNode) leftChild, rightChild;
  integer value;

  TreeNode(ref(TreeNode) l, ref(TreeNode) r, integer v);
  begin
    leftChild := l;
    rightChild := r;
    value := v;
  end TreeNode;
end TreeNode;
```

With the TreeNode defined, we can create and manipulate a binary tree. Example functions include insertion and traversal (in-order, pre-order, and post-order traversals):

```
procedure inOrderTraversal(t); ref(TreeNode) t;
begin
  if t /= none then
  begin
    inOrderTraversal(t.leftChild);
    outint(t.value, 4);
    inOrderTraversal(t.rightChild);
  end;
end inOrderTraversal;
```

Graphs: Graphs are structures composed of nodes (vertices) and edges connecting pairs of nodes. Graphs can be directed or undirected and are crucial for modeling networks, paths, and relationships.

In Simula, we represent graphs using adjacency lists. Here is a snippet for the graph node definition:

```
class GraphNode;
  text name;
  list ref(GraphNode) adjNodes;

  GraphNode(text n);
  begin
    name := n;
    new adjNodes;
  end GraphNode;

  procedure addAdjacent(ref(GraphNode) node);
  begin
    detachif(adjNodes, none);
    attach(node, adjNodes);
  end addAdjacent;
end GraphNode;
```

```
ref(GraphNode) node1, node2;
node1 :- new GraphNode("Node1");
node2 :- new GraphNode("Node2");

node1.addAdjacent(node2);
```

```
ref(GraphNode) currentNode;
currentNode := sub(front(node1.adjNodes));
while currentNode /= none do
begin
  outtext(currentNode.name); outimage;
  currentNode := sub(currentNode.suc);
end;
```

Hash Tables: Hash tables utilize hash functions to map keys to values, ensuring efficient data retrieval. The primary operation involves inserting key-value pairs, searching for a key, and deleting key-value pairs.

We start by defining the hash table class:

```
class HashTable;
  const integer TABLE_SIZE = 128;
  ref(ValueNode) table[1:TABLe_SIZE];

  class ValueNode;
  begin
    text key;
    integer value;
    ref(ValueNode) next;
  end ValueNode;

  integer hashFunction(text key); virtual;
  begin
    integer hash := 0;
    integer i;
    for i := 1 step 1 until (*upb key) do
      hash := hash * 31 + ord(substr(key, i, 1));
    hashFunction := hash mod TABLE_SIZE;
  end hashFunction;

  procedure insert(text key, integer value);
  begin
    ref(ValueNode) newNode;
    newNode := new ValueNode;
    newNode.key := key;
    newNode.value := value;
    newNode.next := none;

    integer hash := this.hashFunction(key);
    newNode.next := table[hash];
    table[hash] := newNode;
  end insert;

  integer search(text key);
  begin
    integer hash := this.hashFunction(key);
    ref(ValueNode) node;
    node := table[hash];
    while node /= none do
      if string(node.key) = string(key) then
        search := node.value;
        return;
      end if;
      node := node.next;
```

```
    end while;
    search := -1;
  end search;
end HashTable;
```

These advanced data structures provide robust tools for effectively handling complex data scenarios in Simula. Understanding and implementing these structures will significantly enhance the efficiency and performance of your programs.

10.2 Generics and Templates

Generics and templates in Simula provide powerful abstraction mechanisms that enable code reuse and type safety. These constructs allow developers to write flexible and reusable code components that can operate on various data types. This section explores the syntax, usage, and best practices for implementing generics and templates in Simula.

To begin with, generics in Simula are achieved through the use of formal type parameters. These type parameters allow the definition of classes and procedures that can operate on different data types without sacrificing type safety. For instance, a simple generic class for a pair of objects can be written as follows:

```
class Pair[T1, T2];
begin
    T1 first;
    T2 second;

    procedure init(f, s);
    begin
        first := f;
        second := s;
    end init;

    procedure printPair;
    begin
        OutText("First: "); OutImage;
        OutText(first);
        OutImage;
        OutText("Second: "); OutImage;
        OutText(second);
        OutImage;
    end printPair;

end Pair;
```

In the code above, the class Pair has two generic type parameters, T1 and T2. These parameters can be instantiated with any type when creating objects of the Pair class. Here is an example of how to instantiate and use this generic class:

```
begin
    ref(Pair[integer, real]) p1;
    ref(Pair[text, boolean]) p2;

    ! Creating instances of Pair;
    p1 :- new Pair[integer, real];
    p2 :- new Pair[text, boolean];

    ! Initializing the pairs;
    p1.init(10, 20.5);
    p2.init("Hello", true);

    ! Printing the pairs;
    p1.printPair;
    p2.printPair;
end;
```

In this example, p1 is a pair of an integer and a real, while p2 is a pair of a text and a boolean. The init procedure initializes the values, and the printPair procedure prints the pair values.

Additionally, it is important to understand that templates in Simula are used to define parametrized classes and procedures that are capable of working with any data type. They add a significant amount of flexibility, especially when designing data structures like arrays, linked lists, and trees.

Consider the implementation of a generic stack class:

```
class Stack[T];
begin
    integer size;
    ref(T) arr[1:size];
    integer top :- 0;

    integer procedure isEmpty;
    isEmpty := (top = 0);

    integer procedure isFull;
    isFull := (top = size);

    procedure push(x);
    begin
        if isFull then
            OutText("Stack is full! Can't push more elements."); OutImage
        else
            top := top + 1;
            arr[top] :- new T;
            arr[top] := x;
        end if;
    end push;

    ref(T) procedure pop;
    begin
        if isEmpty then
            OutText("Stack is empty! Nothing to pop."); OutImage;
```

```
            pop :- none;
        else
            pop :- arr[top];
            top := top - 1;
        end if;
    end pop;

end Stack;
```

The class Stack is parametrized with the type T, allowing it to handle any type of elements. The isEmpty and isFull procedures check if the stack is empty or full, respectively. The push procedure adds an element to the stack, while the pop procedure removes and returns the top element of the stack.

Using the Stack class can be demonstrated as follows:

```
begin
    ref(Stack[integer]) intStack;
    ref(Stack[text]) textStack;

    ! Creating instances of Stack;
    intStack :- new Stack[integer](size := 10);
    textStack :- new Stack[text](size := 5);

    ! Pushing elements onto the stacks;
    intStack.push(1);
    intStack.push(2);
    intStack.push(3);

    textStack.push("hello");
    textStack.push("world");

    ! Popping elements from the stacks;
    OutText("Integer Stack Pop: "); IntOut(intStack.pop); OutImage;
    OutText("Text Stack Pop: "); OutText(textStack.pop); OutImage;

end;
```

In this example, intStack is a stack of integers, while textStack is a stack of text values. Elements are pushed onto and popped from the stacks, demonstrating the versatility of the generic Stack class.

When employing generics and templates, it's crucial to ensure type safety while maximizing code reuse. Advanced Simula programs should leverage these constructs to handle various data types and complex data structures efficiently.

It's also beneficial to use bounds on generic types when applicable. Consider a scenario where a certain type parameter should conform to a specific subclass or interface. Simula supports bounded generics to enforce such constraints, thereby offering more control and ensuring type compatibility.

Generics and templates provide a substantial advantage by allowing developers to write more modular, type-safe, and maintainable code. Proper utilization of these features is essential for advanced Simula programming and can significantly enhance the robustness and flexibility of applications.

10.3 Concurrency and Parallelism

Concurrency and parallelism are pivotal concepts for high-performance computing and efficient application design in Simula. Concurrency refers to the ability of a program to manage multiple tasks simultaneously, whereas parallelism involves the actual simultaneous execution of computations. Utilizing these paradigms can lead to significant performance improvements, especially for applications involving complex calculations or extensive data processing.

Simula, being one of the first object-oriented programming languages, provides constructs that facilitate the implementation of concurrent and parallel programs. To leverage these capabilities effectively, one must understand the underlying mechanisms and proper design patterns suited for concurrent programming in Simula.

Simula Processes and Process Scheduling

In Simula, concurrency is primarily managed through the use of processes. A process in Simula is an independent sequence of instructions that can be executed concurrently with other processes. Processes can be created and scheduled using Simula's process-related constructs.

Processes are declared using the PROCESS keyword and are managed by the Simula runtime's scheduler. The scheduler uses a coroutine-like mechanism to control the execution order of processes. Below is an example of creating and running processes in Simula.

```
BEGIN
  PROCESS PROC1;
    BEGIN
      INTEGER I;
      FOR I := 1 STEP 1 UNTIL 10 DO
        BEGIN
          OutText("Processing in PROC1: ");
          OutInt(I,2); OutImage;
          HOLD(1.0);
        END;
    END PROC1;
```

```
  PROCESS PROC2;
    BEGIN
      INTEGER J;
      FOR J := 10 STEP -1 UNTIL 1 DO
        BEGIN
          OutText("Processing in PROC2: ");
          OutInt(J,2); OutImage;
          HOLD(1.5);
        END;
    END PROC2;

  ! Schedule Processes
  TransferTo(PROC1);
  TransferTo(PROC2);
END;
```

This example illustrates two processes, PROC1 and PROC2, each printing a series of numbers at different intervals. The HOLD statement pauses the execution of a process for a specified duration, allowing the scheduler to transfer control to another process.

Inter-Process Communication

Effective concurrent programming often requires processes to communicate and synchronize with each other. Simula provides several mechanisms for inter-process communication, such as shared variables, condition variables, and events. Shared variables can be accessed by multiple processes, allowing data exchange between them. However, careful management of shared variables is required to avoid race conditions.

The following example demonstrates the use of a shared variable for inter-process communication:

```
BEGIN
  INTEGER SharedCounter;
  SharedCounter := 0;

  PROCESS INCREMENTER;
    BEGIN
      INTEGER I;
      FOR I := 1 STEP 1 UNTIL 5 DO
        BEGIN
          SharedCounter := SharedCounter + 1;
          OutText("Incremented to: ");
          OutInt(SharedCounter,3);
          OutImage;
          HOLD(0.5);
        END;
    END INCREMENTER;

  PROCESS DECREMENTER;
    BEGIN
      INTEGER J;
      FOR J := 1 STEP 1 UNTIL 5 DO
        BEGIN
```

```
          SharedCounter := SharedCounter - 1;
          OutText("Decremented to: ");
          OutInt(SharedCounter,3);
          OutImage;
          HOLD(0.7);
        END;
    END DECREMENTER;

  ! Schedule Processes
  TransferTo(INCREMENTER);
  TransferTo(DECREMENTER);
END;
```

In this code, two processes, INCREMENTER and DECREMENTER, modify a shared variable SharedCounter. The output will vary depending on the execution ordering of the processes by the scheduler.

Mutual Exclusion

To avoid inconsistencies caused by concurrent access to shared resources, Simula supports mutual exclusion using semaphores. Semaphores provide a way to signal and wait on conditions, ensuring that only one process accesses the shared resource at a time. A semaphore is typically defined with an initial count and two primary operations: P (wait) and V (signal).

Below is an example demonstrating the use of semaphores for mutual exclusion:

```
BEGIN
  INTEGER SharedCounter;
  SHARED COMMON Integer Semaphore;
  Semaphore := 1; ! Initial value set to 1

  PROCESS INCREMENTER;
    BEGIN
      INTEGER I;
      FOR I := 1 STEP 1 UNTIL 5 DO
        BEGIN
          P(Semaphore); ! Wait
          SharedCounter := SharedCounter + 1;
          OutText("Incremented to: ");
          OutInt(SharedCounter,3);
          OutImage;
          V(Semaphore); ! Signal
          HOLD(0.5);
        END;
    END INCREMENTER;

  PROCESS DECREMENTER;
    BEGIN
      INTEGER J;
      FOR J := 1 STEP 1 UNTIL 5 DO
        BEGIN
          P(Semaphore); ! Wait
          SharedCounter := SharedCounter - 1;
          OutText("Decremented to: ");
```

```
      OutInt(SharedCounter,3);
      OutImage;
      V(Semaphore); ! Signal
      HOLD(0.7);
    END;
  END DECREMENTER;

  ! Schedule Processes
  TransferTo(INCREMENTER);
  TransferTo(DECREMENTER);
END;
```

The P(Semaphore) operation decreases the semaphore value and may block the calling process if the value is zero. The V(Semaphore) operation increases the semaphore value, potentially waking up a blocked process. This ensures that SharedCounter is correctly updated without race conditions.

Parallelism in Modern Multi-core Systems

While traditional Simula constructs are suitable for teaching concurrency concepts, utilizing parallelism in modern multi-core systems often requires more advanced techniques and libraries that interface with Simula. For instance, leveraging parallel programming libraries and extensions written in languages like C or C++ for computationally intensive tasks can be highly effective.

To interface Simula with parallel libraries, consider the following methodology:

- Identify computationally intensive segments of the Simula program.
- Implement these segments using a suitable parallel programming model (OpenMP, MPI) in a language such as C.
- Use Simula's foreign function interface to call the optimized parallel routines from the Simula codebase.

The careful integration of concurrency and parallelism approaches allows the developer to harness the full power of multi-core systems, providing significant performance boosts for computationally intensive applications, and ensuring that the reader is now equipped with the tools and knowledge to manage concurrent and parallel tasks within Simula, optimizing both performance and efficiency.

10.4 Memory Management and Garbage Collection

Memory management is a critical aspect of any programming language, and Simula is no exception. Proper management of memory ensures that a program runs efficiently, minimizes memory leaks, and avoids unnecessary overhead. In Simula, memory management is handled with a combination of manual techniques and automatic garbage collection, allowing developers to write efficient and robust code.

Simula manages memory through a heap, where objects are dynamically allocated. To allocate memory for an object, the new operator is used, creating a new instance of an object and returning a reference to it. This reference can then be used to access the object's attributes and methods.

```
MyObject m = new MyObject();
```

In the above example, an instance of MyObject is created and assigned to the variable m. The space required for MyObject is allocated from the heap, and m holds the reference to that memory location.

Garbage collection in Simula is an automated process that aims to reclaim memory occupied by objects that are no longer in use, thereby preventing memory leaks. Simula uses a tracing garbage collection mechanism that is typically based on the mark-and-sweep algorithm. This method involves two main phases: marking and sweeping.

To understand the garbage collection process, consider the following example where multiple objects are dynamically allocated:

```
MyObject obj1 = new MyObject();
MyObject obj2 = new MyObject();
MyObject obj3 = new MyObject();
```

If obj1 and obj2 are dereferenced at some point in the program, these objects become eligible for garbage collection:

```
obj1 = null;
obj2 = null;
```

Once objects are dereferenced, the garbage collector starts by marking all objects that are still reachable from the root references. The root references generally include global variables, local variables in currently running methods, and any references in the registers or stack frames. During this marking phase, the garbage collector traverses the object graph starting from the root references and marks all reachable objects.

For instance, consider the following simplified pseudo algorithm in Simula syntax to demonstrate the marking phase:

```
Data: Set of root references
Result: Marked objects
Function Mark(Object obj):
    if obj is not marked then
        Mark obj;
        foreach reference field in obj do
            Mark(reference field);
```

Following the marking phase, the sweeping phase begins, where the garbage collector scans through the heap, looking for unmarked objects. These unmarked objects are considered unreachable and their memory is reclaimed. The sweep phase can be depicted by the pseudocode:

```
foreach object in heap do
    if object is not marked then
        Reclaim memory of object;
    else
        Unmark the object for the next cycle;
```

Simula's garbage collection process ensures that memory occupied by objects that are no longer referenced by any part of the program is efficiently reclaimed and made available for future allocations. This helps in maintaining optimal memory usage throughout the application's lifecycle.

While garbage collection automates much of the memory management process, it is still essential for developers to understand how memory is allocated and freed. Proper coding practices, such as nullifying object references when they are no longer needed and avoiding unnecessary object creation, can assist the garbage collector, thereby enhancing performance.

It is also worth noting that certain scenarios may require manual intervention in the form of explicitly freeing large chunks of memory or optimizing the use of data structures to minimize memory usage.

Simula allows setting user-defined garbage collection triggers, which can be configured to initiate garbage collection based on specific conditions, such as when the available heap space falls below a predefined threshold. These configurations can be useful in fine-tuning the application's performance based on the requirements.

The following example illustrates configuring a custom garbage collection trigger:

```
// Assume a function setGarbageCollectionThreshold exists
setGarbageCollectionThreshold(1024*1024*50); // 50MB threshold
```

With this, the garbage collector will be invoked when the available heap space drops below 50 MB, ensuring timely reclamation of memory.

Furthermore, memory management in Simula can be enhanced through the use of efficient data structures and algorithms that minimize memory footprint and improve access patterns. Optimized data handling routines can significantly reduce the frequency and duration of garbage collection cycles.

Understanding memory management and garbage collection in Simula allows developers to write high-performance and robust applications. By leveraging automatic garbage collection and practicing conscientious memory allocation and deallocation, applications can maintain optimal efficiency despite complex and dynamic workloads. The following chapters will delve deeper into advanced techniques that complement the knowledge acquired here and target specific performance optimization strategies used in professional Simula programming.

10.5 Design Patterns in Simula

Design patterns are established solutions to common problems encountered in software design. They provide a template for how to solve a problem in a flexible, reusable way. Understanding design patterns and how they can be implemented in Simula is essential for creating maintainable and scalable code.

Object-Oriented programming in Simula lends itself well to many design patterns due to its inherent support for classes and objects. We will explore several key design patterns, including the Singleton, Factory, and Observer patterns, and provide examples illustrating their implementation.

Singleton Pattern

The Singleton pattern ensures that a class has only one instance and provides a global point of access to this instance. This is useful when exactly one object is needed to coordinate actions across the system.

```
CLASS Singleton;

BEGIN
   REF(Singleton) INSTANCE;

   IF INSTANCE = NOTEXT THEN
      ! INSTANCE is not yet created. Create it.
      NEW INSTANCE;
   END

   INSTANCE:- THIS;
END;
```

The Singleton class definition above ensures that only one instance of the class is created. The INSTANCE variable holds the reference to the single instance, and checks are performed to see if this instance already exists before creating a new one.

Factory Pattern

The Factory pattern provides an interface for creating objects in a superclass, but allows subclasses to alter the type of objects that will be created. This pattern is useful for creating objects that require a bit of complexity and makes the system more modular.

```
CLASS Product;

CLASS ConcreteProduct1;
 BEGINSUPER Product;
    ! Implementation details specific to ConcreteProduct1
END;

CLASS ConcreteProduct2;
 BEGINSUPER Product;
    ! Implementation details specific to ConcreteProduct2
END;

CLASS Creator;
EXPORT CreateProduct;
PROCEDURE CreateProduct; REF(Product);
BEGIN
    ! Method definition to be overridden by subclass
END;

CLASS ConcreteCreator1;
 BEGINSUPER Creator;
    PROCEDURE CreateProduct;
    BEGIN
       CreateProduct :- NEW ConcreteProduct1;
```

```
    END;

CLASS ConcreteCreator2;
 BEGINSUPER Creator;
    PROCEDURE CreateProduct;
    BEGIN
        CreateProduct :- NEW ConcreteProduct2;
    END;
```

In this example, Creator class defines an interface CreateProduct, which is implemented in ConcreteCreator1 and ConcreteCreator2 classes to create different types of concrete products.

Observer Pattern

The Observer pattern defines a one-to-many dependency between objects so that when one object changes state, all its dependents are notified and updated automatically. This pattern is particularly useful for implementing distributed event-handling systems.

```
CLASS Subject;
REAL PROPERTY;
REF(ListClass) OBSERVERS;

PROCEDURE Attach (obspect); REF(ObserverClass) obspect;
BEGIN
   INSERT(OBSERVERS, obspect);
END;

PROCEDURE Detach (obspect); REF(ObserverClass) obspect;
BEGIN
   REMOVE(OBSERVERS, obspect);
END;

PROCEDURE Notify;
REF(ObserverClass) obspect;
FOR obspect IN OBSERVERS DO
   obspect.Update;
END;

CLASS ObserverClass;
PROCEDURE Update;
! Update method to be overridden by concrete observer classes

CLASS ConcreteObserver;
 BEGINSUPER ObserverClass;
   Procedure Update;
   BEGIN
       ! Concrete update logic here
   END;


REF(Subject) subject;
REF(ConcreteObserver) observer1, observer2;

! Subject instantiation
subject :- NEW Subject;

! Create observer instances
```

```
observer1 :- NEW ConcreteObserver;
observer2 :- NEW ConcreteObserver;

! Attach the observers to the subject
Call subject.Attach(observer1);
Call subject.Attach(observer2);

! Change the state of the subject and notify observers
subject.PROPERTY := 10;
Call subject.Notify;
```

In this example, the Subject class holds an integer PROPERTY and a list of OBSERVERS. Methods are defined to attach and detach observers and notify them of changes. The ObserverClass defines an interface with an Update method that concrete observers will implement.

Understanding and implementing these patterns in Simula enhances the reusability, maintainability, and scalability of code. Further, by adhering to these patterns, developers can more effectively communicate their design intentions, fostering better code comprehension and collaboration across teams.

10.6 Metaprogramming

Metaprogramming in Simula entails writing programs that can generate or manipulate other programs or themselves. This advanced technique is particularly useful for tasks like optimization, code generation, or domain-specific language (DSL) implementations. It leverages the reflective capabilities of Simula, allowing the program to inspect and modify its structure and behavior at runtime.

The concept of metaprogramming can be classified into two main types: **compile-time** and **runtime**. Compile-time metaprogramming involves generating or modifying code during the compilation phase, while runtime metaprogramming occurs as the program executes.

Class Name in Simula provides runtime type information (RTTI) and reflective operations that can be used for metaprogramming. Consider the following example which illustrates the usage of reflective capabilities in Simula:

```
BEGIN
   CLASS Object;
      TEXT Name;
      INTEGER ID;
   BEGIN
      ID := RANDOM;
      Name :- "Object#" & OUTTEXT(ID);
```

```
    END;

    CLASS ReflectionDemo;
        PROCEDURE PrintClassInfo(Obj);
        REFERENCE (Object) Obj;
        BEGIN
            OUTTEXT("Class Name: " & Obj.Name & "\n");
            OUTTEXT("Class ID: " & OUTTEXT(Obj.ID) & "\n");
        END;

        PROCEDURE InvokeMethod(Obj, MethodName);
        REFERENCE (Object) Obj;
        TEXT MethodName;
        BEGIN
            IF MethodName = "PrintClassInfo" THEN
                PrintClassInfo(Obj);
            ELSE
                OUTTEXT("Method " & MethodName & " not found.\n");
            END;
        END;

        BEGIN
            REF (Object) myObject;
            myObject :- NEW Object;
            InvokeMethod(myObject, "PrintClassInfo");
        END;
    END;
END;
```

The ReflectionDemo class in this listing uses a procedure, PrintClassInfo, to access and display information about an object of the Object class. Another procedure, InvokeMethod, demonstrates invoking a method based on its name, providing basic reflective capabilities.

Using metaprogramming for code generation involves dynamically creating code constructs. Consider an example where a list of integers needs to be processed, and optimization can be achieved by dynamically generating specific methods for common operations such as sum, average, or maximum.

```
BEGIN
    CLASS GeneratedMethods;
        INTEGER PROCEDURE Sum(nums);
        ARRAY INTEGER nums;
        BEGIN
            INTEGER i, total;
            total := 0;
            FOR i := 1 STEP 1 UNTIL UPB(nums) DO
                total +:= nums[i];
            Sum := total;
        END;

        INTEGER PROCEDURE Max(nums);
        ARRAY INTEGER nums;
        BEGIN
            INTEGER i, maxValue;
            maxValue := nums[1];
            FOR i := 2 STEP 1 UNTIL UPB(nums) DO
```

```
            IF nums[i] > maxValue THEN
                maxValue := nums[i];
        Max := maxValue;
    END;

    REAL PROCEDURE Average(nums);
    ARRAY INTEGER nums;
    BEGIN
        Average := Sum(nums) / UPB(nums);
    END;
  END;

  REF (GeneratedMethods) methods;
  methods :- NEW GeneratedMethods;

  ARRAY INTEGER nums[1:5];
  nums[1] := 2; nums[2] := 4; nums[3] := 6; nums[4] := 8; nums[5] := 10;

  OUTTEXT("Sum: " & OUTTEXT(methods.Sum(nums)) & "\n");
  OUTTEXT("Max: " & OUTTEXT(methods.Max(nums)) & "\n");
  OUTTEXT("Average: " & OUTTEXT(methods.Average(nums)) & "\n");
END;
```

This code segment showcases a class, GeneratedMethods, where procedures for summing, finding the maximum, and calculating the average of an array of integers are dynamically incorporated. This approach reduces code redundancy and enhances maintainability by generating repetitive and commonly used methods programmatically.

Another powerful application of metaprogramming is building domain-specific languages (DSLs). DSLs are specialized mini-languages tailored to a particular application domain. By utilizing Simula's inherent capabilities, one can create a DSL that translates high-level domain-specific commands into lower-level Simula operations. This further abstracts and simplifies complex tasks.

```
BEGIN
  CLASS DSL;
    TEXT METHOD RunCommand(command);
    TEXT command;
    BEGIN
      IF command = "sum numbers" THEN
        OUTTEXT("Executing: Sum Numbers\n");
      ELSE IF command = "find max" THEN
        OUTTEXT("Executing: Find Max\n");
      ELSE
        OUTTEXT("Error: Unknown Command\n");
    END;

    PROCEDURE Execute(commands);
    TEXT commands;
    BEGIN
      INTEGER i;
      ARRAY TEXT commandList[1:UPB(commands)];

      commandList := SPLIT(commands, "\n");
      FOR i := 1 STEP 1 UNTIL UPB(commandList) DO
```

```
            RunCommand(commandList[i]);
        END;
    END;

    REF (DSL) dsl;
    dsl :- NEW DSL;

    TEXT commands;
    commands :- "sum numbers\nfind max\ncalculate average";

    dsl.Execute(commands);
END;
```

In this illustration, a DSL class is created with a method RunCommand that interprets and executes specific commands. The Execute procedure takes a series of commands and processes them sequentially. This example highlights the potential of Simula in creating powerful domain-specific abstractions effortlessly.

Metaprogramming empowers developers to produce more flexible, reusable, and efficient code. Understanding and mastering this technique significantly extends the capabilities of Simula programming, allowing for the creation of complex and optimized applications.

10.7 Networking and Socket Programming

Networking in Simula involves constructing communication pathways between systems to transfer data over networks such as the Internet or local area networks (LAN). Socket programming is a key technique used to facilitate such communication. Sockets serve as endpoints for sending and receiving data across a network.

The SOCKET class in Simula is among foundational constructs designed for network communication. Understanding the properties and methods of this class is crucial for implementing effective networked applications. Sockets can be represented by two primary types: stream sockets and datagram sockets.

Stream sockets (SOCK_STREAM) rely on the Transmission Control Protocol (TCP) to provide a reliable, connection-oriented communication channel. Datagram sockets (SOCK_DGRAM), on the other hand, use the User Datagram Protocol (UDP) for connectionless communication, allowing for faster but less reliable data transmission.

```
! Example of creating a TCP socket in Simula
begin
  ref(SOCKET) clientSocket;
```

```
  integer port;
  text address;

  clientSocket :- new SOCKET(SOCK_STREAM);
  port := 8080;
  address :- '192.168.1.1';

  ! Connect to the specified address and port
  clientSocket.Connect(address, port);

  ! Sending data
  clientSocket.Send('Hello, Server!');

  ! Receiving data
  text receivedData;
  receivedData :- clientSocket.Receive();

  outtext('Received: ' & receivedData);
  clientSocket.Close();
end;
```

In the example, a SOCKET object is instantiated with SOCK_-STREAM to create a TCP socket. The Connect method establishes a connection to the server at the specified address and port. Data is transmitted using the Send method and received via the Receive method.

For creating a server socket, the process is quite similar, with additional steps to bind the socket to a port and listen for incoming connections.

```
! Example of creating a TCP server socket in Simula
begin
  ref(SOCKET) serverSocket, clientSocket;
  integer port;

  serverSocket :- new SOCKET(SOCK_STREAM);
  port := 8080;

  ! Bind the socket to the port
  serverSocket.Bind(port);

  ! Listen for incoming connections
  serverSocket.Listen(5); ! The parameter specifies the backlog queue length

  ! Accept a client connection
  clientSocket :- serverSocket.Accept();

  ! Receiving data from the client
  text clientData;
  clientData :- clientSocket.Receive();

  outtext('Client says: ' & clientData);

  ! Sending response to the client
  clientSocket.Send('Hello, Client!');
  clientSocket.Close();
  serverSocket.Close();
end;
```

The server socket setup involves binding to a port with the Bind method, setting it to listen for incoming connections using the Listen method, and accepting connections with the Accept method, which returns a new socket dedicated to the client.

For UDP communication, the process is simpler as it does not require a connection to be established beforehand.

```
! Example of creating a UDP socket in Simula
begin
  ref(SOCKET) udpSocket;
  integer port;

  udpSocket :- new SOCKET(SOCK_DGRAM);
  port := 8080;

  ! Binding the UDP socket
  udpSocket.Bind(port);

  ! Sending a datagram
  text message;
  text destination;

  destination :- '192.168.1.1';
  message :- 'Hello, UDP Server!';
  udpSocket.SendTo(message, destination, port);

  ! Receiving a datagram
  text receivedMessage;
  receivedMessage :- udpSocket.Receive();

  outtext('Received: ' & receivedMessage);
  udpSocket.Close();
end;
```

Here, the UDP socket sends data using the SendTo method and receives data without establishing a persistent connection.

Robust error handling is critical in network applications due to the unpredictable nature of network conditions. Common error sources include network unavailability, connection timeouts, and data transmission failures. Implementing proper error handling ensures the stability and reliability of the networked application.

```
! Example of error handling in socket programming
begin
  ref(SOCKET) clientSocket;
  integer port;
  text address;
  boolean success;

  clientSocket :- new SOCKET(SOCK_STREAM);
  port := 8080;
  address :- '192.168.1.1';

  ! Connect to the specified address and port with error handling
  success := clientSocket.Connect(address, port);
```

```
if not success then
   outtext('Failed to connect to server.');
else
   ! Sending data
   clientSocket.Send('Hello, Server!');

   ! Attempt to receive data
   try
     text receivedData;
     receivedData :- clientSocket.Receive();
     outtext('Received: ' & receivedData);
   else
     outtext('Failed to receive data.');
   endtry;
   clientSocket.Close();
 endif;
end;
```

Integrating error handling within socket operations, as demonstrated, includes checking the status of connections and using the try construct to manage exceptions during data transmission.

Understanding these fundamentals in Simula's socket programming opens avenues to more advanced network programming concepts, such as secure communication (SSL/TLS), non-blocking sockets, and multi-threaded network servers. Establishing a solid foundation in these core principles prepares one to efficiently develop and troubleshoot complex, real-world networked applications.

10.8 Graphics and User Interface Development

Graphics and user interface (UI) development in Simula allows for the creation of visually compelling and interactive programs. This section explores the capabilities of Simula in handling graphical output and constructing user interfaces.

Simula provides built-in support for graphics through its Class system. The graphical output can be divided into raster graphics (bitmap images) and vector graphics (shapes, lines, etc.). Additionally, developing a user interface involves managing user input events and updating the display accordingly.

Basic Graphics Operations

Before delving into complex UI elements, it's essential to understand basic graphics operations in Simula. Begin with creating a window and drawing simple shapes.

```
CLASS Window;
BEGIN
  REF (Window) w;
  ... -- Initialization and window management code
  w := NEW Window;
  w.open("My Graphics Window", 800, 600); -- Open a window with title and
        dimensions
  w.setColor(0, 0, 0); -- Set drawing color to black
  w.drawLine(100, 100, 200, 200); -- Draw a line from (100, 100) to (200, 200)
  w.drawCircle(300, 300, 50); -- Draw a circle with center (300, 300) and radius 50
  w.fillRectangle(400, 400, 100, 50); -- Draw a filled rectangle at (400, 400) with width
        100 and height 50
END;
```

The code above demonstrates creating a window, setting drawing colors, and drawing basic shapes like lines, circles, and rectangles.

Handling User Input

Interaction with users is a crucial aspect of UI development. Simula can handle various input events such as mouse clicks, keyboard presses, and window resizing. Below is an example of capturing and processing a mouse click event:

```
CLASS EventHandler;
BEGIN
  REF (Window) w;
  w := NEW Window;
  w.open("Event Handling Window", 800, 600);
  WHILE TRUE DO
    REF (Event) e;
    e := w.getEvent; -- Get the next event
    IF e.isMouseClick THEN
      INTEGER x, y;
      x := e.getX; y := e.getY;
      w.setColor(1, 0, 0); -- Change color to red
      w.drawCircle(x, y, 10); -- Draw a small circle at the click position
    END;
  END;
END;
```

This code snippet showcases a basic event handler that responds to mouse click events and draws a small circle at the click position.

Complex UI Components

Creating more advanced user interface elements such as buttons, text fields, and menus can be accomplished by combining basic graphical operations and event handling. Simula's Class mechanism is powerful in structuring these components.

```
CLASS Button;
BEGIN
  TEXT label;
```

```
  INTEGER x, y, width, height;
  PROCEDURE init(lbl: TEXT; xpos, ypos, w, h: INTEGER);
  BEGIN
    label := lbl;
    x := xpos; y := ypos;
    width := w; height := h;
  END init;

  PROCEDURE draw(REF (Window) w);
  BEGIN
    w.setColor(0.8, 0.8, 0.8); -- Light gray background
    w.fillRectangle(x, y, width, height);
    w.setColor(0, 0, 0); -- Black text
    w.drawText(label, x + width / 4, y + height / 2);
  END draw;

  PROCEDURE click(REF (Event) e) BOOL;
  BEGIN
    IF (e.getX >= x AND e.getX <= x + width) AND (e.getY >= y AND e.getY <=
        y + height) THEN
      RETURN TRUE;
    ELSE
      RETURN FALSE;
    END;
  END click;
END;

CLASS Interface;
BEGIN
  REF (Window) window;
  REF (Button) btn;
  window := NEW Window;
  btn := NEW Button("Click Me", 50, 50, 100, 40);
  window.open("Complex UI", 800, 600);

  PROCEDURE mainLoop;
  BEGIN
    WHILE TRUE DO
      btn.draw(window);
      REF (Event) evt;
      evt := window.getEvent;
      IF evt.isMouseClick THEN
        IF btn.click(evt) THEN
          window.setColor(0, 0.5, 0); -- Change color to green
          window.fillRectangle(200, 200, 150, 50); -- Feedback action
        END;
      END;
    END;
  END mainLoop;

  mainLoop;
END;
```

The above code constructs a button component with a label, position, and dimensions. The click method checks if the mouse click occurred within the button's boundaries. The Interface class manages the window and button's interactions.

Graphical User Interface Libraries

While the basic facilities provided by Simula can be used to create custom UI components, there are existing libraries that facilitate more efficient development. Libraries such as SimView or SimGraph offer higher-level abstractions for common UI components.

Ensure to include library-specific documentation when utilizing such libraries for a comprehensive understanding of their APIs and capabilities.

Performance Considerations

Effective UI development includes considerations for rendering performance, especially for complex interfaces or animations. Techniques such as double buffering can be used to minimize flickering and rendering artifacts.

```
CLASS DoubleBufferedWindow (Window);
BEGIN
  ... -- Inherited attributes and additional buffer management
  REF (GraphicBuffer) buffer;
  buffer := NEW GraphicBuffer(width, height);

  PROCEDURE draw();
  BEGIN
    buffer.begin(); -- Start drawing on off-screen buffer
    ... -- Drawing operations
    buffer.end(); -- Finish drawing
    self.display(buffer); -- Display the buffer on the window
  END draw;
END;
```

In this example, DoubleBufferedWindow extends the basic window class to include an off-screen buffer that is drawn to before being displayed, reducing flicker during updates.

UI development in Simula allows for a high degree of customization and complexity, leveraging both the built-in graphical capabilities and third-party libraries to create responsive and visually appealing interfaces.

10.9 Interfacing with Other Languages

Interfacing Simula programs with other programming languages is critical for leveraging existing systems, reusing code, and integrating with diverse software components. This section discusses various methods for interlanguage communication, focusing on techniques to call external procedures, handle data exchange, and manage interoperability challenges effectively.

One of the primary methods for interfacing Simula with other languages is through Foreign Function Interfaces (FFIs). FFIs enable Simula programs to invoke functions written in other languages such as C, C++, or Fortran. Before delving into specific examples, it is essential to understand the general principles and mechanisms employed in FFIs.

Utilizing FFIs involves the following main steps:

- Declaring Foreign Functions in Simula
- Establishing Data Type Correspondence
- Managing Memory and Resources
- Error Handling in Interlanguage Calls

Declaring Foreign Functions in Simula

To call an external function, it must be declared in Simula using the external keyword. The declaration includes the function's name, argument types, and return type. Consider an example where we call a simple C function to add two integers:

```
/* C function */
int add(int a, int b) {
    return a + b;
}
```

In Simula, declare this C function as follows:

```
EXTERNAL PROCEDURE add(a, b);
INTEGER a, b; VALUE a, b;
INTEGER add;
```

Establishing Data Type Correspondence

Data type correspondence between Simula and the interfacing language is crucial to ensure that the data is correctly interpreted on both sides. Common types such as integers, floats, and characters often have direct mappings. However, more complex types, like structures or arrays, require careful handling.

For instance, to pass an array from Simula to C, you must ensure the array layout in memory matches the expected layout in C. Suppose you have the following C function to sum an array of integers:

```
/* C function */
int sum_array(int* arr, int len) {
    int sum = 0;
    for (int i = 0; i < len; i++) {
        sum += arr[i];
```

```
    }
    return sum;
}
```

Here's how you can call this function from Simula:

```
EXTERNAL PROCEDURE sum_array(arr, len);
INTEGER arr, len; VALUE len;
INTEGER sum_array;

ARRAY arr(1:10); ! Declare an array of 10 integers
INTEGER result, len;
len := 10; ! Set the length of the array

! Initialize array values
FOR i := 1 STEP 1 UNTIL len DO
    arr(i) := i;

result := sum_array(arr, len);
```

Managing Memory and Resources

Memory management is a critical aspect when interfacing with other languages to avoid leaks and ensure data integrity. When exchanging data, especially large structures or buffers, it is essential to manage their allocations and deallocations appropriately.

In Simula, dynamic memory allocation can be performed using new, and it must be deallocated correctly to prevent memory leaks. Consider the following scenario where a Simula program allocates memory for a C function that processes a string:

```
/* C function */
void process_string(char* str) {
    printf("Processing: %s\n", str);
}
```

In Simula, this can be handled as follows:

```
EXTERNAL PROCEDURE process_string(str);
TEXT str;

TEXT myString;
myString :- NEW TEXT(50); ! Allocate memory for the string
myString.SetString("Hello, Simula!");

process_string(myString.Image);
myString.Finalize(); ! Deallocate memory
```

Note that Finalize is used to clean up the memory allocated for myString.

Error Handling in Interlanguage Calls

Error handling when invoking functions from other languages is critical to ensure robust and reliable systems. Foreign functions may fail due to various reasons, including invalid arguments, system errors, or runtime exceptions. It is essential to check for and handle such errors appropriately.

When calling a C function that returns an error code, you can handle this in Simula by interpreting the return value. For example:

```
/* C function */
int divide(int a, int b, int* result) {
    if (b == 0) return -1; /* Error: division by zero */
    *result = a / b;
    return 0; /* Success */
}
```

Simula code to handle this function could be:

```
EXTERNAL PROCEDURE divide(a, b, result);
INTEGER a, b, result; VALUE a, b;
INTEGER divide;

INTEGER res, err_code;
err_code := divide(10, 2, res);
IF err_code = 0 THEN
    OutInt(res, 0); OutImage
ELSE
    OutText("Error: Division by zero"); OutImage;
```

Overall, effective interfacing requires a comprehensive understanding of both Simula's and the target language's calling conventions and runtime behavior. Properly managing data types, memory, and errors is key to achieving seamless interoperability between Simula and other languages, allowing developers to build versatile and powerful software systems.

10.10 Performance Optimization Techniques

Performance optimization is a critical aspect of advanced Simula programming, focusing on enhancing execution efficiency and reducing resource consumption. This section elaborates on optimization strategies and techniques applicable to Simula programs, addressing both algorithmic improvements and language-specific optimizations.

Profiling and Benchmarking

Before initiating optimization, it is crucial to identify performance bottlenecks and quantify improvements. Profiling tools help in pinpointing sections of the code that consume the most resources. A typical profiling process in Simula might involve using a timing mechanism to measure the execution duration of code blocks.

```
integer tStart, tEnd;
text procedure getTime;
  begin text system class OpenTime;
  OpenTime.start;
  getTime := OpenTime.time;
  OpenTime.finish;
  end;

...

tStart := getTime();
!-- Code block to be measured --!
tEnd := getTime();

OutText("Execution time: " & (tEnd - tStart) & " ms");
...
```

Integrating a systematic process for profiling ensures that optimization efforts are directed appropriately.

Algorithmic Optimization

Choosing the correct algorithm significantly impacts the performance. For example, if searching is a frequent operation, using a binary search tree rather than a linked list can drastically improve efficiency.

Algorithm 3: Binary Search Algorithm

Data: Sorted array arr of size n, element x to search
Result: Index of x if present, otherwise -1

```
low ← 0;
high ← n - 1;
while low ≤ high do
    mid ← (low + high) / 2;
    if arr[mid] == x then
        return mid
    else
        if arr[mid] < x then
            low ← mid + 1
        else
            high ← mid - 1
        end
    end
end
return-1;
```

Binary search has a time complexity of $O(\log n)$ compared to $O(n)$ of a linear search, providing substantial performance gains for large datasets.

Memory Management

Efficient memory usage is essential for performance optimization. Simula's garbage collection can induce overhead during execution. Reducing the frequency and volume of memory allocation operations minimizes this overhead.

Suppose a program frequently creates and destroys instances of a particular class. Using object pooling can significantly reduce the impact of garbage collection.

```
external class Pool;
class MyClassPool(Pool) begin
  MyClass freeList;
  MyClass access
  begin
    if freeList == none then
      access new MyClass;
    else
      begin
        access := freeList;
        freeList := freeList.nx;
      end if;
  end Free(p MyClass) begin
    p.nx := freeList;
    freeList := p;
  end;
end MyClassPool;

...
```

Object pooling minimizes the number of allocations and deallocations, reducing the strain on the garbage collector.

Concurrency Optimization

Parallelism can be leveraged to optimize performance, especially on multi-core systems. Utilizing Concurrency in Simula can be achieved via coroutines and detached processes.

```
process P1; begin ... pause; end;
process P2; begin ... pause; end;

...
activator External.Transaction;
proceed(P1);
proceed(P2);
...
```

By identifying independent tasks and executing them concurrently, the overall execution time can be reduced. However, careful attention must be paid to synchronization and avoiding race conditions.

Code Optimizations and Compiler Directives

Providing hints to the compiler can result in significant performance improvements. Unrolling loops and inlining functions are common optimizations.

```
for i := 1 step 1 until n do
begin
  !-- Optimized loop with unrolling --!
  if (i + 1) <= n then
  begin
    Operation1(i);
    Operation2(i+1);
    i := i + 1;
  end
  else
    Operation1(i);
end;
...
```

This technique balances between increased code size and execution speed by reducing the loop overhead.

Efficient Use of Data Structures

Selecting data structures that align with the access patterns is crucial. For instance, using hash tables for frequent lookups or balanced trees for ordered operations detects access time consistency.

```
! Example of optimized hashmap usage
class HashTable n; begin
  ...
  procedure Insert(key, value);
  integer hash := ComputeHash(key);
  bucket := table[hash];
  bucket.insert(key, value);
  ...
end
...

myTable.Insert("Key1", "Value1");
```

Each application case might benefit from a different strategy, and understanding the trade-offs of each structure is imperative.

Engaging these optimization techniques allows for refining the efficiency of Simula programs, ultimately leading to faster execution and reduced resource consumption.

10.11 Case Studies and Real-world Applications

This section explores several nuanced case studies and real-world applications to illustrate the practical aspects of advanced Simula programming. Each example demonstrates the integration of concepts developed throughout the chapter, offering deep insights into sophisticated problem-solving techniques.

Case Study 1: Automated Stock Trading System

Automated stock trading systems demand high performance and reliability, making them an excellent candidate for advanced Simula applications. Key components include data structures for maintaining real-time market data, concurrency to handle multiple trading algorithms, and network programming for interfacing with financial APIs.

Algorithm 4: Stock Trading Algorithm Pseudocode

```
Data: Real-time market data stream
Result: Generate buy/sell signals
Function computeTrends(marketData);
Function SimpleMovingAverage(data, period):
    Data: data: List of market prices, period: Integer
    Result: List of moving average values
    averages := [];
    for i := period to len(data) do
        movingSum := 0;
        for j := i-period to i do
            movingSum += data[j];
        averages.append(movingSum/period);
    return averages;
trends := computeTrends(marketData);
signals := generateSignals(trends);
```

Here, the calculation of simple moving averages is central. Using Simula's capabilities in data management and algorithm execution, such financial models can be efficiently implemented.

Trade objects manage individual transactions, each endowed with specific properties such as timestamp, quantity, and price.

```
class Trade(type, timestamp, quantity, price);
```

```
  begin
    text type;
    longreal timestamp, quantity, price;
  end;
```

Market data can be processed concurrently to maximize performance, evidenced by launching multiple simultaneous algorithms. Simula's co-begin construct facilitates this:

```
co-begin
  algorithm1.run();
  algorithm2.run();
  algorithm3.run();
co-end;
```

```
Output:
Algorithm1 completed.
Algorithm2 completed.
Algorithm3 completed.
```

Case Study 2: Real-time Traffic Simulation

Urban traffic simulation is critical for city planning and intelligent transportation systems (ITS). A real-time simulation incorporates data from various sensors, uses complex data structures for road networks, and involves concurrent processing to simulate multiple vehicles.

Vehicles are represented with objects possessing state information such as speed, direction, and location.

```
class Vehicle(speed, direction, location);
  begin
    real speed;
    integer direction, location;

    procedure move();
    begin
      location := location + speed * direction;
    end move;
  end;
```

Simulating the movement of numerous vehicles concurrently is achieved using coroutines:

```
procedure simulate_traffic();
begin
  co-begin
    vehicle1.move();
    vehicle2.move();
    vehicle3.move();
  co-end;
end;
```

Network data is processed to adjust simulation parameters dynamically:

```
process data_stream();
begin
  while true do
  begin
    read next data_packet;
    update_simulation(data_packet);
  end;
end;
```

Output:
Vehicle 1 at location X.
Vehicle 2 at location Y.
Vehicle 3 at location Z.

Case Study 3: Distributed File System

A distributed file system (DFS) enhances data accessibility and storage management across multiple servers. Simula's object-oriented paradigm aids in encapsulating file metadata, authoritarian control, and replication protocols.

Classes such as File and Directory manage hierarchical data:

```
class File(name, size, data);
  begin
    text name;
    integer size;
    byte array data[1:size];
  end;

class Directory(name, files);
  begin
    text name;
    list(File) files;

    procedure addFile(file);
    begin
      files.InsertLast(file);
    end addFile;
  end;
```

Concurrency and network communication enable replication and consistency across nodes. Data replication employs distributed algorithms like the following:

Simula manages synchronization and communication pathways ensuring consistent data across server nodes.

```
procedure sync_files();
begin
  co-begin
    replicate(node1);
```

Algorithm 5: Replication Protocol Pseudocode

```
Data: File updates
Result: Ensure consistency across nodes
Function replicaManager(fileUpdate, nodeList):
    for every node in nodeList do
        if node has not been updated then
            send update to node;
changes := detectChanges(localFile);
replicaManager(changes, nodeList);
```

```
    replicate(node2);
    replicate(node3);
  co-end;
end;
```

```
Output:
Node1 synchronized.
Node2 synchronized.
Node3 synchronized.
```

These cases reveal the practical application and efficacy of using Simula for complex, real-world problems, leveraging advanced data structures, concurrency, network communications, and algorithmic precision. The detailed explanations and code samples offer a comprehensive guide to advanced Simula applications, enhancing the reader's proficiency and understanding of the language's real-world utility.